Praise for Dina Bennett's *Peking to Paris*

"Like Tim Cahill before her, Dina Bennett brings adventure car travel to a new level. Written by an unlikely (and often reluctant) navigator, Dina's flair for self deprecating humor and insight left me literally laughing out loud."

—Beth Whitman, Founder, Wanderlust and Lipstick

"A couples' willingness to take a stable relationship into unstable lands for a road-trip on map-challenged routes makes for compelling stories. Her tale is rendered with just the right words to make you want to be along on the journey, and all the right words to keep you safely at home instead."

—Rick Antonson, author of *To Timbuktu for a Haircut* and *Route 66 Still Kicks*

"Bennett writes fearlessly on the disregarded aspects of travel: the uncertainties, hesitation, self-doubt. In so doing, she reminds us that travel isn't reserved for the heroic; it's open to all who seek it."

—Hal Amen, Managing Editor, MatadorNetwork.com

Peking to Paris is "a road-trip memoir from an author who has 'a love–hate relationship with adventure.' [Bennett's] writing captures the beauty of the austere landscape, changing social dynamics with other teams, and the nuances of her shifting relationship with her husband. A fun ride, worth the trip."

—*Kirkus Reviews*

"Where travel memoirists tend toward the intrepid adventurer, Bennett is another sort altogether. [*Peking to Paris* proves] it's all about the journey, not the destination."

—*Booklist*

"[Dina] Bennett agrees to the rally despite having no mechanical aptitude and a propensity for carsickness. When it's all over, she misses the cramped quarters of their beloved Cadillac (nicknamed Roxanne) so much that they take to the road again—this time in a rental car. The camaraderie between participants in the race is a secondary character: 'I look around the table and note Americans, Swiss, French, Dutch, Greek. And the one nationality we now have in common: Rally.' Tip: Start at the end. The book's glossary and numerous appendices spoil nothing, but give you a clear sense of what goes into a project like this, which only enhances the fun once you actually hit the road."

—Heather Seggel, *BookPage*

Dina Bennett is "... an adventurous woman, willing herself to ... push up against the outer boundaries of her comfort zone. ... many comedic observations."

—Michael Milne, *New York Journal of Books*

A Travel Junkie's Diary

*Searching for Mare's Milk
and Other Far-Flung Pursuits*

DINA BENNETT

Skyhorse Publishing

To Vivienne

The traveler sees what he sees. The
tourist sees what he has come to see.
—G. K. Chesterton

Table of Contents

HERE AND GONE

Preface

Have you heard of Lost Glove Syndrome? I hadn't either, until I thought for a long time about my life, why I travel the way I do, and made up a philosophy for it. Everyone knows what I'm talking about when it comes to a missing glove (just substitute "sock" if "glove" doesn't work for you). Whether they shield you from frigid weather or add retro personality to an outfit, when one glove is missing you're incomplete. Having one remaining glove isn't bad, but it's not great either. As you search for the missing glove you have time to think . . . about what it means to you and why you want it so badly. So when you do finally find it you understand something profound: you have so much more than two gloves. You have a matched pair.

As applied to life, the quest epitomized by Lost Glove Syndrome is why I've been willing to humble myself during the journeys that follow. Like that perfect pair of gloves, I suspect there are elements of me out there, some-where, which, when encountered, will make me better, in a so-much-more-than-whole way. It's why, for me, travel isn't a quest to see. It's a quest to be.

Because I have Lost Glove Syndrome in a serious way, travel has become more than just passing time or an activity. It's a process by turns uncertain, monotone, exhausting, and sometimes embarrassing, spiked by revelations and encounters so intense they're like a miracle. People talk about travel taking me out of my comfort zone. That's never been my goal. Why would I put myself into discomfort for days on end just to say I was uncomfort-able? Besides, eventually the outside of that zone becomes comfortable enough that the whole term loses its meaning. And then what?

No, the reason I repeatedly am willing to open the door to a car and set off on the sort of road trips that populate this book, is my search for the proverbial missing glove, that element of my character I know is there and without which I feel unfinished. When I travel to likely places in likely ways, I find only a mirror cheerfully reflecting everything I enjoy about myself. It's easy, comfortable—and I'm happy. When I'm in less likely places, though still on a normal trip, that mirror may show me an unflattering reflection of myself, but in ways familiar enough that I can remain unchanged. It's only the radically different methods and environments of these road trips that challenge me to search for an aspect of me which, if I can find it, try it on, wear it for a bit, will enhance me with that laughing "ah-ha" moment of discovery melded with recognition.

The trip that started it all was the 7,800-mile Peking to Paris car rally (which I now call the P2P) I did with my husband Bernard in 2007. Before that year, all I knew about cars as a mode of travel was to stay out of them, because I get carsick. Following that trip, I still knew that cars and I didn't get along particularly well. But I also knew that a specific magic took place when Bernard and I set out on the road together, passports stamped with illegible visas, closed in a car for weeks at a time, seeking the rutted tracks and backcountry hamlets where outsiders rarely go.

The tales in this book are gleaned from ten years of extraordinary and difficult road trips in the world's out-of-the-way places, trips we embarked on after that shattering thirty-five days of the P2P race. The near-calamity of the P2P yielded something surprising—that when concentrating I no longer got queasy—and something very personal as well: that by putting myself through the fire I could come out the other side a little different. And I wanted more.

I confess that, despite the passage of time, a road trip still is a mode of travel for which I remain generally unsuited. I'm like a rat ejected from a grain bin, ripped from the comfortable predictability I crave. In the early days, I clung to the lip of that bin, longing to stay home, mightily resisting the next road trip. Now, while I don't exactly leap from the edge of that bin, I'm genuinely happy to get on the road, even relishing that vague dread about what comes next.

I try in these stories to reveal what happens when you travel not in search of statistics and data, but for whatever happens right around you. You'll see what I see, and I don't hide how, like any friend, I struggle. Sometimes there's an obvious point, but sometimes you'll find yourself getting it, just like I did, because of the truth of the moment.

The stories themselves are organized by subject rather than date. I made this organizational leap of faith without knowing that Mark Twain had already come up with the idea. "Ideally a book would have no order to it," he said, "and the reader would have to discover his own." I don't mean to be obscure in presenting things in this unstructured fashion. It just strikes me as an honest reflection of how discovery happens when traveling and how friendships develop between people who at the start know little about each other.

The travel dream we all have is for something elemental to materialize when we're away from home, something that connects us indelibly to the life around us. Obviously, each story you're about to read took place at a particular time, but more importantly they all are timeless in their human connection. The bewitchment of these tales is that they permit you to suspend the judgment promoted by our time-sensitive society, in which how fast you get things done is better rewarded than the quality of result. I hope that you, too, in dispensing with *when* and in focusing on *why* and *who* and *how*, will find yourself with a fresh perspective.

Mary Oliver, our great American poet, wrote an essay that starts like this: "In the beginning I was so young and such a stranger to myself I hardly existed. I had to go out into the world and see it and hear it and react to it, before I knew at all who I was, what I was, what I wanted to be." This applies to us all, regardless of age, experience, or opportunity. Through my travels, I've learned to find opportunity for connection where others see only strangeness, to feel myself lucky where others see missteps, to know that the grass is greener right where I'm standing, to come back a different me from when I left. I invite you to ride with me in a world without a roadmap, to become, as I have, a travel junkie.

INTRODUCTION

HOW IT ALL BEGAN

B ernard ran over the sleeping policeman at full speed. I didn't even flinch.

This was our third rough road trip through India. I already knew driving these village back roads after dark was a dangerous venture, not just because of people and livestock walking home from a far grazing plot in a darkness so dense it felt like velvet, but because Indian drivers refuse to use their headlights. Neither of us could fathom what karmic rationale could justify the necessity of keeping off the very lights that would enable one to avoid dying and taking a handful of blameless villagers with you in the process. Not to mention the sacred cows. In truth, a speed bump—which I grew up calling a "sleeping policeman" for the obvious work it did slowing down cars—such as the one we'd just jolted over was a minor annoyance compared to other obstacles. For when driving the little-traveled village roads of a country, as we choose to do on our long-distance road trips, our goal is not to challenge the local habit but to survive it.

The jolt sent our luggage, cases of tools, and car parts to the ceiling. They slammed back down like an earthquake aftershock. All the while I stared resolutely ahead. There was a time when such thoughtlessness on Bernard's part would have extracted from me at minimum a shout, more likely a flood of stern words about at least having the consideration to slow down a *bit*. The truth is, given the tens of thousands of miles that we have chosen to drive, in the backcountry of India, China, Iran, Siberia, Tibet,

Mongolia, the former Soviet republics, and more, I've become inured to such bad behavior. Or rather, I've become achingly aware that where there's one speed bump in an Indian village, ten more will likely follow. Just at the village entrance. With ten more at the exit as well.

When it comes to long-distance road trips, I am not to the manner born. I am the one who used to enter a car already counting the minutes before I'd reach my destination. And that was as the driver. As the passenger, road trips were a one-note tune centered on my intense, unrelenting, and unforgiving motion sickness. That is, until one brash, ill-considered but highly imaginative decision changed everything.

It was 2005, five years into our adventure of living on and operating a cattle ranch in the high mountains of northern Colorado. One morning to my delight—and eventual dismay—we received a notice that the entry Bernard and I had submitted to participate in a classic car rally had been accepted. It was the 2007 Peking to Paris Motor Challenge, and we'd be driving a set route from Beijing to Paris in a 1940 LaSalle. This was a competitive rally over open roads, not on a racetrack, in cars built as long ago as 1903. Bernard would drive, something he adores as only a man who rebuilt his first car at age three (well, okay, at sixteen) could. I would navigate, using the provided route book, which prescribed every single turn we had to make the entire way. And don't let me forget to mention that we were timed every day from start to finish, because if fourteen hours a day in a car wasn't stressful enough, knowing that we were perpetually late added to the fun. At my disposal as navigatrix were various gadgets, like a Tripmeter showing how far we'd driven to the millimeter. That I knew nothing about GPS devices, would be considered feeble in matters of technology, and could not look at a screen or page for more than five minutes while in a car without being overwhelmed by nausea, should have fazed me but did not. After all, who wouldn't leap at the opportunity to tell their husband of thirty years exactly where he could go, with him allowed only to nod and say thank you in reply?

Like the other competitors of what I quickly learned was a rather "in" club, I took to calling our epic endurance rally by a short acronym: P2P.

The quicker I could say it, the quicker I could add, "I want to go home." As someone whose every fiber disagreed with cars and driving, I was clearly about to be in the wrong place at the wrong time for a very long time. You can see why the odds did not look to be in my favor on this one. The story of that race would fill a book. In fact, I've written it (*Peking to Paris: Life and Love on a Short Drive Around Half the World*, Skyhorse Publishing 2013).

It's not a secret that we got to Paris. What isn't widely known is that instead of leaping on the first jumbo jet home, I did a surprising thing. There I was in the City of Lights, emotionally and physically shattered beyond any exhaustion I'd ever experienced, yet somehow unable to conceive of any life other than one that kept me in a car with Bernard. Sorting through problems side by side, all day every day, had turned out to be wondrous, in its peculiar way, filling me with a sense of collaboration I missed at home, where we each had our own ranching chores to tend to. I wanted to feel again that frisson of excitement that coursed through me when we left for China at the start of the P2P in May 2007, to revel once more in waves of intense anticipation as we entered a new country. I'd lived what Sir Richard Burton put so well a century ago when he observed: "The gladdest moment in human life . . . is a departure into unknown lands." The speed of car travel also suited me. Under our own power, we could wander at will, a method of travel with innuendos of early explorers for whom the getting there was as much the point of an expedition as the ultimate discovery they sought.

Like any new addict, I was desperate for more. What to do? I'd just spent thirty-five days on the P2P sunk in a bog of cranky jitters, my shyness challenged by two hundred fifty strangers, my talent for fretting summiting new heights thanks to the old car we had to repair ourselves, not to mention the days sweating through a desert with only the old-fashioned kind of air conditioning—open windows. The logical next step seemed to be to create the antithesis of the P2P: find a place we'd like to explore on our own, devise our own route, and use a rental car. Why a rental? Because then any problems that occurred would be someone else's to fix.

We chose Patagonia and called our journey the Anti-Rally. After driving on our own across every tough road and crossing as many isolated borders as we could find between Chile and Argentina, the next decision needed barely a glance and a nod: time to leave the labor of route-finding and hotel-reserving to the professionals again. We joined a social rally to drive from the southernmost point of India to the foothills of the Himalayas roughly along the seventy-eighth parallel, a route tracking the Great Arc Survey of the first half of the nineteenth century, the one that brought a man named Sir George Everest to fame. (Yes, that Everest.) The only competition on this rally was how many gin and tonics one could imbibe and still fit the key in the ignition the next morning.

And so it's gone ever since, with us exploring the world's out-of-the-way places, sometimes by ourselves, sometimes in the company of others, always by automobile. We stick as much as possible to small or unpaved roads used by locals, getting a view of life around us that would be impossible on a train or flying from place to place. In the years since embarking on the P2P our road trips have, to paraphrase Ibn Battuta, a great Moroccan traveler from the fourteenth century, left me speechless and turned me into a storyteller.

Because roads and locations call to mind differing types of vehicles, we've driven quite a variety, some our own, some rented, all of which I've named. I like being on a first-name basis with cars. It's chummy. It makes me feel like the car and I are in cahoots to get where we're going in one piece and with a minimum of wrong turns. It all started with Roxanne, the 1940 LaSalle that carried us fearlessly forward in the P2P and was named for Alexander the Great's wife Roxana. We've used our own stately Bentley Saloon, dubbed La Serenissima because on our first trip with her we were heading toward Venice. Avis in Santiago de Chile assigned us a Suzuki Grand Vitara I called Sprite for the way she could dodge unobtrusively through border posts despite a remarkable absence of appropriate paperwork. There's even been a private loaner, the new-but-designed-to-look-old Mahindra Commando we drove, or rather tried to drive, on our first time in India. This sad sack of a car, with its soft top, half-doors, and Patton-esque mien, I named Sexy Beast, since it was. Sexy that is. Until it stalled for good, since salt water had been put in its radiator. Not by us of course. Because Bernard, the man I married when I was twenty-eight, with whom I built a successful software company, and next to whom I ran that isolated working hay and cattle ranch in the Colorado Rockies, has a particularly appropriate skill for the road trips we do. He's the world's best auto mechanic, a statement I say based on comparative analytical studies of the first-hand sort, and with not the slightest tinge of partiality from loving the man.

When we choose a place for a road trip, I get to pore over maps and understand profoundly where a country is, what's around it, and what it contains. Mountains here, sea over there, friendly or warring neighbors, borders that are violent no-man's-lands versus borders as carefree as a sophomore on spring break. Like a Peeping Tom, headlines about that country suddenly stare at me from every magazine. Even more bizarre, newscasters can't seem to stop talking about the place I'm going. It's like a media conspiracy. Pick a country and suddenly it's everywhere.

In addition to a country's location, I do my best to learn something special about it when I'm there, something not mentioned in guidebooks and blogs, something that, if I'm lucky, will help me avoid mortifying myself with a *faux pas*. By now I have a number of local habits to draw from, such as which hand to use when greeting someone in India, whether it's okay for me to wander unbidden into a restaurant kitchen in China to see what's cooking, and that it's permissible for my headscarf to reveal my hair in Iran, but not in Afghanistan. Somehow, though, each new country finds a way to drive home how the more I think my tutelage is coming to an end, the less worldly I actually am.

One of the unexpected pleasures of being in a car for hours is that it gives me a chance to observe what's happening outside without intruding. I have puzzled about how important this is to me. I also occasionally berate myself for dodging what I think is the essence of travel, which is to engage fearlessly with the foreign place I'm in. Here's a truth about me and travel: sometimes the strangeness of a country overwhelms me. I like being able to retreat inside the car, to watch and think, without always having to react.

The stories that follow are as fascinating and frightening, humorous and humiliating, poignant, pointed, and engrossing as I felt when I went through them. Because despite my pleasure in being comfortable, doing an easy drive doesn't appeal to me. I'm like a baby bird shoved out of its nest, one minute nestled in cozy familiar security, the next flapping frantically as I tumble headlong into a new world. The whole point of these drives is to thrust me into a continual state of amazement, eyes startled wide open, heart pumping madly at the uncertainty of it all.

Since completing the P2P in July 2007, we've logged tens of thousands of miles seeking out the bad roads, the forsaken border posts, and the odd encounters that transform a trip into an adventure. Bernard has twisted the steering wheel around thousands of hairpin turns through the Andes and wrestled it to stay straight over hundreds of washboarded miles across Tibet. We dodged the Tamil Tigers of Sri Lanka's civil war by cleverly staying south of their DMZ. Red dust from Ethiopian roads became one with our skin and my hair, Bernard not having enough left to worry about. We've rambled through half of South America, skirting mudslides and crossing salt flats, despite knowing from that Mahindra experience that salt and cars don't mix. Or shouldn't. In a fit of madness, we left Istanbul on a nine-thousand-mile drive that brought us to Kolkata forty-five days later, having crossed Iran, all but one of the former Soviet republics, and half of China in the process. And then there's Myanmar, where we started out being driven in someone else's car, had to scrap that plan and complete three hundred fifty miles of the journey by riverboat instead, only to return three years later with our sturdy Land Rover, Brunhilde, a vehicle unfazed by even the most rutted oxcart tracks, to finish the road journey we'd imagined three years before.

I'm a person who's rarely satisfied with the way she is. Don't think of me as whiny or difficult to please, though there have been instances of that. Many, in truth. It's more that I see life as an evolving palette with me as the brush, colors, and canvas. I'm also the painter who's continually recreating the image. This mindset isn't a new thing. I imagine this trait stems partly from being the younger sibling, forever seeing ahead of me the competency of my older sister Vivienne, envious of the benefits conferred her, struggling to change myself so I could do what she did despite our age difference. And I'm sure it has a lot to do with my parents, who believed I could accomplish anything, making sure I had every opportunity to prove them right.

Before each trip my mind glitters with possibilities: Will I get sick? Will I be more patient than last time? Will we break down or get lost because of me? Will we find a place to stay before dark? Will it have a sit-down toilet or will I have to aim into a suspect hole in the ground? Somehow, I never seem to grasp that the lessons of the open road will never be what I imagine, having little to do with guidebooks and maps, and everything to do with the ups and downs of long-distance travel. What happens to me on the road is by turns surprising, embarrassing, and more often than you'd imagine, mundane. It's enough to make me wince, grumble, laugh. And cry.

If it's weird and someone's eating or drinking it, I have to try it, whether it's a pucker-worthy three-day *injera* in Mek'ele, Ethiopia, coca leaves in Potosí, Bolivia, or rancid yak butter tea in Nepal. Without fail, Bernard passes his portion to me in these situations, so his ability in Laos to chow down on a grilled rat that looked exactly like a grilled rat left me justifiably astonished. I have a habit of ignoring my better judgment, signing up for spa treatments in places where the word *spa* doesn't exist in the local language. I've gone rogue on a secret visit to an Akhal-Teke horse training stable in Turkmenistan so I could compare these mythic military steeds to my complacent quarterhorses at home, and I've used shameless flattery hoping to purchase the stiff peaked hat bristling with gold braid off a blushing Uzbeki customs officer even before she'd agreed to let us into the country. I've found myself in a bedroom standing knee to knee with an armed border guard, entered Iran bareheaded, been stoned by Indian village women, and let wild hyenas nibble raw meat from my fingertips.

I've never stopped wanting to see if I can bring myself closer to what I imagine I could be. This is something I began to do consciously as early as seventh grade, when my parents shifted me from public to private school, as they had my sister two years before. Back then, reinvention seemed a necessity if I were to find a way to have any friends at all. Now that I can claim that I am, or should be, grown up, the excitement of reinventing myself has hardened into a habit at its best when I travel. Every trip is like early Christmas, with the old me as the wrapping paper and the new me as the gift.

And so the road beckons. Crossing borders behind the veil of a visa has become my guilty pleasure, an addiction plain and simple. Like any addiction, sometimes I find it hard to believe that all this has happened to me. But I know it's the truth. I was there.

BLASTOFF

PREAMBLE

Suitcases. I can base an entire life's philosophy on my suitcase, both what it contains and what it doesn't. It's emotional baggage in the best sense, weighted with potent symbols of hope, joy and calamity, and, it's no secret, dirty laundry. I know a lot about dirty laundry from life at home: a working cattle and hay ranch in Colorado.

Even the shrewdest Ouija board would never have revealed that I would live on a ranch. And love it. At the end of sixth grade, when we made predictions on who would do what in life, I was a slam dunk to be a translator at the UN, because I already spoke French. No one would have guessed I'd be someone with barbed wire rips in her jeans. We didn't even know what barbed wire was.

For me, a child of suburban New York City, and Bernard, a Frenchman growing up in shorts and clogs in the French Alps, life on the ranch was enchanting and captivating. I was passionate about the flow of nature around me, the flocks of robins fluttering in sagebrush bent under a late blanket of snow, moose calving along our river, my horses cantering through fields of tall mountain grasses undulating in a hot summer breeze. Bernard engrossed himself in manual labor, secretly relishing the black grime under his nails and the torn jeans from fixing tractors and fences, as only a man who has spent his life as a software entrepreneur can do.

But the winters at nine thousand feet in the Rockies are long and quiet. They're also filled with snow removal of an amount and relentlessness that led Bernard, driver of the plows, front loaders, and snowblowers rivaling those used by the department of transportation, close to despair. Leaving the ranch to explore other parts of the world during the winter was a no-brainer, if only our brains had kicked into gear sooner.

Despite my fondness for the ranch, packing my bag for a long trip filled me with a particular rapture that only the perpetually snowed-in can share. Getting my suitcase out of its storage closet let me give my imagination free rein, calling up all sorts of electrifying circumstances that could occur on the trip ahead. As with everything worthwhile, I have a system for this, one that can work for any type of trip and any sort of traveler.

First, I fantasize about the wildest array of activities I might experience. Because I'm a pessimist, I begin with catastrophes. Fixing a flat in the torrential rain of Nuwara Eliya, Sri Lanka? Pack the slicker that rolls to the size of a toothpick. Awaiting rescue on the banks of Myanmar's Chindwin River, our passage boat stranded on a sandbar in the fog? Stash wash-and-wear tops, preferably the kind light enough to rinse in a tiny pot and guaranteed to dry wrinkle-free in twenty minutes. Unable to do even that type of laundry in Ethiopia's desiccated Omo River Valley? Pack the pants I can eat, sleep, and drive in for a week, which won't vary in utilitarian perfection whether it's the first day of a trip or the last.

Having snarled myself into a tense ball of nerves by these reveries of discomfort, I switch gears. That I am bargaining with inanimate objects over matters of pure fantasy does not lessen my enthusiasm. Scrounged tickets for the Moscow Ballet? Nothing can match my flame orange Pashmina for glamour and warmth. Invited for tea by the begum of Jaipur's long-deposed nawab? Add those gold strappy flats and subtract two pair of underwear in exchange. Dancing in the streets during the La Diablada festival in Oruro, Bolivia? Make my one skirt a swirly reversible sort, getting two garments in one.

A week before departure, after I've given my imagination free rein, I start packing. I divvy up everything I could possibly want or use into logical piles: shoes on the floor, rugged wear on the bed next to the pillows, lingerie and swimsuit in the middle, specialty outfits for sports or evening by the foot of the bed. Though it's mildly embarrassing to admit, I then communicate with my clothes. "Which of you really wants to go on this trip? You're not all going to be able to fit in that suitcase, so some of you will have to make the ultimate sacrifice and stay home." I am stern, because I absolutely want to know.

Certain garments call attention to their unsuitability right away. Their wrinkled shapelessness after a few days of bedtop lounging unmasks them as prima donnas that need a breather in a closet every night, a closet I'm unlikely to have because of the tiny guesthouse where we're sleeping. Others are too dull to be worth wearing for two straight months. Then there are those that make the cut purely because I don't want to leave home without them. In my years as the senior female executive in our software services company, I developed a style that was voguish without being enslaved to fashion. When I entered a sales meeting, I wanted my green slingbacks and violet shirt to show I was someone to reckon with, so clients not only would agree to sign a contract, but have fun doing it. Make no mistake: I have earned my title as Countess of Coordinated Separates.

I can't be so ruthless as to whittle down my wardrobe on practicality alone. There has to be some joie de vivre in my bag, a few items that make me smile. One such is a white shirt. I always pack a white shirt or four. Nothing brightens my mood more than daring the day to do its dirty worst by donning a white anything. It makes me feel dashing and bold. It says I have the courage to buy my cake and eat it too, even if the cake squirts raspberry filling down my front.

As the piles shrink, I do trial packings, hefting the result onto my shoulder as a reality check for lugging it up four flights of stairs. In between whittling and hefting, I keep an eye on what Bernard's packing, noting what I can borrow, freeing up room in my bag for something else. Finally, I stuff nooks and crannies with the chargers, adapters, and spare batteries that are de rigueur these days. They will add bulky pounds to my bag, but until every gadget maker in the world agrees to use the same size and shape of plug, I have no other option. Then everything comes flying back out of the suitcase as I discover I've forgotten to wedge in the big first aid kit, a rectangular, football-sized object rattling with spare narcotics accumulated from surgeries of yore, antibiotics galore, even my dead dog's morphine. (Yes, literally, my dog. His name was Toby.)

By the time I'm finished, whatever I think I'll need for weeks of unpredictable events is folded, rolled, heaped, and otherwise squashed within my soft-sided duffel. That includes items that I forget about as soon as they're squirreled away in those handy pockets in which modern suitcases abound, only to rediscover them weeks later, after spending a whole day in a strange city trying to buy the very same object. If I've done a good job, my bag will arrive on the other end looking like a dented blue sausage, and I won't need a Schwarzenegger to carry it to my room each night.

It's perplexing then, that no matter how much thought I put into the packing routine, once I'm away I reach a point where I'm dissatisfied with much of what I've brought with me. This happens without fail, about halfway through every trip, usually when I'm looking at my paltry selection of clothes in the cold, clear light of a second-rate hotel room. If I've packed colorful T-shirts, inevitably my taste abroad shifts to a penchant for cool grays and blacks. If I've overindulged my fetish for white, I rue not having brought something vermilion or aqua.

A few weeks into any trip I don't even have to unpack. Like trout rising to the first hatch, the only clothes I'm interested in wearing have migrated to the top of the suitcase. The rest might as well stay below, bottom feeders, till I get home. Yet even though half my clothes will remain crumpled in my duffel, it reassures me to know those garments are there. Amid all the strange customs, unexpected tastes, and odd sounds that assault me on a trip, my clothes are my toast and marmalade, comfort food when I can't face more chapatis and dal. What I put on in the morning is not just a garment. It's a talisman connecting me to home, a wrinkled, short-sleeved, multi-pocketed remembrance of things past.

Blessings

COCHIN, INDIA, 2009

On the first day of any long road trip I'm full of bustle and nerves. The nerves part comes from the unknowability of the future. It clamps me in a vise, squeezing the breath out of me like my seat belt when Bernard slams on the brakes to avoid hitting a wobbly rickshaw. That's why I need the bustle part. The busier I am, the more capable I feel and the less I dwell on my anguish about being able to manage what's coming. My first-day emotions are a toxic mix, one that leaves me walking slightly hunched, so ready am I to apologize for things that haven't yet happened. This conflicted approach to life on the road has been part of me ever since I can remember.

I have character traits, lovable flaws as I like to call them, with which I have made my peace. There's my expectation that I'm right, which can be annoying, but sometimes results in such brilliant insights that I can coast on the outcome for days, despite otherwise egregious behavior. In my twenties and thirties, I could turn from bright laughing companion to grim taciturn drudge without provocation. Thankfully, this was revealed as not a personality quirk at all, but a symptom of hypoglycemia, brought about by not eating frequently enough. Now, when I say to Bernard, "I have to eat soon," he pays attention, on pain of suffering the joys of driving next to an evil changeling for hours.

I try but generally fail to live by the dicta of Lao Tzu, the sixth century contemporary of Confucius. Lao Tzu is reputed by some to be the author of the *Tao Te Ching*, from which we derive phrases like "create nothingness" and "act spontaneously." I confess that for most of my life I've found comfort in the opposite mantra: "create somethingness" and "act with total premeditation." Still, if I wanted to have one phrase tattooed on my body, next to those three little stars which came to live on my right shoulder thanks to a talented Sunset Boulevard inker, it would be Lao Tzu's definition of travel: "A good traveler has no fixed plans and is not intent on arriving."

My need to envision what I will be doing or feeling in the coming weeks does not seem to serve a useful purpose, nor can it be excused as physical weakness. Bernard says to me, "Stop worrying. It's an application of energy that accomplishes nothing." He's right, in a way Lao Tzu would applaud. But that doesn't matter. The need to place myself in the future is like quicksand. The moment I set foot on terrain called "What this trip will be like," I'm sucked into the swamp of nervous uncertainty. Though I've traveled overseas yearly since I was in diapers, those trips were all of the "arrive, settle in, enjoy the immediate surroundings" sort. I didn't have experience with traveling that calls for daily newness, let alone any aptitude for managing daily uncertainties. On early road trips this left me feeling helpless, but not anymore. As my creative powers have matured with experience, I've grown adept at conjuring wonderful possibilities, each further divorced from reality than the next. Nevertheless, thanks to tens of thousands of road miles, I now have experienced a wealth of real discomforts and disappointments to draw from to stoke my nerves. And what's to stop me? On a road trip in a foreign land, anything is possible.

That I tend to expect the worst is a known trap, hence my ability to deploy bustle, or as my mother would say, "Keeping busy, my darling."

I have many useful things to do on Day One of a road trip, like polishing fenders, and checking that toilet paper is handy somewhere in our car's back seat. Inevitably there's tension in the air. Though I feign nonchalance, the truth is I'm on edge, an edge that's as comforting as sitting on a knife.

I remember one such Day One as if it were yesterday. Recently upright after a thirty-six-hour skirmish with Delhi belly, I wobble across a parking lot in Kochi, India, my sandals leaving size-eight imprints in the melting tarmac. It's a steaming January morning. We are embarking on a rally through India, starting near the southern tip of the continent and ending in the foothills of the Himalayas. We're not alone on this trip, nor are we competing for anything other than daily bragging rights. We're with a small, sociable group of people who will be driving a route reconnoitered and defined for all of us by the rally's organizer. The unspoken purpose of this drive is to regale one another with the day's exploits over one or more suitably refreshing cocktails. Sharing the trip with only eight other couples also is manageable for me, far removed from the two hundred fifty strangers in one hundred twenty-five classic cars with whom we undertook the P2P route two years earlier, strangers who turned out to be so clubby, clannish, and cliquish it gave new meaning to the word "outcast."

However, soon we will leave the safe haven of the parking lot where everything is stationary for the cacophonous, jam-packed roads of India. In that outer world, thousands of things will be moving at once, in all directions and all within inches of each other—and therefore of us. Bernard and I are driving a borrowed Mahindra Jeep. It's a black, tough-looking ride designed to mimic a World War II army vehicle. On the side of the hood "Commander" is scrawled in florid gold script. This seems far too seafaring a name, especially on a drive that will have us bisecting the subcontinent along its seventy-eighth parallel, in other words nowhere close to the sea. I dub our car Sexy Beast.

During the years we were building our software company, vacation was a taboo word. This did not go over well with me. I'm a creative sort and my mind needs breaks. Bernard is the opposite. He's Mr. Logic, and his mind just keeps plugging along at the task at hand. His ability to focus was a trait I admired, while his refusal to leave the office was something I bitterly resented, leading to stern words (his) and tears (mine). Despite the struggle I chose to be loyal to him (meaning us) and the cause of business growth (and continued marriage), though I raged silently that my needs could be subverted to an inanimate entity called "the company."

When we did start vacationing, we opted for vigorous trips. Intent on shaking out the stress of sitting at computers and straining to meet tight deadlines, on one trip we rode horses for weeks in the Kenya bush, on another we trekked to the base camp of Kangchenjunga, one of the highest peaks in the Himalayas. Don't think of us gallivanting about, though. Our vacations were as sparse as hairs on a mangy Indian dog. It was only after we sold our company that we could indulge in yearly long trips. By then, our life on the ranch was so active that we relished the idea of sitting. Because, after all, if one is in a car all day that's what one is doing, even if in a vigorous way.

For India, we toyed with shipping over Roxanne, our trusty 1940 GM LaSalle who performed so valiantly on the P2P. There were problems with that idea, though. For one, India is a sizzling country, even during its cool periods. Driving Roxanne, who loves to overheat, seemed destined to give us vehicular hyperthermia. More to the point, India is a right-hand drive country. Roxanne's steering wheel was on the left, as it should be for an American-made car. "I can stick my head out the window and tell you when it's safe to pass," I offered Bernard as we mulled this over. He stared at me with that look of puzzlement and irritation that sets my teeth on edge. It conveyed with one arching of an eyebrow that, "I know I saw your mouth move, but I don't have a clue what you just said nor why you bothered to say it." But then, Bernard had driven around the world years before he met me and he knew things I didn't, in this case, that Indian drivers are famous for cutting it close. Combine that with my well-known imprecision in gauging the speed of oncoming traffic and I could just hear myself: "Go," I'd shout. "No. Wait. Okay, go now. Now! No. *Stop.* Oh no! Go back. *Go back!*" The prospect of my head being squashed like a Halloween pumpkin didn't appeal to me. I hoped it appealed even less to Bernard.

Thanks to the kindness of strangers, the Mahindra has been put at our disposal, a valiant surrogate for our missing favorite. Little do we know what shambles Sexy Beast's bold and shiny exterior hides. At the outset, in that gooey parking lot, we were impressed. True to its origins, the Mahindra makes do with a modest few dials on the instrument panel, sufficient to tell us our speed and how much fuel we have. The rest of the dashboard is a bleak stretch of cracked black vinyl. Though mechanics have installed seat belts, there are no airbags, no glove compartment. Superficially it appears to be a great car to drive, its doorless frame saying, "I'm practical, but I'm fun, too." As for street cred, everything about Sexy Beast says, "Don't mess with me."

Now, on the morning of, I turn with solemn intent to my personal rites of the road. It's as close to a religious experience as an atheist like me can get, and I pursue it with the same intensity of tradition as I imagine a priest following the liturgy. At the car, I put on my cap and sunglasses, even if it's predawn or cloudy. Wearing these two items is the only way for me to be sure I haven't left them somewhere. Next, I plug the GPS into both the antenna lead and the 12-volt charger. It's like tying your dog to a post when you go into a store, an essential bit of tethering that keeps important things in place till you return. Once this crucial instrument for navigation is attached to the car, I don't have to worry about it getting into places it shouldn't.

Since Sexy Beast is doorless, I set my maps and guidebook in the gap separating passenger and driver seats, map folded back to reveal our route, guidebook flagged to wherever we are going on this particular day. Since I began driving in pre-GPS days, the feel of paper in my hands is the ultimate reassurance. Next, the bottle of purified water gets snugged between the map and the seat. Sexy Beast is a WWII knock-off and cup holders didn't exist during WWII, an era when quenching thirst while in a car meant taking a nip of whisky from that flask in your back pocket. My day pack crammed with almonds, raisins, and mini-packs of lemon and cashew cookies gets lodged in the rear, within an arm's length of my seat. Nothing gives me courage so much as having food handy. I store extra water bottles behind my seat, wedge my purse where it can't easily be snatched by an enterprising pedestrian, and put my camera on top of the food for hasty grabbing when something photogenic appears.

Helping to soothe my nerves is the fact that yesterday we were blessed in a proper *puja*. This Hindu ceremony of worship ranges from simple private daily prayers to elaborate rites filled with bowing, chanting, and symbolic offerings of flowers, incense, and fruit. As with many religious rituals, a ceremonial puja is frequently done in a temple. Ours took place on a humid late afternoon under a dull gray sky. In a parking lot.

Inside our semicircle of vehicles was a Brahmin priest, forty-ish, with a lush black beard. His skin a deep reddish-brown that reminded me of old sepia photos and, despite the very public location, was mostly naked, the upper half of his body decorated by a simple strand of black beads around his neck, a short white cotton *dhoti* keeping his midsection decent. The beads glistened from sweat dripping from a fold of neck fat, evidence that life as a priest was more lavish than I'd imagined. Entranced with the spiritual mission of ensuring our safety in the weeks ahead, he delicately placed the following in front of each car: a tiny clay bowl of salt, one hairy brown coconut, and a small brass brazier in which coals of incense burned an ashy red. Tenderly he lodged a pale yellow lime under each front tire, then knotted a garland of marigolds to the front bumper. This done, he gathered his dhoti around his loins and slowly sank to the ground, coming to rest cross-legged, his buttocks support by a thick slab of wood, belly flab sagging gently toward the tarmac. Arrayed within easy reach were brass spoons, saucers holding sacred water, two tiny clay salt bowls for his personal use, a two-foot tall ornate brass incense burner, one tin tureen holding a bunch of mottled bananas, grapes, and peeled clementines, another tureen holding rice, raisins, and almonds, and some large banana leaves heaped with mounds of pink, yellow, and orange petals.

Eyes closed, thick black lashes that I would have killed for curling against his cheeks, he pressed his palms together and raised them to his forehead and his heart in a gesture of humility. He dipped his fingertips in water, flicked droplets in all directions, delicately lofted a pinch of marigold petals in the air. They fluttered to the ground like pastel-hued butterflies. Palm up, his right hand gestured toward the bowls of fruit and rice, then he pinched up some salt and flicked it onto the pavement.

I was thirsty and for a moment wondered whether, with his eyes closed, he would notice if I grabbed some of those clementine slices for myself. But I was quickly lulled, transfixed. As his low humming mingled with the buzz of traffic, the sweet incense smoke seemed to stick in the sultry air, clothing me like a second skin. The priest chanted, nodded, and flung, banishing my thirst, calming my eager excitement until I was leaning against our car in drowsy silence.

After forty-five minutes, our parking lot priest arose. I was so hypnotized my limbs felt like heavy ropes, the kind used to attach ferries to the dock, with equally lax articulation. With the priest advancing I marshalled every Pilates and Zumba command I could remember to get my legs moving. Carrying the container of water that was now properly sanctified, along with a bowl of equally blessed yellow turmeric paste, he approached our car, his attendant tagging along with a woven grass basket full of more candy-colored petals. Moistening his fingers in the blessed liquid, he sprinkled droplets on the hood, flung petals over the roof and thumbed a smear of turmeric paste on the windshield. A facial tic of annoyance made my cheek muscles jump when the assistant stopped me from wiping the yellow smears off. He couldn't know I'd followed my own karmic ritual that morning, Windex-ing bug bodies off the windshield. Now it was smudged again. Not a good sign.

Drive, She Said

When the possibility arose of driving those 7,800 miles on P2P, I would like to say I leapt at the chance. I did not. I shuffled. I lagged. I felt as unsuited for the mission ahead as a tightrope walker with vertigo. Only one thing kept me from quitting: shame. My fear of the humiliation from giving up before ever getting going was greater than my anxiety about what lay ahead.

It's a shame that during the angst of P2P preparation and its ensuing travails my mind deserted me so thoroughly that I did not recall I'd already done a distance drive, albeit one of modest length. That honor goes to Morocco in 2004. Compared to our months-long, thousands-of-miles drives after the P2P, our five days in Morocco were a jaunt, a soupçon of an excursion, not a journey. At the time, I didn't realize that Bernard and I were doing a practice run for things to come. We just wanted to see a broad cross section of the country at our own pace. Even on so short a trip, and with no expectation of applying our experience to something more rigorous in the future, we each fell into what later became our standard roles: Bernard dealt with all things car, from driving to mechanics. I handled the GPS, map, and snacks.

Early in our short road trip, we arrived at a lodge in Derkaoua, twenty miles or so from the edge of the Sahara, the desert which forms Morocco's southern border. The surroundings were as you would expect for the world's largest desert—sandy, barren, parched, the air so hot and dry I thought the skin inside my nostrils would crack with each breath.

Stopping only long enough to check in and leave our bags, we continued along a sand track to a spot known to offer camel treks into the dunes. It was easy to tell which way to go. Someone thoughtful, or tired of searching for lost travelers, had lined the way with whitewashed cobbles. I thought they were picturesque, a bright ellipsis in the sandy forever. I had no inkling of how thankful I would be for their existence a few hours later.

Arriving at the desert trek shack, we pulled in facing a row of parked camels. "Tall beasts," I said to Bernard, as usual compelled to state the obvious. "Cute lips." We approached the supine camels, giving several a broad and wary circle of inspection in case they felt compelled to lurch to their feet. I noticed a number were ribby or scarred. "No skinny ones," I said, feeling that making an undernourished animal work for my pleasure was unfair.

Eventually we found two which were appealingly sturdy and obedient-looking, both lying with gangly legs tucked and folded out of the way Origami-fashion, their heads swiveling curiously on necks like limp celery. A youth squatted lethargically mid-dune above the camels. I assumed he was associated with them, a slim small bedouin of the region's Sahrawi tribe, left to mind the goods while the grown-ups tended to more serious matters, like sipping tea in the shade.

"These two, please," I said, sweeping my arm from him to the two plumpest camels in the row, expecting him then to shuffle over to the big guys with our request.

Looks, as I am continually reminded when traveling, are deceiving. With business on offer, the young man got his legs under him more swiftly than I expected the camels would, scrambling up and handing each of us a red and white checked *keffiyeh* headscarf to wrap around head and mouth. "I am Kamal. *I* will be your guide," he announced, his white *burnous* framing full smiling lips, a pointed chin, and the sort of arched, symmetrical black brows that my cosmetician has never been able to create for me.

"Moustache," he said to Bernard, because he has a big, bristly one. "This is your camel. You get on like this." He held out the mounting stirrup for Bernard to use as a step up, then disconnected it, leaving me to wonder how we were expected to get off.

"Gazelle," he said to me, as I stood in front of my camel admiring the beast's long lashes. Later, when I'd been called Gazelle multiple times, I understood it was merely a multi-national moniker for women used by all guides in Morocco, who find Western names unpronounceable and easy to forget. At the moment though, I was thrilled with my nickname, which I took as flattery of my legs. The boy's gratuity went up immediately. "Do not stand there. He may spit on you. Come around here," he said, luring me with my own personal mounting stirrup.

Kamal secured a lead line to each camel's nose ring. They both crawked out a rough, low groan, like the sound of a falling redwood as its ancient fibers are slowly rent apart. It was a sound of distress, of protest, of resignation. I was fully inclined to lift my voice in sympathy with theirs. Yet the sun shone, the breeze frisked, we were snug in our saddles, ready for our single-humped ships of the desert to carry us forth.

It took next to no time for the camels to bear us beyond the first dunes, after which no sign of civilization was visible. It was just the swaying camels, endless waves of blonde sand, and the enterprising Kamal leading the way. Like all camels, mine preferred to walk, but with legs as long as I am tall we made remarkable progress, even at his don't-rush-me pace. My camel and I were both well-equipped to battle the desert sun. He had boney eyebrow protrusions to shield his eyes from the glare. I had my Ray-Bans. He had self-closing nostrils to keep out blowing sand. I had my keffiyeh. He had thick leathery patches on his knees to prevent sand burns when kneeling. I had on special underwear guaranteed to prevent monkey-butt, scourge of all riders.

It was hot inside my keffiyeh, so when the breeze turned strong enough to whip the ends out of their securing knot, I didn't mind. I dislike being sweaty, and with the keffiyeh pulled up over my nose to keep out the fine Sahara sand, I was becoming not only uncomfortably damp but claustrophobic. Unlike our guide, the last time I'd had my head swaddled, I'd been a baby.

With images of my keffiyeh flying off and spooking my camel into a lunging gallop of the sort destined to make me more seasick than a cross-channel ferry bucking surging seas, I struggled to retie the scarf ends into a windproof knot. The wind would have none of it, untying each knot quicker than Houdini doing an underwater trick. It was pleasant, though, to have the cooling effect of this now stiff wind, and I enjoyed it. That is, up until the moment when Kamal insisted, "Look!" He stood on the crest of a dune, arm outstretched and pointing, white robes whipping around his legs, a miniature Sherif Ali in my personal version of *Lawrence of Arabia*. I expected to see more dunes, or better, a camel train making its regal way toward us. I didn't. I saw a horizon obscured by an undulating wall, battle-ship gray, livid in its turmoil of wind and sand. It spanned the sky and moved so swiftly it was as if a massive hand behind it was impelling it toward us.

"Run," shouted Kamal, his voice small and seeming far away. With a sandstorm looming I had some concerns, though none of them involved my camel. He had two rows of eyelashes, plus the windshield wiper effect of a third eyelid which could move left to right. If any of us was equipped to weather this storm, it was he. I only had my fists to wipe sand out of my eyes, and right then both hands were occupied clinging to the saddle horn as we joggled across the dunes at such alarming speed that after my first glance down I dared not check the distance of a possible fall again.

We got back in half the time it had taken us to venture into the dune-scape. By then, the ashen wall had covered half the distance it needed to reach us. I could distinguish roiling clouds of sand swirling within. The entire hulking mass seemed to gain in density and scope as it heaved down upon us. Camel touts sprinted after flying saddle pads, their feet seeming to skim above the surface of shifting sand. Tourists dithered about whether the torture of sitting out a sandstorm in the open would be worth the brag-ging rights afterward. Camels kneeled in the sand, blinking those wind-shield wiper eyelids and chewing their cud, in their element. Bernard and I slithered off the backs of our camels, not even noticing the absence of that helpful stirrup. I wished my beast luck, stuffed enough bills in Kamal's hand to cover our fee, and dashed to the car, where I jumped into the passenger seat and slammed the door. Safe. Or so I thought.

We had barely reached the track with the white-washed rocks when the sandstorm enveloped us like Dracula swirling his cloak, blotting out the sun and turning the smiling day into a dark, evil, yellow-gray dusk. Howling as if populated by tormented souls from the underworld, the storm invaded the car through every crack and crevice. It coated the dashboard, colonized my hair like an epidemic of nits, and in an instant brought home to me the vanity of wearing contact lenses. I was terrified, as my rankly perspiring armpits attested. Pulling my shirt tails over my mouth I yelled at Bernard, "What are we going to do?"

In our many road trips since Morocco, I've learned if I have a solution in mind I should flat out say it, because Bernard is literal and confident when compared to my premonitory worrying. In this case, I longed to do what everyone else had done: sit in their cars at the camel rental agency, waiting things out. We were the only ones to leave, and now the road ahead and behind was covered with shifting sand. What I wanted to insist was, "Let's hunker down right here, where we'll be found after the storm," leaving implied my unsportsmanlike expectation of "Let's not get stuck somewhere in the miles of empty sandscape between here and our lodge." But I didn't want to hurt Bernard's feelings by suggesting lack of confidence, so I left it to him, thinking with his gallantry he'd intuit what I wanted. Stupid me.

Bernard being Bernard, he replied, "Let's drive!"

For a minute, he pursued that exercise by pressing his nose to the windshield. Too soon he shouted, "I have to open the window. I can't see."

"No, no! Are you crazy? That'll let all the sand in." But then, of course, the sand already was in.

"It's the only way I can find the markers. We have to keep moving. If we stop, that's it!" He ratcheted down the window, stuck his head into the blowing sand, ducked back in as he rammed the window shut. Neither of us spoke. There was too much sand whirling in the car to risk opening our mouths.

Bernard inched us forward, white marker to white marker, for what seemed like hours as the sandstorm shrieked and moaned around us. My body didn't know what to do with itself. The upper part of me sweated, my feet turned to ice, and my mouth outdid the Sahara in dryness. Yet I kept my terror to myself. Bernard was so obviously delighted I didn't want to dampen his enthusiasm. Besides, I knew what awaited us if we stopped, and it wasn't a chilled gin and tonic. The discomfort of slowly suffocating as sand filled my nose and mouth needed no elaboration.

It took us four times as long to get back to the auberge as it had to reach the camels that afternoon. When the vague outline of our lodge appeared in the gloom, I nearly peed myself in relief. We scurried, bent double, into a hotel dining room filled with a brown haze of swirling sand, mini-dunes already shifting on the floor. The owner, being French, brought up bottles of wine, offering each guest a glass of gritty Beaujolais. Though the generator that might have provided fresh air would have benefited from his attention, I couldn't quibble. The calming effect of the alcohol was sufficient proof he had his priorities straight. Thus soothed, and having eaten a cold snack of bread and goat cheese, we went to our sandy beds. Breathing in shallow pants to minimize sand in lungs, I drifted to sleep pretending I was spending the night on a tropical beach. Minus the rum punch. And the waves.

Like a migrating camel, the sandstorm moved on in its own time. By next morning it was so gone it was as if it never existed. If I hadn't been picking sand out of my ears since waking I would have doubted my sanity. The sky, scoured to a spotless bright blue, seemed to shrug its shoulders as if to say, "Sandstorm? What sandstorm?"

Solutions

KERALA, INDIA, 2009

Back in the Cochin parking lot, everything that can be is stashed, stowed, and otherwise secured. Thinking back to Morocco, I find no excuse to offer in favor of staying put. I agree to leave. Besides, we're blessed. Why should my future abound with anything other than good karma?

Within two hours, Beast's flaws appear. In the category of unpleasant but not a showstopper, we discover that the word *hushed* is not one of Beast's attractions. What with being open to the elements and no sound-proofing under the hood, the clamor of the engine envelops me in a mind-numbing din. Top that with a garnish of continuous honking and shouting in the streets, and it's like three orchestras playing John Cage, Ligeti, and George Crumb over each other, at full blast. By the time we arrive at our hotel after the first day's drive, my head is throbbing.

Next morning, I climb into Sexy Beast, my box of French earplugs in hand. I've relied on them for years to guarantee slumber in hotel rooms with cardboard walls, tissue paper windows, and a wedding party of hundreds in the street below. Those little balls of pink wax swathed in a thin robe of cotton, looking all virginal, fill me with hope. Surely they will muffle Beast's roar. When Bernard turns on the engine, I squash the plugs snugly into my ears and urge a pair on Bernard, too. I don't have much hope he'll use them.

Bernard seems to believe use of any lotion or palliative unmanly. At the ranch, it took years before he began using hearing protection muffs around loud machinery, which is why I now talk a little louder than I used to. In terms of skin care, it's nigh hopeless. We've lived at seven thousand to nine thousand feet our entire married life, so the sunscreen conversation is not new. It is, though, brief.

Me: "I'm putting sunscreen on. Do you want some?"

Him: "What did you say?"

On road trips Bernard's rationale as he swats away my tube of SPF 100 Neutrogena is, "I'll be inside the car all day."

"Yes," I reply, sarcasm leaking through the patience I don't feel. "But the sun can penetrate the windshield, which is why you wear sunglasses. Right?"

Bernard's only concession to the rigors of the road is to wear driving gloves, those fingerless soft leather mitts that keep sweaty palms from slipping off the steering wheel. Still, he's more than ten years my senior and I want to be sure he retains what hearing he has left. I shake the two plugs at him as if they were lucky dice. The charm works. He takes them. We head out the hotel driveway and I give Bernard the first direction of the day: "Turn left at the corner."

"What?" he says.

"Turn left at the corner," I say louder.

"Speak up!" he shouts.

"I am!" I shout back.

"What?"

The odd thing about earplugs is that, inside my muffled world, I sound as clear and loud as a cow bell. That's not the case outside my plugged ears, where trying to convey driving directions is an exercise in futility. By the end of the day, my throat is raw from constant yelling.

When I remove the balls from my ears, they are, predictably, as dirty as the rest of me. Ordinarily I would throw them out, but my one box is meant to last me for an entire trip's worth of nights. I didn't anticipate having to use them during the day as well. With some reluctance and much disgust, I pinch the balls into filthy squares and replace them in their box. Bernard hands me his, rolled into perfect, if grimy, globes to distinguish them from mine. Putting grime-crusted hands into the snack sack is fine, but it seems neither of us wants to squash the other's used plugs in our ears.

Through Days 3 and 4 we wear earplugs, shouting until we're hoarse and frustrated. By Day 5, we accept it is our lot to have our hearing permanently damaged on this trip. I return the earplug box to my suitcase. By then I am further deflated by the knowledge that driving in a car designed to blow out my ear drums is the least of our problems. I have discovered that Sexy Beast being open to the elements is not an unadulterated pleasure. At first it strikes us as dandy. We get the benefit of every breeze. We hop in and out with a jaunty sense of daring-do, like Patton inspecting the troops of his Third Army. The drawback is that everything wafting on that breeze settles on us. We notice this at the end of Day 1 when we arrive at our night's hotel. Relieved to have navigated our first encounter with Indian city traffic without creating an international incident, we unbuckle our seat belts and heave ourselves outside. My sweaty back and thighs are so glued to Beast's suffocating vinyl that it feels my skin is being ripped off as my legs struggle to part company with the seat.

Meeting Bernard around the back of the car to get our bags, I notice a black stripe emblazoned across the front of his shirt, like a pageant banner in mourning. "How'd you get that?" I ask, jabbing at his chest. He peers down at his shirt, rubs the charcoal stripe, which smudges it worse. Declaring he'll take my insult and raise me one, he says, "You've got one, too," and jabs me back. It dawns on us that this is a souvenir from the seat-belt strap that's cinched us in our seats for the past seven hours. If there's that much dirt in the belts, it's unsettling to imagine what must be residing on my exposed skin, my clothes, my hair.

The hotel manager, as disturbed by our dirty appearance as we are, volunteers one of his staff to clean our car. That he doesn't volunteer another to hose us down before entering his establishment is vaguely disappointing. We're the last to arrive, a point driven home by the waves of laughter undulating from the open terrace.

At the start of every drive, I still battle the fragile ego that undertook the P2P; although this isn't a competition, there's still an "us" and "them" thing I can't seem to shake. Have we left early enough? Have I packed the right clothes? How could others dispense with border formalities faster than we? There's even an "us" versus "us" element, such as: why is Bernard always able to be so much more cheerful than me? This first evening I suppress my qualms by blaming it on the one who can't fight back—Beast—and attribute our late arrival to the car's overall sluggishness, rather than any particular failing on our part or success on anyone else's.

Throughout the evening, we eye the young car cleaner with his small bucket and meager rag, scrubbing, rinsing, and changing the grimy water over and over again. He's still at it when we turn in for the night. By morning, Sexy Beast is cleaner than he's ever been in his hard life. By midday, when we stop for fuel, the black stripes are back. And for the stretch of days in which we are burdened by Beast, they become our personal banners of foolhardiness. Oh, to be back in Roxanne, a car with doors, with windows that close. A car we know inside out, which has faithfully transported us over some of the toughest roads we've ever driven.

Noise and dirt are mere distractions in light of Beast's third liability, which is also revealed within hours of our departure on the first morning of the road trip. The cool breeze blowing through the open car in the early hours of the day lulls us into believing that as the day heats up we'll have a pleasantly refreshing time of it. By midday, Beast is hotter than a pizza oven. This is because he is painted black, a bad color to be when the sun beats ceaselessly from its perch in a cloudless sky. It is also because Beast lacks anything but the most rudimentary firewall between the engine bay and the car interior. Two hours into a day's drive and the floorboards are sizzling. As their temperature climbs, my ankles balloon like a startled blowfish. To cool them, I alternate squeezing my knees to my chest so I can prop my feet on the dashboard eighteen inches in front of me and hanging my feet through the space where the door should be, hoping they won't be amputated by a truck cutting it close.

The general discomfort of driving in Sexy Beast is something I have to put up with. It's disagreeable but not dreadful. What is dreadful is that Beast was decidedly neglected in his early life. If there were an Association for the Prevention of Cruelty to Cars, I would have no choice but to report Beast's owners for abuse, and demand they never be allowed to own a car again.

The full extent of Beast's failings would have been apparent to anyone who knows cars and who cared to spend an hour checking this one over. That would include us. Except on this trip, we've decided to change our customary MO. Instead of at least eyeballing every last item as we did before the P2P, we have been uncharacteristically karmic. This is India, after all, even though Bernard's acquaintance with the lotus position ended as a one-year-old, when he could still cross his legs. Though we're deeply unsettled when we first meet Sexy Beast a day before departure, we suppress our premonitions in the face of protestations from the car's mechanics. "Yes, sir, the car she has been gone over thoroughly, sir. Yes, we have checked her exceptionally for you. She is in fighting trim!" We want to believe them, because on this trip we are relaxed and happy-go-lucky. Or trying to be. And of course there's the *puja*, meant to cure any lingering maladies of the vehicular sort.

That they refer to Beast as "she" should have been a clue to her condition, since even today there are articles every month about the deplorable treatment of women in India. If there's one incontrovertible sign that no one has given much thought to how Beast will survive traversing 3,500 miles of India, it's the tires. Yet the mechanics who prepared Sexy Beast look at us in astonishment when we point out that Beast's tires are as slick as old gums awaiting new dentures.

"Do not worry, sir," one mechanic says. "In India, these are considered very good tires."

"I see," Bernard replies, startled nearly speechless. "Pardon me if this is not so, but I would have thought even in India these tires would not be used if one could help it."

"Unless perhaps as a playground swing," I can't help but chime in.

"Actually, sir, we recently drove over fifteen thousand kilometers in a different car and your tires look much better than the ones we had."

"Really? And did you get any flat tires?"

"Oh yes, sir. We had a flat tire nearly every other day. But we never needed new tires."

Which is how we notice that an essential bit of equipment is missing from Beast's modest toolkit: a serviceable jack. In a land where the retread rules, jacks should be a popular item, available anywhere. The only jack we can find must have been meant for one of the millions of Indian vehicles that look like a Mini Cooper made out of cardboard. It is so short, it barely raises Sexy Beast a few inches. Two blocks of wood under the jack solve that problem, boosting the jack like a short lecturer at a high podium. Now we are equipped not just for fixing a flat, but also for starting a campfire. My relief knows no bounds.

Two days in and we arrive at our hotel, a dashed line of gasoline streaking the road behind us. Lots of Indians smoke and the street is their ashtray. Being trailed by gasoline could lead to a confluence of events with potentially fiery results. Repairing the hole in Beast's fuel tank strikes us as not only prudent, but the new top of the list. The three Indian rally mechanics agree, then vanish for their eagerly anticipated night on the town.

Morning dawns sunny and warm, a perfect day for car repairs. Everyone else leaves by eight o'clock. We wait. We pace. We phone, leave a message, wait some more. The mechanics drag in around ten o'clock, shirttails loose, eyes bleary, clearly on the wrong side of some dedicated carousing. They begin draining the tank. Fuel slowly fills a gallon bucket, dripping in slow plops like a metronome with a low battery. The full bucket is hauled, sploshing, up a hill behind our hotel, where it is dumped somewhere top secret—probably the local water supply.

Once the gas tank is emptied and removed, the mechanics squeeze a special sealant from a tiny tube onto the offending hole. The tube's instructions, the size of flea footprints, say give it four hours to dry. But the call of the road is strong, as is the need to arrive at the evening's camp before dark. Once night falls, smoke from village fires lays a dense aromatic fog over the land. At this witching hour, Indian villagers emerge to use the roads as their pathway, moving animals and themselves down the middle in perfect obscurity. Driving in India at night is an idea only for the desperate or the demented. As yet, we are neither.

Unsinkable

CHINDWIN RIVER, MYANMAR, 2012

Having briefly straddled the India-Myanmar border from Nagaland in 2009, we'd felt homesick for Myanmar ever since, if such were possible given we'd never been there. But sanctions and the predations of the military regime precluded our planning a trip. But by the first quarter of 2012, pro-democracy fighter Aung San Suu Kyi had been released from house arrest. Then–Secretary of State Hillary Clinton had visited the country, the first such foray since 1955, even proposing the potential for an exchange of ambassadors. Myanmar was beginning to open and we arrived shortly after Clinton left.

Intent, as always, on reaching parts of a country that tourists wouldn't, we were heading into the northeast sector by car, a region of nearly impassable roads where foreigners had only recently been permitted to go. This time we would be driven, as in someone other than Bernard would handle the steering and other car essentials while we sat in the back seat. I don't know which of us was more fussed about this, Bernard, whose body fairly twitches when he has to let someone else do the driving, or me, who would have to sit next to him while he fidgeted. I did not think that directing him to look at the scenery would suffice and I was concerned that absent our usual dialogue of directions, we might run out of things to say. Understand that letting ourselves be driven had nothing to do with preference and everything to do with the still-stringent constraints placed on foreigners, especially those who wished to travel away from tourist sites.

So why was I now sitting on this slender, overcrowded barque, shivering uncontrollably, at eye level with the dark Chindwin River? Contemplating this question, I pressed myself against Bernard, hands jammed between my knees, my T-shirt no protection from the pre-dawn chill. Early in our travels, when I was not adept at managing physical uncertainty, such discomfort would have vexed me. In the years we've been on the road, I've learned a few things. For one, I know if I wait long enough, the sun will rise and I'll warm up. Better yet, I can shrug Bernard's arm around me and cuddle next to him for warmth. Around me, eighty Burmese villagers more physically modest than me—and better prepared—flung towels and spare *longyis* (sarongs) over themselves for warmth. So thick was the unexpected fog that, even had it been daylight, we could not have seen the nearby shore.

On the prow, a thin youth sounded the placid water with a long bamboo pole. Left and right he probed, seeking viable channels among submerged sandbanks, transmitting his findings by hand signal to the captain behind him.

Two hours into our journey, the boat shuddered to a halt. "I don't think this is the usual stop to pick someone up," Bernard said.

"I know. Too abrupt. Plus," I peered into the gloom, "no one's moving. And we seem to be still in midstream."

As we sat in the dark, the sound of the engine straining in reverse reverberated off the invisible banks. And then there was a loud pop.

Settling back on the hard bench, I noticed our guide, Saw, squatting on the deck next to me. "Stuck," he said, not a man to waste words. "Prop shaft broken. But? No problem. New boat will come."

How a new boat would hear we needed help was a mystery. This was remote western Myanmar. That no one had a cell phone was irrelevant. There was no service anyway. I know. I tried.

Usually I am one to take matters in my own hands, regardless of whether it's helpful, but in this case, I decided to mimic the villagers. They weren't making a fuss. Neither would I.

Being on the river wasn't our plan when we decided to get off the beaten path in Myanmar. We were supposed to do a car expedition, exploring the untraveled back roads of northwest Sagaing Region by day, staying near the Chindwin each night. This was our sixth extended road trip. I was a seasoned hand. I'd experienced what Rumi meant when he said, "Travel brings power and love back into your life." I knew that every trip, no matter how it varied from my still incorrigible imaginings, would yield something of value, even if months later.

Our first day's drive went from Monywa to the former British teak depot of Kalewa. On the map it looked simple, a dirt road used mainly by a dozen shared taxis, a few buses, and local oxcarts, crossing a ripple of high ridges along the eastern perimeter of Alaungdaw Kathapa National Park.

"This should take five to six hours, right?" I asked Saw.

"Twelve," he grunted, chewing the packet of *kun-ya* (areca nut, tobacco, and slaked lime wrapped in betel leaf) stuffed in his cheek and sending a stream of red spittle out the window.

"It's barely a hundred miles. How is that possible?"

"Possible," said Saw.

Twelve hours later, after nursing the van's geriatric suspension through bucket-sized potholes, inching over steep hills, and eating the dust of those taxis, we reached Kalewa. The place was bustling with people shopping at stalls packed with housewares and produce, customers at ease in teashops, parents shepherding children home from school.

Our sky-blue concrete guesthouse stood high above the river, now twenty feet lower than during the summer rainy season. Within minutes of arriving we were shown rooms and offered our pick. Mindful of the layer of dust coating our skin, we chose one with its own bath trough, the last such luxury on the Chindwin.

Back outside we found Saw confronted by three policemen, each with holstered gun on hip, all jabbing at copies of our passports and permits. Saw stood in what I came to call negotiating pose: arms crossed, face impassive, wild, wavy black hair escaping from his headband. He looked tense and avoided eye contact with me, which I took as a sign to stay away. Placing ourselves nearby in case we were needed, we gazed longingly at the river, so cool, so peaceful compared to the heat, dust, and dragging ennui of the road.

When Saw finished with the police, we beckoned him over for the story.

"Not used to foreigners," he said. "Nervous. Say we must go."

"So, what do we do?" The thought of getting back in the van was too depressing.

"Not leave. Can stay. Permits say so!"

One conundrum of a road trip is figuring out when to ditch the car in favor of the local way of getting around. This isn't easy, because we both would rather rely on Bernard's driving acumen to get us where we're going. To reference Marshall McLuhan, the shrewd philosopher intellectual of the mid-twentieth century, our car had become an article of dress without which we felt uncertain, unclad, and incomplete. Proceeding any other way but by car left us feeling as vulnerable as a squirrel crossing the interstate.

Sometimes, though, a radical shift is not only expedient, it's downright refreshing. And in this case, since we weren't using our own car and Bernard wasn't even driving, it seemed reasonable to broach what we had discussed while Saw was in the police stand-off.

"If we were to switch to the river for the rest of the trip, would that cause permit problems?"

"Permits for village. Use car. Use boat . . . okay."

"What about the boats. Do we need to reserve in advance?"

"Buy every day, each village. Easy."

Switching to the river was sounding too simple.

"And the van and driver. What will they do if we continue from here on the river?"

"They drive back Yangon. Also okay."

Which is how I wound up hopping riverboats for 350 miles, till the Chindwin got so shallow we couldn't go any further.

Next morning, we were at the docks by 8:30 a.m. Only there was no dock. There were passengers, vendors, and porters swarming among an assortment of boats painted lime and turquoise with red trim, each nosed into the broad sandbank. Finding our boat, we followed pigs in handmade bamboo crates, furniture, and sacks of rice up the one-plank gangway.

Families piled in dragging parcels and babies. A monk sat amidst barrels of oil. Snacks were hawked from skiffs and by deck vendors. And then, impelled by an ear-splitting horn, vendors scrambled to land, skiffs pushed back, and we were away.

The river was its own sort of highway, accommodating everything from one-man fishing canoes to mammoth bamboo rafts floating teak logs downstream. Our boat stopped often to pick up or drop off passengers on the banks below their homes. None of the stops were set, nor could we disembark. Each, though, brought a chance to see river life up close, like peering in a neighbor's window from the sidewalk.

The Chindwin is narrow enough you can see what's happening on the banks when you're midstream. We passed fields of sunflowers and corn tended by farmers in traditional conical bamboo hats. Naked kids splashed about the river's edge next to women doing laundry. A farmer swam with his zebu ox, then the two of them clambered, refreshed and dripping, up the steep sandy bank, the zebu's hump towering over the small, bandy-legged man. White *stupas* with gold spires poked through the palms as the setting sun turned the dusk to orange. Myanmar is strongly Buddhist and these structures for meditation and housing relics, which look like portly sitting Buddhas with spiky hats, were everywhere.

Life simplified. There was river time, spent visiting, reading, and watching the scenery. And there was shore time, finding the lone guesthouse with its stall-sized rooms, choosing a teashop for cold beer and peanuts, roaming village streets.

In Mawlaik, our first stop, Saw was again confronted by the local police, an authoritarian welcome repeated in every village. When he finished persuading them our permits were valid, I asked if he needed to come if we went for a village wander. "Go," he said. "Anywhere okay."

"Where will we find you when we get back?"

"I find you," he said, and gave a rare chuckle. "You only white people here. Everyone know where you are!"

We walked quiet roads rimmed with broad-leafed shade trees where sows rooted in the vegetation. Schoolgirls squeaked along on rusty bicycles.

A colonial mansion of dark teak listed, slowly dragged down by flowering vines. Each village faded into farms where water buffalos grazed and white egrets pecked for bugs. If we liked a village, or the next day's schedule didn't suit us, we'd stay another night.

Evenings, we'd pick a restaurant for a dinner of fried rice, noodle soup, or my favorite meal-as-adventure: Burmese curry. Burmese curry has nothing to do with Indian curry. It's served everywhere and here's how it works.

The restaurant will have a glass case with bowls of cooked food. Some contain proteins, like pork, chicken, or fish. Another five (or more, if it's a prosperous restaurant) hold vegetable and bean dishes. At the case, choose your protein and return to your table.

A number of small dishes will be brought, one with your pork or chicken, the rest with *every* vegetable on offer. Along comes a bowl of peppery broth, a large tureen of rice, and, sometimes, a plate of cucumbers and tomatoes.

Serve yourself some of everything. Splash spoonfuls of broth on anything that seems dry. Refill your plate often. There's no extra charge, as good an indication of the open generosity of the people of Myanmar as any.

Our morning routine matched the villagers'. Rising around six o'clock, we'd see women heading to market, Naga villagers hawking grass brooms, a procession of monks with silver or lacquered bowls seeking food offerings.

Breakfast was strong black tea with sweetened condensed milk, plus freshly fried doughnut sticks with a few spoonfuls of lentils. I might go to the kitchen and gesture for fried eggs. At a street stand, we'd get cool rice noodles smothered with sauces, greens, and a chopped hardboiled egg, blended with chicken broth.

Street markets, the heart of each village, offered an astonishing variety of food: eggplants, bitter greens, immense gourds, onions, cauliflower, carrots, peppers, thumb-sized bananas, chicken, quail and duck eggs, slick silver river fish, brawny catfish, scrawny chickens, more beans than I knew existed. And rice, from premium at two dollars per kilo to the dregs for half that. Weighing was done with hand scales, the goods on one tray, D-cell batteries on the other.

As the only foreigners in villages where no travelers had been for decades and only the elderly, born before the end of British colonial rule in 1948, spoke English, we were greeted with a wave and smile but otherwise left alone. Unlike in places that depend on tourism for income, no demands were made of us. And so we were able to join village life as much or little as we wished.

I always headed for the local beauty salon. I discovered this indulgence in a Mawlaik teashop, where the traffic into a curtained area made me curious. The smell should have been a giveaway: the flowery scent of shampoo mixed with an acrid odor of bleaches and perms. Pulling back a drape patterned with cartoon ducks, I discovered a five-foot-by-twelve-foot alcove where a young woman was having her hair straightened while her boyfriend had his hair bleached. Intrigued, I gestured for a hair wash and then waited my turn.

While a beauty shop's smell is instantly recognizable, what happens in Burmese salons is unique. You lie on your back on a padded table, head over a basin as cool water is scooped from a nearby bucket and splashed over your hair. Expect your hair to be washed two or three times. In between, your scalp will be plucked, pinched, and squeezed in a head massage that will have you in raptures.

It took only one hair wash for me to be hooked on this way of spending a blissful hour blending into village life. That I could do so while supporting women entrepreneurs *and* getting my long hair clean was a bonus.

Life on the river was good. So good that on the day we got stuck, I didn't care that we waited three hours for a boat, called by our captain via radio, to rescue us. I didn't even care that it, too, got stuck, twice more, stretching a twelve-hour day to nineteen. I would have been happy to sit or drift on the Chindwin forever.

But even rivers come to an end, and when the Chindwin got too shallow, we had to fly from Khamti to Mandalay. At the airport, I asked Saw, "When the water's higher, is it possible to go farther up?"

"Possible," he said.

EATING

PREAMBLE

Road trips are an involuntary alternance of feast and famine. On days when the latter is in force, the road is so long and empty that I inhale cookie crumbs and reluctantly peel the blackened skin from an old, bruised banana in between searching a plastic bag for stray remnants of the raisins and almonds I bought at a street market a week earlier. By no means is this starvation, and I'm not complaining. And yet it highlights something I find especially interesting about long drives, which is that a road trip meal is more than just a rudimentary necessity in the course of life. It's a chance to look at both sides of Bernard's face at the same time rather than his profile, to think about something other than rights and lefts and roundabouts, to watch others on their way to somewhere they'll surely get to before me.

The sometime absence of meals drives home just how full a sensory pleasure food is, replete with smell, taste, and texture. It's something I can study minutely that doesn't move, or at least it shouldn't. And if I've ordered smartly, it even gratifies my hearing, with a crackling oil or sigh of escaping steam. For me, everything about food is hooked so deeply into indelible taste memories that regardless of which one I yank to the surface it makes me salivate.

Despite the haphazard lack of food during our road trips, don't imagine me as obsessed with finding the most fabulous food or the best-kept secret café in a village. That would be futile, since the places we drive through don't even have a word for *bistro* in their language, let alone *café*. Or a direct translation of *fabulous*. And if one is into wish-fulfillment—and, by the way, isn't travel itself the ultimate in that regard?—it's important to start with a wish that has the possibility of being fulfilled. Or, to quote that magnificent tenor Luciano Pavarotti, a man who clearly knew more than a thing or two about food, "One of the very nicest things about life is that we must regularly stop whatever it is we are doing and devote our attention to eating." Now that I am more practiced at road trips, part of me does look forward to that first day getting on the road, because I know that the sooner we get moving, the sooner I can stop to investigate the local fare.

What am I looking for? Something to eat in the simplest of terms. I am happiest when I can eat whatever everyone else is eating at that moment. Accompanying my chewing with a beverage other than warm bottled water is a plus. I'm joyful about a bowl of homemade soup at a windy outpost before crossing the Straits of Magellan at Chile's Punta Delgada. Freshly fried seeds and rice from a corner *chaat* stand in Kolkata provide just the right mix of salt, spice, and crunch to quell the belly gremlins screeching, "Feed me." Handing a quizzical chef a few thumb-size eggplants and a fistful of slimy brown orbs from grimed baskets lining the dank, dark corridor of a café kitchen in Golmud, China, satisfies my lust for food novelty. And danger.

Vivid as my own taste memories are, of my father bribing me to sample strong cheese by showing me how to squeeze a house shape from its waxy rind, or my mother tearing off a small orb from her pastry dough so I could roll and fill for my own apple tart, it is no wonder that food is the binding with which I can blend my life with the locals. The fizzy foulness of home-brewed barley beer offered by a hospitable farmer in Bahir Dar, Ethiopia, does nothing to hydrate me and everything to quench a spirit thirsting for friendship after weeks on the road. That said farmer claimed to be a former Black Panther, with the stories to prove it, surely helped me down a beverage otherwise intent on making me retch.

It all comes down to this: The rituals of mealtime are a refuge—an opportunity, dare I hope—to clean my hands with water and soap instead of moisture-sapping, skin-desiccating, antibacterial wipes. An interlude of rest and calm in a cool, quiet space, a space that, best of all, is stationary.

Sacrificial Lamb

RÍO GALLEGOS, ARGENTINA, 2008

We're making two nice ladies sweat. They're in the kitchen at Estancia Monte Dinero, a sheep station a few miles back up the road, likely wondering if we're coming back as promised. I'm equally anxious, as, if my wishful thinking becomes reality, there's a home-cooked meal awaiting our return, albeit one that, given our tardiness, is now cold.

That morning, on our drive down Argentina's Atlantic coast from Río Gallegos to see the penguins at Cabo Virgenes, we stopped there unannounced, more for an impromptu leg-stretch than with any expectation of a meal. As we approached down a long dirt driveway, we could see metal sheds with rusting tin roofs and wood barns with paint peeling off splintered boards. Farm tractors listed on flattened tires with seats sprung like a jack-in-the-box, the barnyard littered with engine and gearbox detritus so oxidized by salt air that whoever was attempting that lube job years ago was right to give up. Everything appeared on the losing end of a wrestling match against gravity, abetted by the sharp breeze blowing off the nearby Atlantic. Bernard, as usual, was driving. I, as usual, was fretting. There wasn't a sheep in sight.

"Looks abandoned," I said by way of encouragement. "Maybe we should just go on to the penguins." Bernard, as he often does when he disagrees with where I'm suggesting he go, replied by pressing on the gas. As we rounded the base of the driveway, we saw a red and white clapboard house set on a swatch of lawn under the gnarled branches of a giant, twisted tree. It cast such deep shade the grass looked black. The cottage was

33

like a fairy tale, freshly painted, surrounded by a white picket fence protecting a well-kept bed of yellow and orange marigolds. Clearly, the bungalow was still in use, though it looked out of place, being so fresh and clean amidst the derelict, dried up rest of the property. As a child, I read all of Hans Christian Andersen's works as well as Russian fairy tales and the Brothers Grimm, so I know my cottages. And this one had nothing foreboding about it. It was benignly inviting in its cheerfulness, speaking to me of plump gray-haired grannies cooking lovely nourishing things. The only thing missing from the picture was me, eating.

During its heyday in the 1990s, Estancia Monte Dinero used to welcome guests to simple rooms and home-cooked meals. When two women stepped onto the veranda to greet us, lured, I suppose, by the crunch of our tires on gravel, it was a good sign. Wiping floury hands on their aprons, they introduced themselves by their jobs, not their names: cook and assistant. The cook, in a starched white chef's jacket, had dark curled hair and rosy cheeks. Her assistant was short, strong, with tawny skin, her hair swept under a floral head kerchief. At first I was puzzled to be greeted by the kitchen help, but as we stood chatting about the usual topics, such as where we were from and where we were going, the two struck me as proficient in more than just cooking. There was something in their bearing and the way they met my eyes that made me think they were probably running a larger operation than just a seasonal tourist kitchen. Yet despite the floury hands, a dead giveaway that they were in the midst of making something dessert-like which surely needed attention, they seemed uncommonly eager to talk, to do whatever they could to keep us from leaving.

The story of the place was a classic tale of immigrant success. In the mid-1800s, the Greenshields family of Scotland emigrated to the Islas Malvinas (the Falklands) as part of a wave of thousands of immigrants drawn to economic opportunity provided by the British government, which regained possession of the islands in 1833. In 1884, a family son, Thomas, left the security of his family's sheep ranch in the Malvinas for the mainland of Patagonia. Though cattle couldn't thrive on the short dry grass, sheep could, and did. Between 1880 and 1914, the Patagonian

Austral became one of the world's premier locales for raising sheep, following the pattern of New Zealand. Thomas prospered as a sheep rancher despite the hardships of climate, remoteness, and predators. Perhaps tiring of only sheep for company, he married Anne McMunn in 1889. Unlike some of his fellow Scottish Malvineros, who became very wealthy, Thomas died at age twenty-nine, a few months after his wedding. Anne's grief was short-lived. Or perhaps she simply was pragmatic as only a pioneer needing to survive can be. She remarried swiftly, to a local doctor, Arthur Fenton. It was Fenton who chose the name Monte Dinero, "Money Hill," though not to crow about his newly wedded fortune. Monte Dinero was already the name of a hill on the property that was used as a reference point by ships entering the Straits of Magellan. Some of those ship captains apparently were too near-sighted to notice landmarks, haplessly running their galleons aground, spilling the gold doubloons in their hold into the ocean. Thus the hill also became the reference point for land-based treasure hunters.

Five generations later, on the sunny day we arrived, the Estancia was still in the Fenton family, pasturing twenty-three thousand sheep on its sixty-six thousand acres. "Our prize Merino ram is at the livestock fair right now," the chef said. "In Río Gallegos this weekend. Please, you must go to see them." Her voice entreated me, as if their ram expected to welcome us to his pen personally, would be desolate if we didn't visit. "This year our rams have won the award for Most Handsome. This has been so for many years." Despite these pleasantries, I had a strange feeling that there was more to be told than she was saying. She seemed sad. Maybe also lonely.

"Is Monte Dinero still serving lunch?" I inquire. Her face crestfallen, the chef says, "No. Now we only have the oilfield workers. And when they get back here, well . . . They're tired. And they only want to drink." So that was it. No more accolades from visiting travelers, just drunk wildcatters at her table who couldn't distinguish soufflé from slop. She straightens her shoulder and sighs, as if to imply the decision would have been different if left up to her. I, too, am dejected, because the spruced up old house seemed to promise a wonderful lunch to come.

We stand there looking at each other, none of us ready to leave. Which gives enough time for a brilliant thought to appear, something I learned from traveling to Europe with my French mother every year of my youth. My sister and I still fall into hysterics as we mimic our mother inspecting any hotel room assigned to us, pursing her lips, her head unconsciously shaking a genteel "No" as she opens a closet door and peers into the bathroom. "But this will never do," she would say, her aggrieved tone registering shock more appropriate to a concierge at the Four Seasons suggesting we sleep outside on the dumpster, than for a perfectly adequate room at a perfectly nice hotel. Though when my sister was twelve and I was ten our mother's behavior left us cringing in the hallway, her aim was clear: if she refused the offered room, maybe she'd be given something better, if only to shut her up. Since then I never hesitate to ask for what I want. At Estancia Monte Dinero, the opportunity fairly screams. Where Bernard would chat for an hour until the chef could do nothing but offer us lunch of her own accord, I am too impatient for that. Besides, penguins are waiting. "Would you make lunch for us?" I ask. "We love good food. And I know Monte Dinero is famous for that." I'm hoping flattery will get me everywhere. From the way she gives our bodies a quick once over, it seems she might base her answer on whether our small size warrants her culinary efforts. But if she wants to cook, we're the only ones around willing to eat.

"Yes," she says. "With pleasure. Of course. What time will you be back?"

"What do you think, Bernard? Noonish?" We go through a rapid calculation of drive time plus penguin spotting time and then tell her to expect us around 1:00. We can barely suppress our grins. Lunch cooked to order just for us. What delicious luck.

It is shortly after 2:00 when we pull back under the century-old tree that shades the ranch house. Stepping onto the wraparound porch, I quickly brush myself off, but Bernard is more thorough, clapping his hands on my waist, turning me around, and whacking dust off my butt. "Surely we're not as filthy as oilfield workers," I say. Bernard agrees but keeps slapping and brushing. "It doesn't matter if they've seen worse," he says. "They've made a special lunch for us." In a further attempt to appear worthy of their efforts, I run my fingers through my hair to settle the strands loosened by the Atlantic breezes.

We step through the screen door into the hush of another era. Sepia photos of early sheep ranching operations line the walls, populated by sturdy men in wind-whipped baggy trousers, odd old trucks and leggy, scraggle-maned horses, corrals holding what seem like thousands of fluffy, fat sheep. Chunky wood-framed sofas and chairs, piled with overstuffed leather cushions, fairly ooze with a century of citrus, beeswax, and pine soap that saturates the air with a tangy aroma. Inhaling it now, I seem to swell with comfort and a warm, suffuse happiness that only the best childhood memories can provide. The stillness is broken by the *tock, tock, tock* of an ancient grandfather clock in the formal dining room and faint radio tunes from the back of the house. I'm transported back to those old-world inns of my girlhood family trips, on which faint smells of tomato, onion, and caramel wafted from a hidden kitchen, where the hush was broken only sporadically by the swish of a dust rag on a mahogany bannister rail or the clack of low-heeled pumps as a receptionist strode by to attend a guest.

Closing the door quietly behind us as if we've entered Westminster Cathedral mid-mass, we approach the long-burnished wood table on the screened porch with reverence. On it are six little earthenware bowls, holding cashews, cheese squares, cubed ham, chips, tiny saltines, and cheese sticks. We each try to hide our dismay from the other. "Oh," says Bernard. "Nuts. I like nuts." And he takes a handful.

"Cheese. That's good."

We munch a bit. "This isn't much," says Bernard, just as I say, "Do you think this is it?" We look at each other in disappointment. Apparently the chef set out some packaged tidbits for us and left to take care of her other work. Not even a refreshing beverage is offered. I can't actually blame her. She probably had no supplies on hand and had been too ashamed to say so. "Well, let's sit down. It's at least something." Our chairs scrape the wood floor, resounding loudly through the old house as we pull them out.

We have just put napkins on our laps when the kitchen door slams open and out comes the chef, cheeks red, smiling with relief. "Ah!" she exclaims, gratitude evident in her voice. "Here you are. Wonderful. Wonderful!" Because, in fact, the poor lady has suffered her own disappointment, that she cooked a meal for people who didn't care to return for it. We had said one o'clock and here we wandered in after two. I kick myself for being so rude. Now, to put herself at ease, she introduces each of the little snacks she'd set forth. She points to the crackers, "These are crackers." Next, she points to the cheese, "This is cheese." And so on for the ham and the rest of the tidbits. She smiles with pleasure, standing next to the table twisting her hands as if she can't quite believe we're real.

Suddenly she's a whirling dervish, dashing back to the kitchen, to return in seconds bearing larger bowls of freshly made cold appetizers: chicken breast in olive oil with pickled carrots, vinegary slices of lamb heart with onions, and preserved chunks of young lamb with peppers. "To help you be patient. While you wait," she explains.

"Bernard," I whisper. "This isn't even the real meal. Which means there's more to come!" I stab a lamb heart with a toothpick.

Hustling back to the kitchen, the chef skids to a stop, her hand flying to her mouth in mortification. She's just realized her honored guests have nothing to drink. She spins around so fast her white poufy cap nearly falls off her head. With three strides she disappears into the pantry, returning immediately with two bottles of wine clutched in one hand, four wine glasses in the other. She pours us both a glass of warm red and a glass of chilly white, pale as straw. "So! Try it, try it!" she orders, arms crossed, chin tucked into her neck as she waits. Her black hair pokes in wisps from under her cap and her equally black eyes are flashing with pride. Who are we to say no to such generosity? We each raise a glass to each other and to her, sip happily, and only when we put the glasses down, satisfied, does she return to the kitchen.

Hungry from our penguin crawl, we dig into the appetizers but have only a few minutes to make an impact before a parade of hot dishes appears. One after another, the chef and her assistant carry warm entrees in thick glazed ceramic bowls to the table. In a delirium we tuck into succulent stewed lamb liver with caramelized onions followed by juicy lamb brochettes, crisp lamb schnitzel, delicate empanadas stuffed with oregano lamb stew, and the pièce de résistance: lamb pizza, a creation far superior to the pizza we had in Ulan Baatar or Novosibirsk. "Do you think they have rooms?" Bernard asks in a rare pause between bites. And again, I'm amazed how on this journey we seem able to read each other's mind. "We could stay a few days. They'd be happy to cook for us."

When the chef returns to observe us eating, red face gleaming, I raise the idea. She seems as sad to reveal their rooms are occupied full-time by the oilfield crew as I am to hear it. Though it's probably a good thing for the fit of my travel clothes. I feel bad for her. She's a generous, gregarious woman whose circumstances have changed beyond her control. "No go," I tell Bernard. "We'll have to eat as much as we can now and that's the end of it."

The grandfather clock tocks stoically as we delve into the food in front of us. We leave no dish unsampled and would have wiped each bowl clean had not the chef returned with the query Bernard is hoping to hear. "Would you perhaps like dessert?" she asks. Does a Frenchman want dessert? That's like asking if a baseball fan wants a beer. I explain to her that Bernard would crawl to Río Gallegos on his knees for dessert, a statement which does not translate well, leaving her gaping and eyeing me with suspicion. So I revert to the classic enthusiastic "Sí!" Neither of us has said much to the other through lunch, apart from a continuous chorus of yums. But when the chef and her helper return with three desserts, it's an embarrassment of riches that shocks us into total silence. One by one they present us with a flan in caramel sauce, a fresh fruit salad, and torta negra, an Argentinean specialty made with three layers of dense cake slices spread with dark dulce de leche and sprinkled with chopped walnuts. Neither of us can bear to hurt their feelings so, full though we are, we accept a heaping helping of each.

To prepare ourselves for the hour and a half of washboarded road taking us back to Río Gallegos and our rendezvous with Mr. Handsome Merino of the 2008 Livestock Fair, we take a long walk down one of the dusty ranch roads. The land is flat, covered with scrappy dead grass, the sky a washed-out blue. It's not pretty. And if indeed there are twenty-three thousand sheep here, they're doing a good job of blending into the landscape. The desolate scene starts to seep into our bones and the walk does little to settle our aching overstuffed stomachs. It feels to me like we're both low, perhaps a bit depressed. Not in that post-prandial way, but as if the whole experience has been disquieting rather than satisfying. "This is a sad situation here," I say to Bernard. Even as a child in the single digits I could slip into someone else's skin as easily as into my footie pajamas. I think this came from being a sometimes sad, frequently moody youngster, my vibrant imagination nagging me that others' lives were infinitely gayer than my own, and that my life could be cheerier too, if only I could figure out what they knew that I didn't. Projecting myself into the white jacket and practical plastic slippers of our host chef happened without calculation. Our lives were totally dissimilar except for one facet: we both derived immense satisfaction from feeding other people, she professionally, me casually. Food has formed a central part of my life's experience, placed almost at the chromosomal level by my mother, for whom generous hospitality of the culinary source was a hallmark of civility. I knew if I could never again face a friend across the table, her face beaming, exclaiming, "This is delicious!" I would be a sadder person for it. And so, I suspected, might our chef.

Though he doesn't cook, Bernard pitches in at home with every meal, chopping, stirring and, best of all, cleaning. Not leaving others to tackle a job alone, adding his efforts in wherever he can, was his hallmark as a businessman and then a rancher. Bernard has always admired hard work, and his willingness to assist in any endeavor is why everyone in our company loved him and why the surrounding ranchers accept him. He sighs now, straightening his shoulders resolutely. "I know," says Bernard. "Such a great cook, and apart from us, no one to enjoy it anymore. What's the world coming to." That last statement is a Bernard standard, expressing everything about which he despairs, which in this case means good people not being appreciated.

I'm thinking about what I'm going to tell my friends about this lunch, doing my best to memorize every dish set in front of us. Then, a small hope intrudes, distracting me. It's not a big deal, but it does turn inside out the way I've been looking at things. I stop my recitation of foodstuffs and dwell instead on this: as surely as the chef has given us joy, perhaps the immensity of what we've eaten may lift her dejected spirits. Perhaps we will become *her* story, the one she recounts to others, regaling them about the travelers who arrived out of nowhere, for whom she cooked a feast, and who sat at her table eating for hours.

Pads

DUNHUANG, CHINA, 2011

China's Xinjiang Province, stripped bare by mineral mines and huddled hard against China's northwest borders, is home to the Taklamakan Desert, the ultimate in desert paradoxes: one hundred thirty thousand square miles of shifting sands imprinted in the north *and* the south by the Silk Road. As part of our nine-thousand-mile drive from Istanbul to Kolkata in 2011, we were about to have the pleasure of crossing it.

Normally, a desert is traversed by one track and one only, and for good reason. Desert journeyers like to ensure they are safe and well-watered on their trek through the wastelands. For some reason, which ignores the potential for stumbling onto the previous idiot's bones, following someone else's footsteps seems to offer that security. Not so with the Taklamakan. This is a desert so barren that travelers kept searching. I can see that intrepid camel caravan leader, white *dishdasha* whipped round his legs by a ground breeze, checkered *ghutrah* cinched over his forehead by a ropey black *agal* to shield against the sun's brutal rays. He looks at the track, wipes away a bead of sweat, squints in thought, then mutters a profound question: "They *really* thought this was the best way?" before setting off to find a better route. Eventually a northern route and a southern route proved viable, both doing a decent job of skirting the worst of the desolate interior.

The Taklamakan has more to offer than just desolation, however. It also has desert cold, which is an oxymoron if ever there was one. Finding itself thousands of kilometres from the warm embrace of water, this desert allied itself with the frigid north, cuddling into Siberia's armpit, the better to make subzero temperatures common in winter. Not only that, but its sands are in a depression, hemmed in by the Tian Shan mountain range to the north and the Kunlun Mountains to the south. Thus, the sands are constrained to doing an endless vicious swirl within the same concavity, rarely rising above the depths to create new dunes elsewhere. If that were my condition, I'd be depressed, too.

If by now you're inclined to agree with those who ascribe Taklamakan to *taqlar makan*, a Turkic phrase meaning "the place of ruins," wait one more minute. Because I'm not done yet. As we drive through the Taklamakan, I discover that my research hasn't revealed the worst of it. Unlike most deserts, which vie for ranking as the world's best dark-sky areas (because most countries don't want to pursue the folly of creating another Phoenix, Arizona, in their midst), the Taklamakan is smothered in leaden haze. This desert is coal-fired power plant heaven. The sludge with which they've been replacing normal air is now so dense I can't even see the towers from which that sludge spews. But I can feel it. It's painful to inhale, each breath as if I'm trying to suck oxygen through a mask of Thousand Island dressing. I cough even though I am not sick—yet. My eyes are having problems, too, watering so continually I try to find something to be sad about, just so I won't waste the tears. The air is murky enough to obscure road signs until we're nearly upon them. I assume it's a clear day, though verifying the weather by looking at the sky is futile. I take it on faith that there's even a sky up there.

We entered the Xinjiang autonomous region through its border with Kyrgyzstan, staying briefly in Kashgar to complete China's vehicle entry and driver formalities before pushing eastward on the long drive to Tibet. This is Uyghur country, and Uyghurs are a people cursed with being in the wrong place at the wrong time. First off, they're Turkic, with roots in Mongolia, both regions thousands of miles from where they live now. Second, though they originally were Christian they are now Muslim, neither of which wins them the lottery in China, an overwhelmingly Buddhist country. I'm not surprised to hear that Uyghurs feel more kinship with their neighbors in Kazakhstan and Kyrgyzstan than with the Han

Chinese. This doesn't please the Chinese, the result being clashes and jailings throughout the region.

We drive a broad strip of gray highway for hours, passing neither an exit nor a turnout. It's as straight and unswerving as a West Point cadet on parade. When I need to pee, Bernard stops on the highway itself. I squat in the desert sand on the shoulder, which by definition continues to shift. Pants lowered around my ankles, I'm unable to scuttle aside as a tumbleweed the size of Kansas bobbles toward me. This is the local edition of Russian thistle weed, a highly invasive species, much like the country whence it came. Beset by visions of my nether parts being invaded by the prickly orb, it's all I can do to keep my knees from clapping together like magnets. Behind this one I spy others heading my way. It's alarming that these roaming dead plants, with no stake in any patch of ground, think I've invaded theirs. Or maybe they just know I'm vulnerable.

The driving days in the Taklamakan are monotone to an extent that leaves us dreary and drained, unable to alleviate the ennui. This is China and even in matters of driving, the government has decided what the experience will be, by designing a highway with no exits. There's a steel divider painted robin's egg blue, separating us from the occasional truck or car in the oncoming lane, etching a solid, pastel line to the horizon without an opening for hundreds of miles. I clench my teeth at a road building philosophy that seems to declare if you're going in one direction, that's all you're allowed. But it doesn't matter. We have no intention of ever doubling back the way we've come.

When we finally are able to leave the highway for a side road linking regional villages, my joy is the joy of the wrongfully jailed, suddenly released on bail by an anonymous benefactor. Even the omnipresent speed cameras constraining us to progress at twenty-five miles per hour cannot dampen my enthusiasm. Inevitably we are stopped by a traffic cop, part of a roadside operation complete with a squadron of policemen in full regalia. They are small men in straight-legged pants with creases as sharp as the prow of the Titanic, gray jackets cinched with wide black leather belts complete with holster, and gray caps with black patent leather bills. They're frighteningly efficient in the way of a candy dispenser at an automat, no personal discretion needed to issue tickets as all the data is right there on their laptops, transmitted from those aforementioned cameras. When we are shown a photograph of us defying death at thirty miles per hour on a smoothly paved, straight, empty road, we swallow a brief laugh and stare at the ground.

It takes only a brief upward glance at our red-faced traffic functionary waving a thick wad of tickets, each waiting to be filled with a litany of vehicular misdeeds, to remind me that impatient is a word that's suddenly left my vocabulary. I turn Zen, exhaling peacefully at the prospect of looking at people, stretching my legs, rummaging among the detritus that has mounted in the back seat to find the bag of biscuits I know I put there three days ago. When a local miscreant of the road peremptorily demands the return of our passports and loudly shames the policeman for ticketing these pleasant visitors to their country, we are speedily on our way once more, speedily being of course a relative term.

The best part of leaving the highway is that we can now stop to eat. Road food on our drives is the inverse of the United States, having every-thing to do with eating whatever local people eat, and nothing to do with the wrinkled mauve hotdogs and pallid microwave burritos of American gas stations. Here in Uyghur country, kebabs are ubiquitous, as is the clay oven, tandoor cooking commonly associated with India. Though at first puzzled, I decide the tandoor isn't the purview of Indians at all, just a simple transportable way to bake whatever one has on hand. As we creep down the road, spotting a café is easy: anyone willing to sell travelers a meal hangs a raw haunch of lamb from a lattice shelter. It's a roadside tautology. If there's raw meat, someone must be around to cook it, and if there's a cook in the house, it implies someone who'll want to eat, hence one should hang meat outside to attract the hungry traveler. And that would be us.

We pull off the road next to a long table set under the interlocking branches of several gasping trees. A ripped white plastic cloth covers the top. Splintery benches line either side. The rest of the village appears to be populated by tire and engine repair stalls, the ground saturated to an opaque blackness by years of drained oil and hydraulic fluids.

As soon as we park, a man emerges from a nearby doorway, knife with long, curved, oxidized blade in hand. I point to the haunch. He unhooks it, slaps the blade on his trousers, and slices a plateful of red slivers, to be speared for the grill with pieces of lamb liver, onion, and fat. His chopping block is sodden and slick with blood and grease, a chunk of wood that has only rarely known the sweet caress of a swab with clean damp rag. This delights the flies, who in their delirium can't seem to decide whether to suck on the wood or nibble on the haunch.

In the kitchen, a fire roars, flames leaping out of a blackened stove pit with such intensity there's no smell of cooking foods at all. Over the heat, a grizzled wok proportioned to fry an ostrich egg for a giant sizzles with oil, whose splatters goad the flames to leap higher still. A young Uyghur man stands ready to orchestrate my order, shovel-length spatula lifted. Beyond him, two men pulls gobs of dough from a tureen, hand-rolling noodles as fat as garter snakes but as long as a python. The stir-fry cook eyes me, raising black beetle eyebrows. His T-shirt and stained trousers also are black, as is the long wood bench behind him on which he has mounded chopped vegetables and long beans. Though soot rules the day and cleaning doesn't seem to be a point of pride here, the kitchen is so hot no flies have survived and I figure bacteria won't either. To add to our kebabs, I choose a mix of eggplant, onions, and cabbage from the ready-to-cook piles. The lightly seasoned mix of vegetables, which is brought to our table with large plates of cold noodles, arrives just after the kebabs. A Parisian restaurant couldn't have timed it any better.

From Kashgar to Lhasa, I inspect the markets of one rural Chinese city after another as we drive our way through the desert via Aksu, Korla, Turpan, Dunhuang, and Golmud. Gourds are plentiful. Sacks of various dried fungi lounge next to bins of gelatinous brown wood ear mushrooms, while enormous oyster mushrooms cluster nearby. There's bitter gourd, which looks like a prickly cucumber, three-foot leeks, all sorts of greens, pale purple eggplants the size of a baby's foot, and many roots that I can't identify. Plus, plentiful ginger and ropes of garlic. There are melons, apples, bananas, and clementines, and piles of deep purple grapes, which are large and sweet and make a refreshing if sticky road snack. Alongside the highway are miles of mats on which pale jade-colored grapes are laid out for the sun, weak though it is, to transform into tender golden raisins.

The back of most markets is the poultry arena, where crates hold ducks, chickens, and pigeons, necks wrung to order. A dark alley houses troughs of carp, the silver kind that is a delicacy in China, not the orange and pink kind that laze in hotel koi ponds. Water burbles into the troughs and overflows, keeping the air moist and fishy and the rough concrete floor in a perpetual state of puddles. The moving water makes it look as though the fish are swimming. At first, I think they are alive, then realize it'd be unlikely for a fish to swim belly up of its own accord. A young woman lifts a heavy, silvery fish by its tail and it hangs limp. She grabs a thin-bladed gutting knife, waving it at me in a way that would be threatening if I were facing a Congolese rebel but here is meant to invoke temptation. The fish heads piled on a platter do not entice me. They stare unblinking, mouths agape, as if no one told them they no longer need gasp for air.

The market street-front is for meat displays, each vendor willing to use a practiced cleaver to hack off a chunk of mutton or pork on a wood block turned purple and shiny with fatty gore. Here, the air is heavily scented with the tang of rancid meat mixed with a tinny, back-of-the-throat slick of clotted blood.

As long as I can remember, I've loved smells, using them to link me to experiences in a visceral way. To this day scent is one of my travel touchstones, informing most of my memories from childhood to the present day in all its savory, spicy, even stinky glory. So I inhaled deeply, even though this particular stench was not exactly the fragrance du jour at a Bloomingdale's perfume counter. I was never a Bloomingdale's shopper, but my mother was.

While my mother charged toward the escalator to the first-floor juniors section, cheering us on with an eager, "Come on, darling, let's see what they have for you!" I took the long way, sauntering through makeup instead. This puzzled my mother; she marveled at her daughter, a child of the sixties, who eschewed makeup with a sense of mission that would have served a Benedictine nun—well, except we were Jewish. I didn't care about the powders, creams, and lipsticks, all of which fell into my personal teen-ager category of "gross." Instead I kept my eyes out for the pretty lady holding a shapely glass bottle aloft, spraying whoever came within range. I'd stroll nonchalantly into her orbit, feeling the cool aromatic mist alight on my hair and skin, then scurry to catch my mother before she stepped off the elevator lip. She'd sniff the air gently as I arrived behind her, perhaps nursing a faint hope that a soupçon of her French sophistication had indeed rubbed off on me.

The smells around me in the Dunhuang market speak of all the rich-ness of life. At the edge of the meat lane are villagers in kerchiefs, long dresses, and embroidered caps selling bowls of homemade curdled milk, which might or might not be yogurt. One tells me he's walked in that morning. When his milk is gone, he'll walk home. Beyond them, on roomy corners where logs can be stacked, are wood-fired bread ovens from which golden pizza-like crusts embellished with pin-prick designs emerge every few minutes. People walk away with teetering stacks of ten at a time.

Somewhere in the middle of all this are carts mounded with varieties of black, brown, and golden raisins, almonds, sunflower seeds, and walnuts. And there are dates now, fresh dates, which are yellow green and the size of miniature pears. They taste like an unripe pear, too. It's hard to believe that they will eventually dry and turn into the pasty, honey-sweet brown Medjools I am used to. Stalls offer a host of spices and ground chilies, which make me sneeze. Those evil, tiny, red peppers that have been hiding slyly in my food, sneaking into my mouth under cover of gravy are every-where. In the markets, they fill the air with a fierce and pungent bouquet which slips unbidden into the back of my throat, coating it with a warmth that soon turns fiery.

Since I do not have a kitchen in which to experiment with market ingredients, I am partial to the sector offering cooked foods. Every market has one, in tacit acknowledgement that shopping for food is a hungry business. In Dunhuang, I find the best of both worlds, a thriving open market next to an outdoor food court in which twenty local entrepreneurs have opened restaurant-ettes with names like Wang Strotters Bubble Up, a tiny place with a few red plastic stools around tables bolted to the floor. The locals know something about Wang and his family's generations-old recipe for Strotters Bubble Up, giving his shop a wide berth. I follow their lead, sampling steamed pork buns, dim sum, and stir-fry elsewhere.

Entrepreneurial cooks who can't afford permanent walls set up stoves and roasters in the open alleys outside. A tantalizing breeze of caramelizing sugar and strong coffee pulls me to a blackened wok the size of a manhole cover, half-filled with an unruly gallon of oil. It spits and hisses, tamed by a broad-shouldered woman, sleeves rolled up to reveal arms speckled with years of oil burns. Her skin is tawny, her smile welcoming, her black hair tightly bunned under a white cap. As I watch she takes a twist of sweet soft dough, rolls it into an oval pillow and drops it into the sizzling oil. In a minute, it has puffed like a balloon, rising to the surface where it bobs, buoy-like, till she scoops it out with a wire ladle and rolls it in a bowl of coarsely ground sugar. Nearby a coffee vendor stirs beans in the ashy coals of a brazier. Not only is the coffee freshly made, the beans obviously are freshly roasted, too. Even though it's mid-afternoon, no sane person could argue that now isn't the perfect time for breakfast.

Fortified, I turn to my main goal, a desire to taste camel pad. I first encountered Bactrian camels in the Gobi during the P2P and have felt fondly about them ever since, their two humps reminding me of rainy childhood weekends in which Dr. Doolittle's menagerie played an important part. So I was dismayed, in a way one can only be when a childhood favorite turns up on one's plate, to learn that camel pad is a delicacy in Western China. It takes some objective talking-to to remind myself that in this part of the world the Bactrian is not a fictional animal of disarming cuteness. It's food. It's income. It's clothing and shelter. Through the Taklamakan I've been looking for Bactrian camels. Recent desert surveys have found fewer than fifty wild camels left. I have no hope of seeing those, as they stick to where the desert is deserted, but I do see herds of domestic Bactrians raised for food and fiber. And I give silent kudos to the

Chinese herders for making sure they use everything that camel offers, right down to the soles of their feet. More properly called pads. And if ever there's a place to sample camel pad, I'm in it.

In the thriving small metropolis of Dunhuang, still linked to its desert denizens by tradition and proximity, I have a feeling camel pad should be sold. Puffing on my scalding doughnut I walk around the corner to the meat stalls. Right away I see it: two bones sticking straight up from a fat-encased, pad-shaped lump of muscle. The whole thing has been fried or roasted till the fat forms a crackling golden brown skin. The vendor, a middle-aged man whose face glistens as slickly as the fatty products around him, lifts up the chunk and slices me a thin sliver of pale brown meat. This time around there is no scorching fire to sanitize the cleaver or the wood slab permeated with the drippings from a generation of bloody carcasses. I pop the sliver in my mouth and chew, savoring what could be my last bite before armies of bacteria attack. It's mild, slightly unctuous. The taste reminds me of something. I swallow and think. I've never eaten camel, not pad nor hump nor anything in between, so I'm not in a position to recognize the taste of a Bactrian. But camels use their feet for every step, and I have a notion that camel pad should be more muscle-y and less fatty.

I gesture for a bit of paper from the newsprint in which the butcher wraps his sales. He tears off a strip and hands me his pen. Normally I have trouble drawing a straight line and can barely make a respectable showing when playing hangman. Travel has cured me of any shyness about this limitation, and over tens of thousands of miles I have made great progress by fearlessly drawing toilets and other daily necessities. Now I tackle my most ambitious project to date: the Bactrian. A quick few pencil slashes for two humps, four legs, plus an arrow pointing to the feet, and I reveal my cartoon to the butcher. Looking at it, his shoulders start to heave with laughter. He shows the drawing to his partner, who leans back emitting cackles and gales. They oink a Chinese oink at me. I oink back in English. Then we're all laughing, as I realize what I thought was a camel's pad was actually the front shoulder of a pig, placed upside down so the flesh looked like a broad round foot.

Now the vendor picks out a chunk of meat which is so dark red it's almost black. He points to the drawing and hefts the blob as if it were a shotput. He saws off a splinter and hands it across the counter, the flesh of his fingers smeared with bloody bits from other orders, the rims of his fingernails crammed with gunge. This is my moment of truth. I prepare myself mentally for the psychological impact of placing a piece of camel pad in my mouth. In goes the sliver. It's the texture of a tasty tire or half-dried beef jerky. The flavor reminds me of liver mixed with something like chicken, part cloying, part like an old penny, and part sweetly mild. It strikes me as exactly what a foot that's ambled the dunes of a vast desert should taste like. "Very good," I say, nodding my approval while I chew for several minutes more.

I buy a pound. The butcher wipes his knife on the bloody apron skirting his thigh, slashes at the pad and holds up a flake to show me what he will do with the rest. My intense chewing must have blocked blood flow to my brain. I give the OKAY, realizing too late the irrationality of that yes. His knife and its attendant hordes of bacteria shave that lump faster and more evenly than the Slice-O-Matic I almost bought when I was ten, an age when I still believed infomercials. In sixty seconds a drift of red meat is all that's left of the dense blob, every sliver tainted with whatever has been germinating on that wood block, those fingers, that blade.

Back at our hotel, I say nothing about this. I am so aglow with triumph that even Bernard, who normally will not eat what he doesn't recognize, can't resist sampling my prize. In one of the miracles of the road which occasionally anoint us, neither of us gets sick.

Bottomless Pits

ZAOUIA AHANESI, MOROCCO, 2004

Back in 2004 when we drove through Morocco I knew nothing about long-distance driving. I never needed to strategize about the how, what, where, or when of eating. Before Morocco I had never done a drive longer than sixteen hours and that within the two coasts of my own USA. On those drives the most pressing issue was where to stop to buy another bag of Cheetos. Equally relevant to someone whose first thought on getting in a car is when I can get out, they had a defined end about which I could do nothing. On reaching New York or LA, it was either park or nose dive into the ocean. Even I didn't need a GPS to understand the consequences of that. So when we embarked on our five-day drive, my thinking was limited to this: we have a car, it runs, let's use it.

The sandstorm of our second day was now a pleasant memory, all the shifting sand picked from my hair and flicked back into the dunes where it belonged. We were nearing the end of our journey and decided to head onto a little-used road toward the cliffs of Cathedral Rock and the red clay casbahs and hamlets beyond. This was plain rugged country, its lack of ruins unalluring to the average tourist, its rocky, winding roads keeping it inaccessible to mammoth tour buses. It was the perfect place for us. We'd sleep in the hamlet of Zaouiat Ahansal, with Marrakesh and its airport within easy reach the next day. That we had neither sleeping bags nor food along was immaterial. Never having winged it before I didn't know enough to become unraveled at the thought of what could lay ahead. I'd scanned our map. It showed plenty of other villages, and since I was oblivious that font the size of ant footprints could mean a village in name only, I remained unconcerned. It looked adventurous, but not dauntingly so; remote, but with a neighborhood feel that reminded me of when my sister and I pitched a tent in our backyard and spent a night of sleepless suburban terror roughing it between the azaleas and the patio furniture.

Perhaps sensing slow going ahead, Bernard urged me into an early start. When we stopped to refuel in Kasba Tadla, a city seamy in its burgeoning prosperity, we decided a hefty lunch was in order. It might be our last sit-down meal for a while. That eating in a restaurant would also provide a flat surface on which to peruse our map was all to the good.

Dodging through traffic hand in hand, we establish a beachhead at a stained plastic table on the deck of an ordinary restaurant fronting in a sea of honking, belching buses, cars, and motorbikes. From a menu offering more Moroccan specialties than any ordinary kitchen should be able to produce, Bernard chooses lamb chops. I ask for lamb meatballs then push back my plastic chair to seek out the bathroom. "By the kitchen," points our waiter, indicating a splintery plank door to which cling bark-like strips of once-bright-blue paint next to the unscreened cooking area. Approaching, I see men in stained aprons wield heavy cast iron pans in a ballet with leaping flames. Their back muscles ripple inside thin T-shirts as they twist around for ingredients, shaking a pan vigorously, tossing cooked items onto waiting china plates. Black hair curls with sweat, dripping into the eye or down a cheek, to be swiped on a slick bulging forearm with a quick duck of the head. I pause to watch one of them grab a fistful of raw meat. He slams it on a greasy cutting board, whacks it into chunks, flings them into a pan where they sizzle and spit. Without even a cursory wipe of his hands, he then grabs a fistful of salad vegetables and starts chopping them on the same board. With the same knife. For reasons that baffle me even now, the only thought that registers as I watch this is, "How wonderful. A freshly prepared meal."

Closing the creaking bathroom door behind me, I assess the toilet situation. Warm sunlight filters through cracks in the planks, enough to illuminate a hole in the ground made sophisticated by raised platforms of dank wood on which to place my feet. Looking a little closer, I see not everyone here has great aim. There's a sink, but a quick swivel of the taps yields nothing. A thought flits, ephemeral as a darting hummingbird: is running water available for washing dishes? I return to our table just as food arrives, steaming and savory, the plates garnished with lettuce, tomato, and cucumbers.

Big mistake and hard lesson learned, which I now share with you so you can memorize it. It starts with the mantra all mothers, including mine, pound into their children as soon as they're old enough to walk: wash your hands with soap before eating. I was raised in a family of exceptional order. Everything in our house had its place, every activity its time. The gilded bronze sculpture lived on the china cabinet in the dining room, a multi-color vase of Murano glass on the third shelf at the back of the library, across from the Steinway. We ate dinner in the dining room at 6:30 every evening, after I'd practiced the piano for an hour. At the round table set with Limoges china on a delicate embroidered tablecloth, each of us had our place, my mother seated at nine o'clock, my father at three, my sister and I respectively at noon and six. We didn't trade seats. Even after my parents divorced, leaving just my mother, sister, and me at the table, no one ever sat in my father's spot. Three o'clock was his forever. At meals we conversed, discussed, joked and laughed, all four of us participating. I used a headband to keep my long hair from dragging in the food on my plate, held my fork and knife in the proper continental fashion, hid my used Kleenex on a thin ledge under the table rim. And I washed my hands before meals in the powder room off the front sunroom, the one with tiny white hexagonal tiles on the floor and a bar of Dove soap at the ready. So yes, I knew better. To which I'll add a bit of current lore which I soon learned on my own: When in strange places, eat only what you recognize. Never, ever order food made of mystery ingredients.

Would that we could have such hindsight available to us instantly, that we could live with the glory of the future, the purity of the present, and the comfort of the past simultaneously. But no, I dig in, enjoy my lunch immensely, and think nothing more about it. All is well as we drive high into the mountains, heading, unbeknownst to us, to a road that was severely eroded by floods the year before. Initially we make reasonable time, reaching Cathedral Rock with plenty of daylight. Around us are stony hills covered with fragrant cedar and sage brush, juniper and the briar-like thuya. Village walls are flounced with red and white oleander; feathery pink tamarisk line the sandy creek banks.

On we press, bumping along an increasingly rocky, potholed road, squeezing past cargo trucks after hairpin turns, breathing in the fine ochre dust scented with wild rosemary, juniper, and cedar. The going is slow but not particularly hair-raising, until we reach a narrow gorge, now made all the narrower by those floods. With a cliff of pale granite rising on Bernard's side and a sheer drop into the shallow river on mine, we slow to the pace of a Galápagos tortoise with a hundred more years to get where he's going. The road, once paved, is now undercut and crumbling. My eyes, which should be studying the map, instead sneak glances out the window to help my brain assess how much it will hurt if the road gives way beneath us. Soon we have no recourse but to abandon the road altogether and take to the gravelly riverbed. Though it's unfortunate for the farmers, it's quite fortunate for us that it's a drought year, for the riverbed is relatively dry. Our progress improves significantly as Bernard slaloms around boulders, fording rivulets and gliding across sandbars without once getting stuck.

On this, my first driving trip, the unpredictable nature of going away from the beaten track is like the jolting unknowns of riding a roller coaster facing backward. At first, I'm flooded with relief that I've avoided the unpleasantness of sitting in the car while it toppled off the road. This lasts about two minutes. Another few minutes pass as I relish the new adventure of finding our way through the riverbed. Do the math and you can see I allow myself all of five minutes of good feelings before beginning to worry that we are progressing at so slow a pace we'll still be in the riverbed, so recently my savior, at nightfall. None of this pleases me. I now want nothing more than to abandon that riverbed, lurching back onto anything that'll allow us to drive straight and at consistent speed, so I can get out of the car forever.

It is early evening when we reach our shelter for the night, a gîte d'étape housed in a century-old granary. We're on a hill above the village of Zaouiat Ahansal, its casbah roofs blending so perfectly into the surrounding sandstone cliffs that at first I don't even notice it, though that could be because I'm fixated on the granary, which looks hospitable for grain and livestock, but not especially so for people. The silo is built of buff stone crudely chiseled to approximate bricks, flanked by one-story wings of the same stone. Together they form a two-sided shelter to the sandy courtyard in which we now park. A few goats wander around, nosing for scraps, sprinkling glistening black fecal pellets like onyx pebbles on the orange ground. The windows of the living quarters, or perhaps they're goat sheds, seem to be staring at me, each glassless square a glaring eye, the white shutter next to it a Picasso-like vertical eyelid. There are no curtains, no pots of flowers. The place is simple and utilitarian, which is understandable. Threshed wheat has no interest in its accommodations.

If I'd had a crystal ball to tell me this was a training run for the P2P a few years later, I would have made more effort to hide the fact that I'm frazzled and exhausted. Luckily for Bernard, the hearty welcome we receive from our host goes a long way toward improving my mood. We're the first guests this middle-aged shepherd-innkeeper has had in months, and he's so delighted to see us that I can't stay grumpy for long. In gentlemanly fashion, he offers us his best accommodation, a large white-washed room facing onto his goat pen, bare of any furniture except a diminutive engraved wood table squatting on six-inch legs. A few religious icons are displayed on the wall. When we explain that we have no sleeping bags, he pillages his own bedroom, returning with a generous armful of cotton quilts and their resident fleas.

At midnight, my lunch decides to make a second appearance. Not keen at the prospect of picking my way in darkness down a flight of stairs to the outhouse, I scrounge about for a handy receptacle. In the barren room, the only solid, bowl-like thing I can find are the plastic bags that cover my shoes. That's when we realize that, in addition to sleeping bags and food, a flashlight would have been handy. Ever courteous and hoping to help me upchuck with a modicum of neatness, Bernard strikes a match and lights the room's only candle, which casts lurid figures onto the white walls.

I've never felt at ease throwing up in view of others. To me, there's something intensely private about the whole miserable affair. It isn't long before I stagger forth to make my way to the privy. A gibbous moon casts sharp shadows in the courtyard, one silvery ray illuminating steep stone steps leading to the long-drop hole. If I thought the day was tough, I'm doomed now to spend much of the night in more unpleasant surroundings. I find myself kneeling, like a penitent at the altar, in front of a rough board with a black hole in the center. The stench fills my nostrils, and even though it is two in the morning, flies buzz around my head. Opening my mouth, I stick my index finger into the back of my throat to make myself retch. It works, the poisoned contents of my stomach burning my throat on their way into the soiled pit below.

The next morning, I ignore Bernard when he asks, "What took you so long last night?" He doesn't want to know. And I keep to myself the one evident benefit of spending my night over a cesspool: Bernard is covered in flea bites. I have nary an itch.

Food Fair

GRAN ISLA CHILOÉ, CHILE, 2008

I t never occurred to me that Chile would be foodie heaven. I guess I was blinded by the country's history of dictatorship and neglected to think about the fact that Chileans needed to eat.

On our first solo drive following the P2P, we flew into Santiago, from where we planned to peruse as much of Patagonia, both Chilean and Argentinian, as we could fit into a month. After an eventful few days en route from Santiago, including Pucón's Volcán Villarrica, we headed for Isla Grande de Chiloé, Chile's second largest island. It's February and we're looking forward to what we expect, at this time of year, will be a calm and deserted island. Cruising south on the Pan-American Highway, we see a horizon dotted with volcanoes' summits piercing a cool morning mist like cone cakes covered with vanilla icing floating on a creamy bed of custard sauce. The road narrows, bordered now by waving beach grass, as we follow signs pointing toward the ferry docks. The day is pure golden sunshine, and I roll down the car window to let the salt-tinged air fill my nostrils. I'm almost intoxicated with elation that we'll soon be boarding an island ferry.

Boarding a boat for an island hop is a visceral experience for me, reminding me of the many times we took ferries to visit friends on Fire Island when I was a child, and of how much I loved those trips. Ours was a household of friendly routine, one readily understandable and indeed often reassuring to my sister and me. Still, like all children, we chafed at what sometimes felt like restraints, thrilling to those times when we stepped beyond the boundaries set by adults. On Fire Island, we'd be untethered from our home routine in every possible way. With no cars allowed on the island, my sister and I were able to roam at will. The prospect of mornings dodging waves and picking up horseshoe crab carcasses on the beach, of eating lunch later than my mother's strictly observed noon meal, of watching in horrified fascination as friends' kids engaged in spit fights from their bunkbeds, filled my body with such happiness it made me jumpy.

To this day, ferries thrill me. Gulls wheel and cry in a jubilee chorus, celebrating as cars clang over the steel ramp to be packed bumper to fender in the ship's damp hold. There's the continuous thrum of the engine, which strains and belches water to keep the ferry from drifting away from the dock too soon. The slightly fishy, oily, rotten food muskiness of all docks slips up my nose and I inhale it deeply. Then there's the bustle and press of imminent departure as the shore hand catches each thick, hairy coil of rope flung back from the ship across a widening stretch of water. Passengers rush up top to get a glimpse of the crossing, hair whipped by the stiffening breeze as the ferry gathers speed. Soon the deck is lined with a parody of the lonely lover, everyone standing with their arms tightly around themselves, ruing the jackets left behind in the cars below deck. As the wind snarls hair into a frizzle, only the brave or the impervious to cold continue to lean on the railing. Too soon, though, the ferry reaches the other side and everyone clambers back down the steep stairs in search of their vehicle. I still feel the same twinge I did as a child, when I'd wonder if I'd find someone already installed on my side of the back seat, the front being taken by picnic materials and my mother's red plaid thermos of hot black tea. Then the excitement of disembarking would take over as the ramp hit the new dock with a bang, and one by one the cars rolled off.

We've just passed a sign that says it's two kilometers to the docks when Bernard slams on the brakes, screeching to a halt behind a car whose occupants, dressed in festive beachwear, are standing by the roadside, talking on cell phones. Other car occupants ahead have hauled out bright canvas and plastic beach bags. I see them bent double, busily digging through their satchels, extracting drinks and snacks. We're at the end of a line of cars a mile long, none of which are moving. Obviously there's been a major accident, but what a strange habit Chileans have, to start a party when far ahead people must be suffering. I listen for the sound of ambulance sirens, look for police cars with flashing lights.

"Creo que vamos a esperar aquí un poco tiempo, no?" I say in Spanish to the women snacking in front of us. I studied Spanish for all six years of high school, and I'm good enough at it to hold decent if not hugely philosophical conversations. For days now, I've secretly swelled with pride that it's me getting us out of trouble, not just getting us into it. I also have observed in myself an unexpected benefit to speaking in a language not my own, aside from the ego boost I get in showing myself to be an above average foreigner. To say anything in Spanish I first have to contemplate things like gender, conjugation, and sentence structure. And that forces me to take a breath or two. As any good meditator will tell you, breathing has a benefit aside from keeping you alive. Done with awareness, it calms you down. Speaking in Spanish has allowed me to quell my usual impatience, and that makes me happy. Having a contented travel companion has made Bernard happy, too.

"Ay no. No te preocupes," one replies, to put me at ease. "El comité de transporte siempre se organiza bien las cosas." I'm relieved, but I don't know why, since if there's a connection between a transportation committee and the immediate need to evacuate injured accident victims, it escapes me.

"Entonces eso ocurre mucho?" I ask, not knowing how to figure out what she's telling me, but hoping that, by making this a dialogue I will eventually learn something pertinent that informs the situation.

"No, no, solo por los días del Festival Costumbrista," she tells me happily. Seeing my perplexed look, she offers me her bag of chips. Chile is a country where food is the answer to all questions. As if to support her statement, the long line of cars now takes a great leap forward and the ladies nod sagely at me, to convey this is no divine miracle, simply evidence that another ferry has loaded. We all jump back into our cars, drive forward a heartening number of yards, then cut the engines and get back out to resume our conversation. Within minutes there are cars extending far behind us. This makes me especially glad. I hate being last in line.

We adopt the mood of the convivial Chileans in front, taking out our own drinks and snacks, offering them to our neighbors. There's another reason I'm happy. My new friend in the car ahead has said a word that fills me with delight: festival. Added to that is a word I don't know but which makes me think of local customs, another personal thrill. "Bueno," I say, wiping chip crumbs from my lower lip. "El Festival Costumbrista, qué es?"

"Primero, es por todo el weekend. Hay muchísima gente que vienen, porque hay tanto a comer, cosas muy ricas, y también muchas cosas a hacer!" It takes me a moment to absorb the fact that the island will be thronged with festival revelers from all over the country this weekend. My roadside companion is so giddy thinking about it that she has to eat some more before she can continue. Fortified, she explains that the festival committee, knowing that thousands will come to the island that particular weekend, arrange for five times the number of ferries to ply the channel separating mainland from island. Out the window go our plans for a peaceful retreat. In flies exuberance that we have found ourselves in the middle of a native holiday celebration that seems geared to enable us to eat as much as we can for as long as we want.

The crossing is everything I wish for. There's salt air and a boatful of holiday revelers and cars parked in their orderly ferry fashion. There's even enough breeze on this sunny day to tangle my hair and lift the fishy scent of seaweed to my nose. Not even the slow traffic from the docks to the mid-island town of Castro dampens my mood, though we have to inch along behind so many cars that it takes twice as long to get there.

Castro itself is a bit of a letdown, and that's putting it gently. But this is the brave new post-P2P world, in which I'm determined to overlook such flaws. I feel I'm shining a spotlight on myself, in which I must learn to behave better. From my near-calamitous descent into despairing grump-hood on the P2P I knew what would happen to me—and hence to Bernard, who'd have to bear my ill nature—if I let myself backslide. The simple truth is we're not only on a trip I agreed to embark on with senses wide open to what a long-distance drive could be, we're on a trip I personally helped craft as an equal partner. Optimism isn't a natural state for me. Up till our

"Anti-Rally," I'd been comfortable going through life in "I told you so" mode. This allowed me to accept a pat on the back if things turned out well but to dodge culpability if they didn't. Now I wanted to pull that particular root out and plant something new. I was determined to start stepping up as an active player, despite not yet knowing quite how to walk that walk.

"How ugly," is all I say about how dismal a city Castro is, mainly to be sure Bernard still agrees with me. I avert my eyes from the plastic soda bottles and empty detergent tubs floating in the turgid bay, instead of counting them and announcing triumphantly exactly how many offending bits of litter are bobbing about. My spirits lift only when I see our hotel, the eccentrically named Unicornio Azul (Blue Unicorn), whose four stories cling to the steep hillside above the polluted bay like a leech on a choice bit of skin. It's painted pink. Not shy pink. Bubblegum pink. This seems appropriately free-spirited and a good emblem of what I want our trip to become. And what's not to love about an entire island that devotes itself to nothing but food and drink for two days a year?

Next day we arrive at the fairgrounds early, appetites in tow. As soon as he's out of the car, Bernard spies a fire truck with ladder fully extended. "A ladder with a view," he exclaims. "I must climb it." This is a pay-to-play ladder, in support of the local *bomberos*, Castro's busy firefighters, who are delighted to strap Bernard into a safety harness in exchange for a few pesos. From the looks of the fragile old wood houses we passed on our drive down island, the bomberos must be the most popular fellows around, and indeed they're happy to fill me in on their fire exploits while Bernard climbs. "Ah, Dina, it's wonderful up here," he calls down to me from his perch one hundred feet in the air. I get queasy just looking up at him swaying at the top. His hair would be whipping in the breeze, if he hadn't again shaved his head for this trip, as he did for the P2P.

After this short diversion, we're off into the capacious, welcoming heart of the festival to inspect the fifty-five booths where more than three hundred pigs, lambs, and steers have given their lives, creating the most extraordinary display of wood-fired barbecue skills I've ever witnessed. The trusty little red Weber that sits on the flagstone patio outside our dining room at home, ready for Bernard to grill the occasional brace of bratwurst or single ribeye on a dry summer evening, would be green with envy. These barbecue stalls are hosted by everyone from the local girls' basketball team and the Red Cross to all seven of the aforementioned bombero companies. Each one offers whole sides of lamb or hogs roasting on fifteen-foot-long spits that take four people to heft over the coals. Sturdy men in overalls and plaid shirts take it in shifts to turn the red-hot stakes.

We literally masticate our way through the fair. We're in a food delirium, and we're not choosy in what order we put food in our mouths. First some sweet fried rolls. Then savory bread made from a flattened dough of potatoes and flour wrapped around a hot cylinder, barbecued over wood coals, finished with a schmear of shredded seasoned pork and folded in thirds. Next a copious slice of berry pie and a cup of scalding coffee at the Red Cross stand. No longer hungry but unable to stop, I sit at a wood plank with a host of gregarious Chileans and dig into a plate heaped with a big chunk of lamb, steamed potatoes, and sliced tomato, washed down with the local *chicha*, a fermented apple cider. Bernard is suddenly feeling reasonable, so he sits this one out. But then we're both back at it with gusto. When we pass a booth offering baked salmon, he insists on a generous piece that he justifies by saying, "I want to support the locals." Nearby is a pastry stand boasting a seven-layer chocolate cake too luscious to resist, so Bernard doesn't. Cake secured, he plunks himself down on a nearby seat, right arm circling the iced marvel as if he's Frodo protecting the One Ring from the Eye of Sauron, while I act the part of Gollum, my stomach coveting just one bite while I pretend indifference with a "No thanks, not hungry anymore." This is one of the marvelous things about being married for nearly thirty years. We know each other so well, but we still give each other license to act as if we're on our first date.

Finally, I have to call a halt to the gluttony. "Bernard, I don't think I could put one more bit of food in my mouth. At least for a few minutes."

"But we're not done eating, are we?" Bernard knows a good thing when he sees it, and with over forty booths still left to sample, he's not yet ready to cede the territory.

"Let's go work off some calories, make some room in our bellies. So we can eat more!"

In the light drizzle that's been sprinkling since late morning, we inspect the crafts stalls, a visual feast of colorful but scratchy hand-knitted wool socks and caps, cuddly fleece barn animals with painted fabric heads, jars of amber honey with sections of the ivory wax honeycomb in each, a jeweled array of fruit preserves in tones of amethyst, ruby, and topaz, yellow rounds of handcrafted sheep's milk cheeses, garlands of purple-white pork sausages, and more. Next we wander the field exhibits, our shoes soaking up water droplets that cling to the tramped-down grass. Each shows how hard life actually is here on Chiloé, where sheep are sheared by hand, cows are milked by hand, hay is threshed by hand. Having just drunk my share of the local brew, we linger a while at the exhibit that shows how chicha is made. The main task seems to be smashing apples into a pulp. I have no particular experience at this other than whacking my birthday piñata as an eight-year-old, but I see a chance to expend some calories, and apple thrashing looks easier, and less scratchy, than the option of packing hay into a bale-sized rectangle, which is being offered nearby.

Bernard and I each grab a ten-foot-long wood paddle, which resemble what you'd use if you were in an ocean-going canoe and needed to get somewhere before the next squall. The apples reside, yellow, red, and green, in a shallow trough that's paddle-wide. I raise the paddle over my head. It's surprisingly heavy and I wobble precariously, thoughts of toppling over backward in front of a crowd serving to steady my legs just in time. Bernard hoists his with ease and we begin bashing the innocent apples in alternate strokes. After ten strokes my arms are shaking and we've barely broken half the apples, let alone mashed them into a pulp. "Bernard, holding maps for hours a day is not doing my biceps any good. I don't think I'm designed for this," I gasp, leaning on my paddle and wheezing while he gives the apples a few more whacks. "I'm better at drinking chicha. In fact, I'm getting thirsty again." We hold up our paddles in a bid to declare ourselves the winners in a knockout victory over the apples. The crowd standing behind the rope gives us a spattering of skeptical applause. We move on.

Late afternoon we drive to Bahia Cucao on Chiloé's west coast to inspect the Pacific, which we will soon be crossing on a long-distance ferry. The morning's drizzle has turned to slashing sheets of rain, a good first test of our rain gear. Stupefied by the number of calories he's ingested, Bernard has trouble thinking straight, leaving the car park with only his anorak on. I'm stupefied too, but also naturally wary of conditions that might make me uncomfortable, so I don my full rain suit. Thus attired, we toddle a mile or so down a sandy path through woods of scrub oak, pine, and the occasional prehistoric-looking Chilean shrub. We walk in silence broken only by intermittent burps, until we clamber panting and sweaty to the top of the low shore dunes. Crashing breakers pummel the deserted beach in front of us, roaring, spitting foam, and clawing at the gray sky. The ocean, a steely green, blends seamlessly with the heavy clouds that press on the horizon. A broad swath of fine, fawn-colored sand melts into the misty distance. If this were the Gobi, grit would be flying, but the beach sand has been compacted into a dense pancake by the heavy spray lifting off the waves. Now that we're actually on the island's edge, I feel obliged to touch the ocean, as an act symbolizing I've indeed gone as far west as possible. We walk briefly on the hard-packed sand, our feet barely leaving a trace as we head toward the pounding surf.

I'm no wave rider. In fact, big waves terrify me, stirring up visions of tumbling helplessly as I'm pummeled by tons of water. This stems from actually tumbling helplessly as I was pummeled by tons of water in an early childhood episode. For me, a proper beach experience is one in which I can stroll along under a benign sun, waves lapping at my toes, searching for shells, and daydreaming of the tuna sandwiches and cucumber spears chilling between icepacks back at my beach towel. Now, with the wind pushing me forward like a boot in the small of my back, it feels like work to be here. I dip my fingers in the ocean, raise them to my lips, and taste the salt. Then I turn back into the wind, wiping away fine strands of seaweed that cling to my face like a damp spider web.

We pause again on the crest of the dunes and turn around for one last look. Several gulls wheel low, eyeing clumps of brown kelp, searching for a fish or crab tangled within. In the fading afternoon light, it's a wild and seemingly untamed coastline, and we're the only people in it. I exult in the empty passion of the Pacific pounding the shore. I want to laugh, to whirl with my arms open till I fall to ground, too dizzy to stand up. If only I could proclaim as did Simone de Beauvoir: "I am awfully greedy; I want everything from life ... to have many friends and to have loneliness ... to travel and enjoy myself, to be selfish and to be unselfish." But I'm me, and it's raining harder, and I see Bernard's look of tender frustration, which says, "Come on, silly one, let's get going," because he knows I'm not Ms. de Beauvoir and if I get wet and cold I'll turn sulky.

Back at the Unicornio Azul, I fold my perfectly dry clothes on a chair while Bernard squeezes water out of his pants and hangs them over the shower rail to drip. We curl up together, the pull of a nap in a warm, dry bed too strong to resist. The feeling is reassuring in all the right ways, comforting, peaceful, and homey in its ordinariness. Just like at home, it takes me some time to fall asleep. Before I doze off, my mind spins as if the comfortable bed in that pink hotel were swirling. I want to turn to Bernard and rejoice at how opposite the P2P our experience on this Anti-Rally has been, to revel in the happiness I feel, which is due both to the travel itself and that the two of us have created it together. *Look at it all! We've eaten, ridden horses, hiked, eaten, talked in the local language to local people, climbed ladders, eaten, been in and out of a hospital, eaten. All without effort. And in such a short time. Can you believe it?* But he's turned on his back, his arms flung over his head like a baby. Already, he's snoring softly.

Mare's Milk

NARYN, KYRGYZSTAN, 2011

I am on a quest to try mare's milk. My thirst for this beverage took hold five years ago, on day five or six of the P2P, as we drove at breakneck slowness across Mongolia's Gobi Desert. I'd finally seen a few of the horse-back herders for which Mongolia is famous, their horses as small as ponies elsewhere, the horsemen more skilled than any I'd ever encountered. It all started me wondering how I could sample fermented mare's milk, *airag*, which is Mongolia's national beverage. Sadly, as we continued our limping progress across the Gobi, finding our way through the bland sand tracks took all my attention, leaving none for spying out yurts with mares.

Recently, when I found myself in Kyrgyzstan, it dawned on me I'd been granted a second chance. The Kyrgyz are semi-nomadic, conquered eight hundred years ago by that famed Mongol-on-horseback, Genghis Khan. Ever since, their culture has been entwined with the horse and, apparently, much affected by Mongolian thirst. Driving across Kyrgyzstan, I was in mare's milk mecca, assuming, that is, someone did the milking for me.

When we sold our software localization company in 1999, we moved to a two-thousand-acre working hay and cattle ranch high in the Rockies of northern Colorado. For much of the year we were crazy busy ranchers, as nature's deadlines are just as immutable as Microsoft's, with equally vexing results if missed. During the work season, we devoted ourselves to irrigating, fixing fence, haying with the crew, and loading trucks with twenty tons of premium forage for the fancy horse barns dotting Colorado's Front Range. In the off months, our work is modest enough that we can hire someone else to do it. That's how it happened that we could do the P2P and that's how we've managed our lives ever since, heading overseas during slack time, in this particular case on a nine-thousand-mile journey by car from Istanbul to Kolkata.

It's not easy to milk a mare. Unless you're an experienced nomad, the job takes two, plus a handy foal. The foal is a teaser, four legs with a set of lips to get the milk flowing. After that, one of you has to pull the foal off and hold him, squirming and wriggling, next to his mother's shoulder, so she doesn't panic and neither does he.

The other has the riskier job, kneeling on one knee by the mare's haunch, as if proposing, while balancing a bucket on the raised knee to catch what you're about to squirt out of the mare's teats. Remember though, horses are adept at kicking things. And that arm you've wrapped around the mare's hind leg to steady yourself? It could be flung away like limp spaghetti if she chooses to shake you off. But the risk is worth it if you're a nomadic horse herder, because in the four months of the milking season, you can extract three hundred gallons of milk (2,650 pounds), only half of which has to go to keeping your pump primer, that frisky foal, well fed. The rest can be sold.

The best place in Kyrgyzstan to get mare's milk is the narrow, verdant Suusamyr Valley, near the border with Kazakhstan, where nomads have summered their horses for centuries. Day 1 of my quest is cold and gloomy as Bernard and I drive through Suusamyr on our way from Osh to Bishkek. Slashing rain at lower altitude has turned to sleet at 7,200 feet. Fingers of fog drift over the valley floor, camouflaging the nomad yurts, whose white canvas is soaked to a soiled-looking gray. Yurt stovepipes, like so many landlocked periscopes, release curls of smoke into the wetness; the warm plumes of vapor lay low, hovering around the roof, too sodden to rise.

By the roadside are small tables displaying each nomad's milk offerings in reused Fanta bottles, larger quantities filling gallon cooking oil jugs. Each yurt also has equine advertising: a group of small mares, heads drooping and backs humped against the rain. Their foals are nearby, but not close enough to suck.

Today could be my chance to fulfill the quest, yet there are obstacles. For one, there's the 385-mile drive to Bishkek. It should take twelve to fourteen hours. We'd like to complete it in ten, despite two eleven-thousand-foot passes and winding mountain roads iced with the year's first snow. Then there are those soda bottles filled with an opaque white liquid akin to bleached Pepto Bismol. Who knows how long the milk's been there, its temperature rising, bacteria starting happy little families.

My quest for mare's milk is a solitary endeavor, as Bernard has already made it clear he has no intention of supporting me other than being willing to apply the brakes if I ask him to stop at a stand. His abstinence doesn't surprise, as his disinclination to be adventurous with food and drink is long-established. I much prefer he be honest with me and true to himself about this, and I no longer urge him to join me on my gustatory adventures. I've had more than my fair share of rancid, bitter, or otherwise unsavory beverages thanks to Bernard deciding politeness to our host trumped being considerate of me. "Yes, thank you very much, I'd love a cup," he'll say jovially. Then he sniffs it cautiously when the host's back is turned, quickly tipping his half-full cup into my mine. Our host smiles with pleasure eyeing Bernard's empty cup, regarding me with suspicion as I sip and sip and sip, trying to drain my double portion.

Regardless of these incidents, I do wish I could have Bernard's enthusiasm backing me up, especially since I feel uncertain. As it is, I'm naturally more a follower than a leader, and it suits my temperament to know that I have a companion in misfortune, not just a chauffeur. A willingness to stand with me and take just a little sip would suffice, even though on this latest quest I have no inkling whether I'll be able to drink my own glass of mare's milk once I find it, let alone his.

Today's rain doesn't do much to stoke my enthusiasm. Absent any vivacity from Bernard, I droop, any oomph I had succumbing to the weather. Despite it being early afternoon, the low blanket of storm clouds makes it as dark as dusk. When I take my first sips of equine dairy, I want to savor it, not huddle in a downpour. Besides, if no nomad is milking his mare in the rain, that tells me something. We drive on.

Day two finds me at a Bishkek hotel talking with the concierge. "Where can I get a glass of mare's milk?" I ask, expecting to have a choice of places within walking distance.

"Oh, this is not possible in Bishkek."

"But the nomads are just over the pass. Don't they bring it to the city for sale?"

"Never. It doesn't transport. You have to drink it fresh."

"Really? So the only place to get mare's milk is back three hours toward Osh?" We're heading the opposite direction, toward Kyrgyzstan's border with China.

"Suusamyr is the main place for mare's milk." She pauses to consider. "Here in Bishkek, though, there is one café, a very special place, that sells kumis, but . . ." her voice trails off.

"Kumis?"

"Mare's milk that is . . . how you say . . . fermented. I will show you how to get there." She unfurls a city map with a smart snap, jabs a furious dot with her pen to denote our hotel, and skips a dashed line several blocks up and over. "Here it is," she exclaims, scribbling a wild circle of happiness around the location of the kumis café.

I find the café midway down a quiet, tree-lined side street. It's patronized that Sunday by Kyrgyz families, a couple of men indulging a tableside snooze and a crone swaddled in layers of clothing doing some timid begging. Settling in at a well-shaded iron table by the sidewalk, I barely have time to look around before a harried waiter slaps a menu on the table. "Kumis, please," I say.

"Kumis?" he echoes, in a tone that should have filled me with doubt.

"Kumis," I repeat, trying to mimic the confidence with which the concierge said it that morning.

He whisks the menu away, turns on his heels and departs, swiveling his hips through the crowded tables in a blue-ribbon cha cha cha. Five minutes later he's back, carrying a tray with one glass and a clear carafe filled with a viscous white liquid. Taking a filthy rag from his back pocket he swishes it around and inside the glass, which he places in front of me with a flourish, heavy pitcher alongside. He lingers, raises his eyebrows in expectation, perhaps hoping I'll pour and gulp in his presence. For reasons I couldn't then explain, I sense it's important to take my first taste of kumis in private, so I wait him out till he's called to another table. Only then do I scoot my chair in, lean over the pitcher and inhale deeply.

My nostrils fill with a scent reminiscent of vomit.

There is only one thing to do in these circumstances: rely on my taste buds. I pour a drip, sufficient to taste, but little enough to pass for the dregs of a once-full glass. To bypass my nose, I exhale while I sip. Smell aside, I see no reason why milk from a mare shouldn't produce something similar to the sweet-sour deliciousness of other fermented milk drinks, like Greek kefir or Indian lassi.

I am wrong. Horribly, gag-worthy, wrong. But I'm in a public place, a guest of a foreign country, so I swallow the thick, sour, fizzy stuff. It does not go down easy. Abandoning my afternoon of kumis-sipping, I hand the waiter appropriate currency and leave. On the next corner, I buy a bottle of water, which I drain.

Now that it's clear kumis will not satisfy my mare's milk quest, there's only one thing for it. I must find the real thing.

Day three and we are driving west to Naryn, our last stop before reaching China and after which all hope of mare's milk will be lost. The Naryn Region (called an oblast) is the most definitively Kyrgyz of all Kyrgyzstan, with plenty of livestock of the sort that produces wool and meat, but not milk. Through 125 miles, I see small flocks of sheep, scrawny cows, plenty of spunky black goats, but no lush pastures, no yurts. No mares. The countryside alternates flat and dry with hilly and dry, neither conducive to horse nomads. Until, that is, we crest the pass above Naryn and discover we'll be descending through a rumpled landscape of grassy gullies and meadows.

Immediately I see horses, but they're geldings, only useful for travel and transport. I go on high alert for picketed mares. We round a hairpin curve and there, snuggled in a narrow gulch of green grass, I see a square black tent. A young woman with red cheeks and a dark kerchief over her hair stands in front. She places the toddler she's holding onto the ground, where he wobbles like a dashboard doll while she wipes her hands on her apron. The family granny has placed a low three-legged stool on the grassy edge of a wrinkled rise, where she rolls balls of white cheese, tossing them onto a sagging net awning to dry in the sun. Grazing behind them, foals nearby, are mares.

"Mares!" I shout to Bernard. "Stop, *stop*. Pull over." Though there are no roadside tables sporting soda bottles filled with white liquid, I have no doubt I can get what I'm after. Where there are mares and where there is cash, a transaction can be made.

Jumping a small stream, I walk up the short grassy slope, trying to keep my excitement from quickening my stride into something aggressive and too obviously foreign. Being out of my element is now very much my element. I'm not just seeing, I'm becoming part of what I see, my arrival changing the lives around as they part to allow me in, shifting from being a voyeur to a participant. I no longer care whether I speak the same language as those around me, because I know that gestures can convey paragraphs and a smile can open doors.

Seeing that the woman has moved to the tent entrance, I give her an Esperanto smile and she holds open the flap, as if I'd called in advance. Inside, the one-room summer living quarters of her family is crammed with a wood stove, table, chairs, a pile of sleeping quilts, horse tack, and the accoutrements of daily living. Light filters through a plastic window onto a stack of small enamel bowls on the table. She picks one painted with faded flowers, removes the lid from a slender wood churn, and ladles out white liquid. Her outstretched hand offers me the full bowl. "Mare's milk at last," I think, stepping forward to take it. Then she says, "Kumis?"

I parlay with myself. "Try it! This is homemade. It's probably completely different from the city stuff." "Leave it! Kumis is kumis." I look down at the contents of my bowl, taking a discreet sniff. There it is, that odor of things one should not be drinking. Smiling, I hand the bowl back to the woman and shake my head apologetically. Without hesitation, she pours the contents back into the churn.

"Milk?" I ask, hoping other travelers have used the same word. She looks at me blankly, then ushers me over to another churn, this time removing the lid for me to peer at the contents before ladling anything out. I bend low for a whiff. I detect the beginnings of the same sour smells. Adolescent kumis, not yet fully ripe.

"Milk?" I ask again, my voice meek, at a loss for what else to say. She returns the same apologetic head shake I've just given her and opens the tent flap to usher me out. But when it comes to food experiences, I am not a quitter.

My parents never babied my sister and me when it came to food. There was none of this, "Eat two peas for Mommy." I ate peas, I ate beans, I ate carrots, I ate pretty much everything put in front of me. My sister did, too. It wasn't just the specter of "those starving children in China" parents presented in the 1960s that haunted our every bite. My mother, reared on fish and vegetables of France's Côte d'Azur, and my father, fed with the schnitzels and goulashes of Vienna, were serious gourmands who loved delicious food and knew how to prepare it. Raising us as if we were in pre-World War II Europe where they grew up, they injected every interaction with traditions of civility and culture, instilling in me a sense that food and eating were as noble an adventure as climbing a mountain. Every activity had its food component. It might be the sandwich of cold chicken in layers of crisp lettuce and creamy mayonnaise that we took on our Saturday hikes to New York's Lake Mohonk, or the vanilla sundae at Schrafft's ice cream parlor where my elegantly dressed mother happily sat at the counter with me, offering me an icy dairy treat while she sipped her coffee, to buck us up after the exhaustion of inspecting the Christmas displays at Bergdorf Goodman. It might even be the pleasure of picking strawberries in the fields of Long Island on our way home from a day at Jones Beach. In every instance, my parents' happiness in the food they ate was shared with my sister and me. Food was not just eaten, it was analyzed and, above all, adored. We were a family unashamed to moan with culinary pleasure.

I have a memory palace that's actually more like an overstocked larder in the castle kitchen. Whether I'm eating a juicy hot dog or a sizzling porterhouse steak, drinking a glass of apple juice or champagne, I have taste memories that require only a bite or sip to come flooding back. Food speaks to me of love, family, sadness, joy, being young, getting older. It's everything. So now, in Naryn, my moment of hesitation vanished. If there was one thing I was certain of, it was this: where there are mares and where there is kumis, there *must* be mare's milk.

The two of us stand in the sunshine, woman to woman, wanting to understand each other. And then it hits me. I go on one knee as if proposing, curling my fingers into two gentle fists which I raise and lower while opening one, closing the other. Though I have only milked a cow once in my life, even a clumsy milker is an understood milker.

Nodding vigorously, my hostess goes to a large black bucket at the corner of the tent, which I'd walked by without noticing. Wiping her own bowl on her apron, she pours in a full ladle and offers it to me. I stare at it. I squint at the sun. I take a deep breath. At my feet, the little boy tumbles onto the soft ground, somersaults, picks at a pebble, oblivious to the significance of the occasion.

Raising the crock, I pick up a clean, faintly grassy smell. For a second, worrisome thoughts intrude, about unsanitary conditions, about the bucket sitting outside uncovered day and night, about what else her apron may have been used for. Then I open my mouth to let the liquid spill in. It's cool, not watery, but not fatty either. The woman's eyes are on me. I swallow, tasting a creamy sweetness with a mildly sour finish. I want to savor each drop, I want to gulp it down and ask for more. I want to shout, "I found it!"

Handing the drained bowl back to her, I turn to admire the mares. The foals are sucking.

INSIDERS

PREAMBLE

Almost everyone's taken a road trip in their life. But there are road trips and there are *road trips*. The ones I do are to the average take-the-car-to-visit-Uncle Bob drive as a Borneo jungle trek would be to a walk to the mailbox. Though the means of locomotion is identical, the experiences have nothing in common. When given the choice, we will take whatever route is less traveled by foreigners. If a trip works out right, I have a chance not only to become something other than I was, but to find a mirror reflecting all the more clearly the beauty and richness that is my life back home.

On these drives, we are eternally hopeful that we will not encounter tour groups nor, for that matter, others like us. Travel writer Paul Theroux captures it precisely when he says as travelers we want to be at large in an exotic setting, for every one of our senses to confirm that we are far away. We're seeking differences in landscapes and people, not repeated versions of our own lives across someone else's border. If we do things right, we're hoping not just to see the story, but for a moment become part of it.

On the ground, this means we avoid the obvious road that is shortest, swiftest, or smoothest. This makes the driving harder, and the days more protracted than they otherwise could be. It is also more nervous-making for one of us. In my normal life, which means my life on our Colorado ranch, I do not choose a stressful existence. There's already enough that can go wrong when you're ranching at 8,500 feet on the fortieth parallel.

For instance, if a lightning storm is forecast for a summer afternoon, we distance ourselves from anything steel, having personal knowledge of friends who got, shall we say, too charged up. But things don't always go well, even for the most experienced among us. One day a thunderstorm blew in early. Desperate to finish loading and tarp the stack of hay on his truck, our hay hauler raised his steel hay hooks preparatory to picking up a bale, turning himself into an instant lightning rod. He became airborne, blown off his semi, falling thirteen feet and breaking his back and pelvis as he hit the ground. And then there was the rancher who forgot the first rule of solitary cowboying: let the storm pass. Born and raised on this ranch, he certainly knew enough to leave his cows grazing where they were one more day, and he understood without even reflecting on it that he could finish stretching the last bit of fence line around the next field the following morning. We'll never know what did or didn't cross his mind. He was found dead next to his steel fencing tools, electrocuted as lightning coursed through the barbed wire he was gripping with them.

Where I live there are plenty of hazards in the wintertime too, which is long, cold, and white. It's seventy-five miles of empty road and no cell service to get from our ranch to a pharmacy. If a blizzard is forecast, I'll cancel the drive to pick up a prescription. I'd rather live with my flu symptoms another day than risk spending my night in a ditch as snow drifts over me. Whisky with honey and lemon, or what I call Rancher Advil, works like a charm.

Despite my pleasure in being safe and comfortable, doing an easy drive doesn't appeal to me. The whole point of these drives is to thrust me into a continual state of amazement, eyes startled wide open, teeth clenched and heart pumping madly at the uncertainty of it all. Committing ourselves to the less-traveled roads means we can get to parts of a country where even the residents might wish they were elsewhere.

In the Peruvian Andes in 2010, we swooped over long, empty altiplano tracks, alongside young girls in pastel dresses and striped wool shawls herding white alpacas from a watering pond to a field with grass as cropped as a Marine's high and tight. South of Nuwara Eliya in Sri Lanka we took a sharp right off a forest road onto a dirt lane hugged by rhododendrons and stalked by towering wild fig trees. The lower we went, the narrower the road, until turning around wasn't an option. When the forest suddenly ended, we blinked in confusion to find ourselves in the middle of a tea estate, the steep slopes to either side covered in a green gleam, as if cloaked in patent leather. Just as startled were the ladies picking tea leaves. We had only a brief interlude for them to admire our car while I admired the gold ornaments piercing ears and noses.

In a nameless hamlet in central India in 2009, we stood on a packed dirt sidewalk waiting for a flat tire to be repaired at the local bike shop. The air was torpid, abuzz with flies. There was no shade. Looking around, I noticed a wizened elder doddering slowly toward us on thin, bandy legs, his tiny grizzled head supporting a preposterously bulbous white cotton turban. Arms extended, brown parchment hands out to grasp and shake mine by way of welcome, he rasped out in a hoarse whisper, "Osama! Osama!"

Was this an ideological rant? It couldn't be. We were not in a Muslim part of India; in fact, we'd driven by the village's Hindu shrine. Yet the joyful fervor with which this citizen greeted us, his face nearly split with a toothless grin as I took his hands, was apparent. More villagers gathered, looking from him to me, seeking a reaction. I'm averse to crowds generally. As such I'm highly attuned to threatening behavior from even one person, let alone a group. I don't need my college psych minor to know that a heaping helping of crowds plus a dollop of ideology gives a winning recipe for a quick-rise threat. With this crowd, though, I sensed nothing but geniality. Eying the people around me I saw them nodding in agreement as he touched his palm to his heart, showing reverence and gratitude. Osama bin Laden? Here? Really? And then things clicked. I realized the man hadn't said "bin Laden." What he'd said was "Osama," plain and simple. Mimicking his gesture of hand to heart I corrected him with a name held in higher regard that year. Yes, yes, he nodded, as his smooth gums mouthed the name he'd meant all along: "Obama!"

Omo Beauty Queens

OMO RIVER VALLEY, ETHIOPIA, 2011

It's been a week since we reached Ethiopia's Omo River Valley, and my standards of beauty, conduct, and dress are undergoing serious reshuffling. I have never been a slave to fashion, but I do clearly recall my mother's horrified expression when, at the self-absorbed age of fourteen, I appeared for a visit to my effortlessly chic French cousin in Manhattan wearing a faded work shirt tucked into ragged bell-bottom jeans cinched with a fringed orange suede belt. It was the late 1960s, and in my longing to be a proper hippie, I was proud that I had been polite enough not to put a flower in my hair. And to tuck in my shirt.

Though at a loss for words, my mother's shock was instantly visible. Her everyday facial tics went into overdrive, cheek muscles spasming her eyes into rapid blinks, the right corner of her mouth twitching downward, her fingers tapping at each other, thumb to forefinger, thumb to middle finger, thumb to ring finger, back and forth, back and forth. Finally, she said the words she knew would make me fume, "But darling, you can't wear *that* into the city. You must change." I glared hard enough for my hatred of social strictures to burn a hole in her Loewe quilted purse, then stomped back to my room where I put on the simple A-line skirt and light sweater which I knew, had always known, would meet with her approval.

Pico Iyer says, "Travel is like love, mostly because it's a heightened state of awareness, in which we are mindful, receptive, undimmed by familiarity and ready to be transformed." In this regard, I confess part of my heightened awareness falls on how different I am from those around me. There's the obvious distinction that I am white and reasonably well-padded compared to those around me who usually are sinewy from hard work and darker skinned from various ethnicities other than Caucasian. And then there's clothing, or lack thereof. I view outerwear as representative of all sorts of aspects of a person's life. I'm not talking fashion. I'm talking such things as whether locals can afford a change of clothing, or how far away the standpipe is, where they can fill a five-liter peanut oil tub to cook food and wash cookware, clothing, themselves, plus water animals and a small garden if they are so fortunate.

The fact that I look so different from those around me screams, "outsider," a state with which I am profoundly uncomfortable. Even in elementary school I was aware of my otherness; I knew that our mother who'd grown up in France dressed us differently, fed us differently, and organized our lives differently from everyone I knew. Things didn't improve for me when I was switched from public to private school starting in seventh grade, bused from the suburbs while everyone else took the subway from midtown Manhattan, finding myself excluded from cliquish groups and clubs until I became one big bundle of yearning to belong.

When we travel, my inner child emerges, less along the lines of "playful" and more "please let me be one of you." Despite this, you will never find me wearing a sari in India or a longyi in Myanmar. Wrapping myself in the local garments strikes me as the ultimate pretense. Residents dress to suit their needs, I dress to suit mine, always being sure to be respectful of religion and custom, in particular covering whatever parts of my body the local norms decree. This philosophy is particularly suitable in the Omo River Valley where, as it turns out, women are mostly naked.

As we drive along, I consider a Hamar woman walking the roadside. Her hair, in tight ringlets coated with the Omo's ochre earth, glistens with fat that runs like greasy tears down under her jaw, staining rusty red the chunky steel band cinched around her neck. She is bare-breasted and stunningly beautiful, yet her torso displays a crisscross of large welts, which makes me wince. This is the ultimate insider versus outside moment, the welts a source of pride for her, testimony that she has been chosen for marriage in a centuries-old tradition in which women flagellate themselves with thorn branches as an act of devotion to their husband-to-be and his family. As an outsider I choose to leave my preconceived notions of "proper" and "acceptable" in exchange for an open mind about what is meaningful to those around me.

After six weeks in the north of Ethiopia, we've now reached the south, close to the border with Kenya. We're driving orange dirt roads that curve over gently rounded hills spread with a lacy coverlet of thorny acacia trees, dipping down now and then for an abrupt crossing of a desiccated stream bed. The countryside is nearly barren, even though from a higher vantage point those acacias help it look impossibly green, surely home to a thriving human and animal population. In fact, green groundcover here is impossible, because rainfall in this southern region of Ethiopia is usually less than ten inches a year. Even ignoring lack of forage as cause for the absence of anything moving, most of the wildlife in the region is gone anyway, hunted to the brink of extinction by the local peoples to supplement dwindling livestock.

Omo tribes such as Mursi, Hamar, and Karo depend on the Omo River's annual flood, which in turn depends on rains that fall to the north over Ethiopia's western Shewa highlands. It's this annual flood that enables farmers to cultivate maize and sorghum along the river banks and pastoralists to graze sufficient cattle for the nourishment of their milk, dung patties for their fires, and as livestock to sell or trade at market. This hand-to-mouth existence makes the river both secular lord and spiritual god, capriciously ruling the life and death of its dependents. While the river tribes may still believe in the river's omnipotence, in truth the Ethiopian government now controls whether there's a flood or not. Even when rainfall is good in the highlands, the upstream Gilgel Gibe III Dam captures the life-giving water and restrains it. The government has tied this lifeline into a deadly knot, squeezing it tight to prevent any errant drops from dribbling down the once flush riverbed. Arriving level with the deceptive greenery, I can see the policy's impact as we raise broad plumes of pastel dust and skirt herds of bony cows heading to a shallow shrunken watering hole. The acacias are widely spaced on the salmon-colored earth, their thin brown trunks and spidery branches casting a filigreed shade over bleached blonde grass. It's not lush at all. It's parched.

Rolling the window down to let the hundred-degree air blow through the car, I decide this life is not for me. I like deodorant. I have a photofacial twice a year. I wash my hair if not daily, at least often enough to keep it from oozing like a piece of badly fried chicken. And then there's the bare-breasted aspect of things. What would the supermarket bagger do faced with a naked me at the checkout counter, and all those frozen peas and canned tomatoes?

On the road, what people wear and how they live is the ultimate definer of their insiderness. Intent on getting beyond the nakedness, we stop in an Arbore hamlet of eight huts, set among the acacias. The arrival of our Land Rover generally is an event, but in this case no one runs over the hard-baked flat ground to greet us. The hamlet appears empty except for a pert-breasted young woman talking to a saggy-breasted old woman. They're standing outside a stick and thatch hut that looks more like a slash heap, someone's pile of kindling, than a home. I walk toward them, my place slow to give them time to adjust to the fact that a white woman with long straight brown hair dressed in quick-dry polyester pants, is approaching.

After the first awkward exchange of nods, waves, and smiles, I turn to Bernard and say, "Let's see if we can look inside their hut."

"Hmm," he says. "Maybe. Well, um, no." Bernard is more a stickler for polite reserve than I and is often chagrined by my unambivalent curiosity about others. My forwardness embarrasses him, until it gets us some-where special and then he's glad of it. Mostly though, I live with comments like, "Dina, you're staring!" or "Dina, stop listening to them!" That I'm leaning dangerously close as I eavesdrop on strangers, or have lost track of our own conversation because I'm looking so intently at someone, is something I don't even realize. I am so unreservedly curious about other people that I forget what I'm doing.

I have observed, though, that people, especially local people, also are intensely curious about us, and also are looking for a way to extend our encounter. When customs are so foreign I can't even get a toehold in something appropriate, I've learned that a compliment, no matter how vaguely offered, is always a good way to move to a next step. I smile and gesture at the hut, waving my hand around and doing my best to exude pleasure and approbation. This is a woman-to-woman thing, because every woman is house-proud. Whether an element of female solidarity arises or simply because they were heading there anyway, the women smile at my endorsement and motion us inside.

I expect to find one large room in which everyone lives and all activities take place. What I find instead is a thoughtfully laid out home. It's not a McMansion, but it works. We enter the foyer, which in my childhood home was a carpeted entry filled with light from the sunporch, accented by a tall white clay vase with three stems of bird-of-paradise. They never died. They were plastic. That, however, was suburban Westchester County. In Arbore hut terms, foyer means a six-by-ten-foot area with food prep on one side, men's and boys' lounge on the other. The stick roof is barely six feet high, a lattice of leafy branches that provides speckled shade but also lots of light. No need for chandeliers or windows here. The airy lattice that works as a roof is also used for the walls, making windows irrelevant while keeping out intrusive gazes as effectively as a suburban fence.

Like women the world over, I'm most curious about the kitchen. To me, because food sustains life, a kitchen, no matter how meager or lavish, is the center of all households. It's always been the center of mine. During our years in Boulder, it was a place where Bernard and I would have a quiet pre-dawn breakfast going over the day's plans before heading to our office in town. It was also the scene of an informal parade of meals with friends, family, and neighbors. During our fifteen years on the ranch, it's where I learned how to prepare the elk, goose, and occasional beaver Bernard had dispatched to our deep freezer, and where I cooked three meals a day due to the absence of anywhere to go out to eat except a bowling alley in the tiny county seat, population 560, sixteen miles down the road.

Now, I peer discreetly about, wondering what an Arbore woman uses to cook, though the more salient question should have been what food does she have to prepare. The chief's wife, a crone of indeterminate age with polished mahogany skin and a head of sparse hair neatly woven into around fifty tiny braids, comes over, nodding her head in greeting. She kneels in front of a shallow granite mortar. Sprinkling a handful of millet, she puts her shoulder to the task of making flour, scraping the pestle back and forth along its length. Her breasts swing in time to her movement. They're not cantaloupes; more like giant brown bean pods on a windy day.

I stand still, sweating like that proverbial pig, while she works, not a drop of perspiration beading her thin upper lip. I swear never again to take for granted those microwavable dinners in my freezer, organic or otherwise. Besides the mortar and pestle, the only other items for food prep and storage are a couple of plastic bottles and a few large gourds. In the lounge, the males of the group concentrate on what men do best while women slave in the kitchen—lying around on the charpoy and laughing. They chew on sticks, shove each other on the shoulder, talk and shout. *Charpoy* is Hindi for couch, and apart from the absence of a flatscreen TV, there's only one difference between these guys and their American counterparts shooting the breeze on a Sunday afternoon: no one here has a big belly.

Stooping under an opening about four feet high, we enter a window-less, high-ceilinged space, part of the hut proper. This is where the cooking and eating are done. There's enough smoke from smoldering embers that my eyes sting, causing rapid blinking of the sort which would make me think I'd lost my glasses. If I wore them. I can barely make out the ebony-skinned chief in a nearby corner. This black on black is great for a painting at the Guggenheim, but in here it creates difficulties. It's useless to don my attentive expression when no one can notice it. The one benefit of being in this shadowland is that no one can see the stains spreading on my super-lightweight, quick-dry shirt, as sweat slicks my armpits and drizzles from the back of my knees down my calves.

In the pervasive shadow of the room, the chief's arm appears, bony finger crooked, beckoning me forward. But there are hot coals somewhere on the floor and I have no desire to be a firewalker, never having believed in the benefits of singed soles, so I skirt the densest plume of smoke to get close enough to the chief to see what he wants me to see. He's squatting on a tiny stool, but not just any old stool. He smacks his chest to tell me it's his personal stool then raises himself a few inches off it so he can thump it up and down, illustrating it never leaves that particular spot. He's the chief and he sits where he wants, evidently always in the same place. His wife's stool, lower than his of course, is set beside him, but is allowed to move around. This is clever, as without such a decree, she'd never be able to cook and serve him. And it's not worth being a chief if you're not going to be waited on.

Standing, he hoists his ranking seat out from under his bottom and displays it for us to admire. It's a three-legged affair with a roughly sawn slab of tree trunk about butt-wide tacked on for a seat. Still, in a place where most have nothing but dirt to sit on, being the possessor of the high chair, low though it may be, is a thing of which the old gentleman is rightly proud and protective. He puts it carefully back in its spot, implying "Mess with my chair, and you mess with me."

Behind him, he gestures by placing his hands palm to palm and holding them alongside his cheek, is his bedroom. This is private, shared only by his wife. Separated from his room by a cloth is a similar sized space for his children and their spouses. And next to that is the room for unmarried girls and children. The chief's suite has a ragged floor mat, woven from grasses. That was it. At least I think that was it, what with the blurry view of my tearing eyes and the distraction of my perspiring body parts. Regardless, I stayed patient and attentive, and indeed I thought I managed the heat and smoke reasonably well, going with the flow even when what was flowing was me. Not so Bernard. He became desperate, wiping globules of sweat from his cheeks while uttering pointed statements about how it was now time to move back outside. No one paid him any attention, continuing our mimed discussion of the relative height of stools and the merits of pushing the pestle versus pulling it. I knew why he wanted to get outside, and it had nothing to do with his disinterest in food prep or manly lounging. Through the walls I'd noticed a knot of village women peering intently at the lattice, hoping to glimpse the visitors . . . us. Strikingly handsome, necks draped in the tribe's signature necklaces of long strands of beads in primary colors, they are a photographer's dream. And Bernard is nothing if not a photographer at heart.

I'm happy with our hot little tour. There's a nice voyeuristic element to it which appeals to my inner Peeping Tom. At home I always look into windows when I walk down a neighborhood street. If someone wishes to promenade bare-assed while I walk by, that is their decision and no reason for me to avert my eyes. Of course, nakedness in suburbia has different connotations from in the Omo. Here, naked promenading is normal; it's finding any Arbore fully clothed that would be cause for staring.

Divine Intervention

PEMAYANGSTE MONASTERY, SIKKIM, INDIA, 2009

Three weeks of driving through India has placed us in a novel situation: we have a private driver. The signs leading up to this were unmistakable. No longer was Bernard sanguine in the face of an onslaught of vehicles, whether with two wheels or twelve, all honking. No longer did he chuckle at the obstacle course of moving machinery through which he threaded our car. Now from the moment we sailed out of a parking lot into morning traffic he was cursing, growling at the clutch, clenching the steering wheel. I didn't need the bland statistic that India has the highest traffic death rate of all countries in the world to make me clench my teeth. I realized I was holding my breath only when I suddenly felt faint and a rush of air escaped my lungs.

So it was that after reaching Mussoorie, the onetime home of Sir George Everest, we abandoned our rally loaner car, hopped a flight from Delhi to Bagdogra Airport, and hired a driver to accompany us into the hill country of Darjeeling and Sikkim. Sitting in the back seat and holding hands with Bernard, leaning slightly toward each other despite a smooth drive, is my current idea of heaven.

That was four days ago. By the time we enter Sikkim, we have ditched Driver #1 as too slow and are on Driver #2, an enterprising and robust man who handles the steering wheel as if he were plowing a field with a brace of oxen. That Driver #2 is a bit too fond of his evening entertainment, and likes to hug the sharp corners of Sikkim's serpentine roads as if he were clutching a lady of the night, has made me uneasy. It's one thing for him to let two wheels skirt an abyss if he wishes to meet his maker; it's quite another for him to take us with him.

This miscalculation of what it would be like to have someone drive us around isn't our only obstacle today. An unseasonable fog has enveloped Sikkim's highlands in a damp, chilly veil. By all rights, we should have a spectacular view of the snowy slopes of Kangchenjunga, the world's third highest peak. Instead, the horizon is obscured by thick, smoky mist, and though I sniff the light breeze, I don't pick up even a whiff of a village campfire.

We're here to visit to Pemayangtse Monastery, one of the oldest and most revered monasteries, sometimes called *gompas*, of Tibetan Buddhism. Below me, elongated prayer flags in autumn colors line the dirt road, undulating in that breeze, their brisk flapping like so much applause for my arrival. Above me, I can make out low white-washed walls hugging a large, brightly painted, square building. A crumbling cement stairway bisects the wall, inviting me to advance but to watch my step. Even to an atheist like me, it feels serene and sacred.

This is the first gompa I've ever visited. I'm excited and circumspect in equal measure. Pemayangtse means "perfect sublime lotus," and the monks here are *ta-tshang*, of pure Tibetan lineage, celibate, and devoid of any physical abnormality. But Pemayangtse also simply is home to them, since many of the monks have grown up here from the age of nine or ten. As I mull over the niceties of how to be reverential while also feeling at ease, a boy with a shaved head appears around the side of the building. He freezes like a deer in the headlights, startled to see me, giggling. Then he bolts around the next corner, his blue Crocs slapping the walkway as his maroon robe flutters and balloons about him.

I'm unfamiliar with gompa protocol, an absolute greenhorn in matters of what I can do, and where I should do it. Can I can wander around freely? Do I need someone's permission to explore the grounds? While I stand at the steps pondering where to go next, a small car crunches to a halt on the gravel. Out tumbles a hodgepodge of middle-aged Sikkimese, dressed in neat pastel slacks and blouses. The women begin chattering, bustling about their menfolk like shepherd dogs corralling skittish sheep.

Edging away from their commotion, I enter a small, whitewashed building, each wall cut by an archway. It houses only one thing: a giant wood *mani* (prayer wheel) perhaps twelve feet in diameter, garlanded with small prayer flags in primary colors, embellished with carved inscriptions, gilded holders filled with prayer scrolls trimming its edges. It is said that the larger the prayer wheel the more powerful it is, because it can hold more prayers. If so, I am in the presence of one mighty mani.

Another adage about prayer wheels is that they are used to accumulate good karma and to purify bad karma. I'm all for that, so I start my slow circle around the mani's perimeter, choosing, for no particular reason, to walk clockwise. This turns out to be fortuitous, as later I learn that a Buddhist practitioner spins the wheel in the direction the mantras are written, which matches the movement of the sun. In a word, clockwise. There's no one around for me to ask whether nonbelievers are allowed to touch it. I walk studiously, hands clasped behind my back, so they don't get me in trouble.

It's a relief to have gotten in ahead of the large group that just arrived, whose babble nevertheless filters through the foot-thick walls. Finished with my circumambulation, I emerge to see the Sikkimese in various ungainly poses, like a flock of chubby storks, wobbling on one leg or the other to remove their shoes. They stare up at me in shock followed by flickers of, dare I say it, anger and disdain. What have I done? Perhaps nonnatives are forbidden entry here? I stand in the archway, my face feverishly overheated from a wave of self-consciousness that leaves me unable to move even if I could decide where to go.

But they're ready to come in, so I have to come out, which I do on tiptoe, smiling meekly. They all stare at my feet. I follow their gaze while one of them holds up her shoes and motions vigorously for me to step outside. For the nanosecond before I understand what I've done, I'm thinking she wants to trade her tiny, faux-leather loafers for my hiking shoes. What could she be thinking? Her shoes will never fit me. And that's when I realize the nice lady isn't trying to swap shoes with me. She's pointing out that I've just desecrated the prayer wheel house by failing to remove my shoes before entering, an obeisance which should have occurred to me, this being a sacred place, but which somehow never entered my mind. What could I have been thinking? Or more precisely, why had I *not* been thinking?

I hop briskly over to the threshold, bowing and nodding my head in shame as I go. Even though I've already been around the prayer wheel and am now back outside, I don't know what else to do besides remove my shoes then and there. It's after the fact, but it's the only gesture I can think of that might assuage the group's indignation. Now barefoot, I stand humbly while they file into the prayer wheel temple and begin slowly, prayerfully making their way around it. Then I scamper, clutching socks and shoes in hand. Padding barefoot down the cool stone walkway feels divine.

At the main entrance of the gompa I hear chanting from behind monumental heavily carved wood doors. The deep, haunting drone, cut now and then by a lilting soprano call from one of the child monks, gives me the shivers. No fool, I place my shoes with the pairs already scattered in a corner of the portal. A young boy peers around one of the curtains that shield the monks at prayer from the outside world. It's the scamp who scooted around the building earlier. He disappears for a second, then pops his head around the curtain again, this time gesturing for me to enter.

Sticking to the shadows on the perimeter of the prayer hall, I sidle around to a low wood bench behind that of the young novice monks. The boys are beside themselves with excitement at my arrival, twisting to look at me every few seconds, followed by elbow nudging and whispering. This is an important occasion—one of the Nyingmapa lamas is here to bestow blessings—yet I seem to be upstaging the venerable man just by the novelty of my presence. I feel I am looming like Gulliver in the land of Lilliput.

Despite our weeks in India, I had not grown more at ease with my foreignness. If anything, I'd grown less so. Having covered several thousand miles of road I'd observed how even a woman living on the street managed to keep her hair well-braided and her sari clean. The more stained and wrinkled my clothes became, the more unkempt my hair, the more overtly different I was from those around me. I had come to despair of the conspicuousness inherent in being a stranger and a foreigner and I was weary of how isolated it made me feel despite the throngs around me.

Turquoise drums are beaten, accompanying the braying of fifteen-foot-long brass and copper horns. The tones flow over and through me, a vibration at once ancient and alive penetrating my body. There's a faint scent of butter, sugar, and incense, slightly sweet, slightly sour, centuries old. The boys keep peering over their shoulders, a nod and smile, followed by the eruption of bashful giggles as they turn to one another and comment on my presence. For a time, the chants lift me outside myself as the spirituality of the three-hundred-year-old building seeps into my bones.

One of the boys leaps up, scurries into the obscurity at the back of the hall, and returns with a tin platter heaped with gaily wrapped candies, peculiar-looking Indian chocolate bars, and assorted twin-packs of biscuits. Smiling, he bows low, lays the platter on my knees, mimes eating, and scuttles back to his cushion, where he pulls a candy bar from under his robe, raises it in a toast, unwraps it, and takes a surreptitious bite while his brethren continue their chant. His innocent acceptance soothes my mortification like a balm.

When the prayers and blessings are complete, the monks heave themselves off their cushions, and visitors are invited to approach the lama. Feeling I've already trampled on their welcome, I stick to the wall, where I can admire intricately petaled flowers carved from butter for the occasion.

Back outside, I see the Sikkim group again hopping about. This time, they're putting their shoes on, each with a fluttering *kata*, the white silk scarf which the lama has blessed draped over their shoulders. They're all abuzz with the pleasure of their close encounter with holiness. I lean against a far wall to tie my shoes, a safe distance from these people I have so offended. They look up. Though I have no *kata* of my own, it appears nonetheless that I've benefited from divine intervention. One by one they smile at me. All is forgiven.

Garbage and Dogs

USHUAIA, ARGENTINA, 2008

A vis in Santiago de Chile has caused us another headache. This one is in the migraine category, a real showstopper. Our journey through Patagonia, with its attendant distractions of coastal ferries, food fairs, even impromptu hospital visits, has taken us nearly two thousand kilometers from Santiago, if we were crows. We're not crows. If you were to plot our vehicular path it would resemble that of a puppy in a new neighborhood. We've been easily distracted, tugging hither and yon to nose everything in case it's interesting. It's likely that by now we've covered enough terrain to get us to Santiago and back again, if we wanted to go back there. Which we don't.

The night before the calamity there's no inkling of the troubles to come. We spend it in San Sebastián, Tierra del Fuego, on Chile's side of its border with Argentina. It's quiet here for one significant reason: San Sebastián is a town in name only. The hush is actually noisy, wind gusts pressing on my ears like hands shutting out bad news, before booming across the road to slam the half-hung doors of dilapidated wood-sided sheep sheds and swirl uninvited through gaping glassless windows. There are no services and no inhabitants in San Sebastián aside from the owners of a solitary *hosteria* a hundred yards from the border, where we rent a room.

A few cars pass before the border closes for the night. After that, there's nothing around but wind, stars, us, and our hosts, who, from what we could see through the guesthouse windows on the way to our room, appear to have recently invested considerable sweat equity renovating their café. The low clapboard structure has a fresh coat of white paint. The wood strips separating multiple panes of glass in each window are scarlet. Door and window frames are a bright egg yolk yellow. "This looks like a nursery school," I say to Bernard, as we hop through dry weeds back to the café for supper. We skirt a red and white jungle gym made of steel pipe from which hang two swings with blue wood seats, a low-slung yellow trapeze and a blue plastic slide. "This isn't a place where there will ever be masses, children or otherwise, lining up at the door."

"I know. And everything in our room is new, too." The wind whistles, hollow and lonesome.

"Yeah, we're it. We better give them some good business."

"They might not see more for a while."

The café has a long white counter, white linoleum floor, and ice-blue walls. Echoing the exterior motif, the counter stools are plump orbs of cherry vinyl. The name Coca-Cola emblazoned on the plastic chairs snugged up to each table explains why they, too, are cherry red. Even the frames of photo montages decorating the walls are red. There's so much red it reminds me of the day my father's ice skate snagged in a fissure on Twin Lakes, our local skating pond. What with sun during the day and frost at night, the exposed ice heaved and buckled, creating a ragged surface that only kids in the 1960s could adore. Unless you were my father, who loved anything he did out of doors with his children. One moment he was gliding, gloved hands swinging along, a Hans Christian Andersen fairytale come alive, and the next he was sprawling, hands unavailable to save him from hitting the ice face first. I saw it happen, in that comedic slo-mo that all skating falls seem to have. I gasped out a laugh, gulped back the second cackle about to explode from my mouth, watched in fascination as droplets of blood spangled the ice, their warmth melting the surface to form a soupy red map resembling the state of Texas. I was perhaps eight years old and knew two things clearly. One, I could not lift him up to get him back to shore, and two, my mother would be displeased if I stained my white skating gloves trying to block the blood gushing from the laceration on his forehead. Instead I did what any self-respecting kid would do in a situation like that. I covered my eyes with barely parted fingers, like I would when watching zombie movies on TV. Then I closed my fingers hoping it would all go away. I opened them to discover my father sitting up, soiling his own gloves to staunch the flow of blood, and then I started to cry. I feel a similar giggling melancholy suffuse me now. The effect of the overly bright café is one of such brave, wistful hope it makes me want to cry on their behalf.

Señor and Señora are elated to have us, though the mask of joy on their face is betrayed by the anxiety in their eyes. That we're here is cause for relief. That we're the only ones here at all is cause for despair. They're both middle-aged and so earnest we want to hug them as if they were our own parents. Señora, in her white butcher's coat trimmed with red piping, plastic shower cap covering her hair to illustrate how sanitary the premises are, falls all over herself serving us. She plies us with plates of mysterious cuts of lamb, all equally tough. True to his word, Bernard orders a bottle of red wine to bulk up our tab. The elation on Señora's face when she brings it to us is a sign that not many people have been ordering anything in her new restaurant for some time.

Photos decorating the walls clue us in that Señor may have an airplane, may even be a pilot himself. "Repeat after me," I tell Bernard while we both chew the lamb leather and try to clear it with gulps of vinegary wine. "Piloto, avión, helicóptero. Now go, and make airplane conversation with the man." Eventually all four of us cluster around a table, as I scroll through photos of our ranch on my laptop. Sharing the wine with them loosens all our tongues and when my Spanish fails, they smile charmingly, pretending to understand our English.

The next morning, we complete our exit of Chile within a few minutes, cross a short stretch of no man's land and enter the Argentinian border offices, where the first tentacle of disaster reaches out to strike, but is neatly dodged. Or so we think. Reviewing my documents, the border official politely reveals that our car insurance papers, the ones provided by Avis Santiago, which we need if we're to cross back and forth between Chile and Argentina as planned for the next six weeks, expire at midnight that day. "No es posible," I declare, as much to myself as to him, shocked at what he's saying.

"Si, señora, así es," he replies, ever mannerly, pointing to the offending date. He proposes that we return to Santiago to correct the problem. Backtrack two thousand miles? I don't think so. I thank him profusely for his time, smack my forehead to mime shameful forgetfulness and foreign stupidity at leaving the correct document in the car, and stride purposefully out the door pretending to scrutinize my papers to avoid further eye contact.

"Let's go," I tell Bernard, shooing him forward with my hand. "Onward. Down the road. Into Argentina." He eyes me doubtfully. I never tell him when to drive, so my eagerness to move forward is suspicious.

"Everything fine?"

"Well, no, but it doesn't matter," I say. "We have no choice. Unless you want to drive all the way back to Santiago. Two thousand miles in the wrong direction."

Bernard has little patience for my sarcasm, especially since I haven't explained the problem.

"Santiago? Back? Why?"

"No insurance. The papers lapsed. Today." The more distressed I feel, the less my lips want to cooperate by forming words to explain the situation. "Anyway, just go. *Go,*" I hiss. "I don't want that border guy to think he should come out and check if we really do have valid papers. We'll figure things out while we drive."

Bernard's face becomes a stop-animation cartoon as he alternates between wanting to know every detail, needing to be in charge, and having to trust me. I busy myself storing our obsolete papers back in their waterproof pouch. Finally, he starts the engine. As we drive down the washboarded road I explain that we're now in Argentina with lapsed insurance papers. There's no way to get back into Chile with what we have on hand. We either have to get corrected papers or a different car. And we have to do so that same day or we'll be driving without any insurance at all.

Instead of the leisurely perusal of Tierra del Fuego we'd planned, we hightail it the three-hundred-fifty-mile length of the island in one day to reach Ushuaia, where, in theory, a well-run Avis office exists. Stopping briefly in Río Grande enroute, to fuel up, we ask the Avis agent there to speak to the Santiago office on our behalf about proper insurance papers. "Yes, yes, I will call right now. Please, sit," and he gestures to two gray metal chairs in front of his gray metal desk, a man whose need for company is not satisfied by the wilting potted plant in the corner and whose need for more business is evident from the uncannily empty desktop between us.

We perch on the edge of our seats and listen. From our side of the phone it all sounds civil. Indeed, Avis Santiago promises to fax the correct insurance documents to Ushuaia that afternoon. Or so he assures us. I'm suspicious, but can't pinpoint what's wrong. The way he rubs his hands together should have been a clue that all he wants is for us to be happy, that he'll say anything to make it so. The clock with thick black hands tocking on the wall above him should have been a further clue that his main interest now is to get rid of us so he can leave for lunch. I need him on our side, don't want to agitate him, because none of this is his fault. And I can tell from the large belly challenging his belt that lunch is an important element of his day. I flash him my best fake grin, which I perfected by imitating the rictus of a corpse on *CSI*.

"Por favor," I plead. "Could you possibly call them again, after lunch, and make sure they've done what they say?"

"Yes, of course I will call them. Of course. I do my best to make sure they do what they say." He pats his belly a few times, clasps his hands over his paunch. "Ay, those Chilenos. You know. Our work here is very difficult." And he heaves a sigh that ripples through his body, from his curly brown hair down to his scuffed imitation-Gucci loafers. "Because we don't control them. They are a separate company. We are a separate company." He shrugs, is embarrassed, raises his hands in helplessness. "Argentina. Chile. Very separate countries." This does not bode well.

We all wave goodbye. I am quite certain that he's off to a long, leisurely Argentinian repast, before, during, and after which nothing will be accomplished. We press on. My mind is racing like a dog chasing its tail, fretting because the darn thing keeps getting away, which causes me to lose track of where we are. We get lost, right on the outskirts of Río Grande. Bernard winds up driving halfway back to the border before we find a spot to turn around. I sit hunched, shoulders tense, neck rigid, waiting for Bernard to erupt about how I need to pay closer attention to map, GPS, street signs, landmarks, anything, everything, to keep him on track. How that's my only job and it's a pretty simple one compared to his, in which he has to contend with the difficulties of watching traffic, avoiding pedestrians, swerving around cyclists, all while maintaining the proper speed limit, a job in which a lapse of attention could cost someone's life. He says nothing. It seems our agreement for the P2P, that he would not lose his temper with me when I messed up directions, and I would not bellow when he got too close to another car, still holds.

Reaching Ushuaia, we park our car at the airport Avis office in a form of nonviolent protest, hoping the sight of a Suzuki with Chilean license plates will elicit the sympathy, or horror, needed to get us swiftly out of the way. By now, I am more familiar with Avis's cheerful red sign than I ever planned or wanted.

Our newest Avis agent, however, is a breath of fresh air. A raven-haired pixie of a sexpot, she is nothing if not empathetic to our plight. Informing us that no papers have arrived from Avis Santiago she raises a manicured fore-finger to the air as if to bring down the wrath of God—and picks up the phone. Within seconds she's arguing ardently on our behalf. The Chileans seem to divine her beauty through the phone lines. I can almost see them cringing in the face of her passion. "Yes," they tell her. "Of course we'll fax you the necessary insurance papers. Of course we'll get them to you by five this afternoon if that's what you wish." When she mouths to me that they claim this is the first they've heard of the problem, I roll my eyes and tsk to show what a lie that is. Despite her verbal abuse, which is lavish and all of which I can understand, they're falling all over themselves to comply and they can't even see her. But when she turns her kohl-rimmed green eyes on us and says "Come back later," I get the queasy feeling victory is anything but assured.

Argentina has labeled Ushuaia the southernmost spot on the South American continent. This is without the consent of Chile, which turns up its nose at Argentina's marketing baloney. Chile knows full well that its territory includes a minuscule island, Isla Navarino, farther enough to the south to put Argentina's claim to shame. Nevertheless a happenin' spot on the cruise circuit, as well as the jumping-off point for trips to Antarctica, Ushuaia sits on a hill overlooking a sweeping blue bay fronting the Beagle Channel, not a sop to the Westminster Kennel Club, but to Charles Darwin and his boat of exploration, the *Beagle*. Now that we have some hours to look around, I notice that Ushuaia might more aptly be named Rubbishville, or, since this is a Spanish-speaking country, Punta Basura. The town is a dirty hodgepodge whose general problem with litter shocks me only until I see Río Gallegos up north several days later.

For a while, I try to dismiss how pervasive the garbage is. But it's like trying to ignore a python intent on squeezing you to death. It's all around. As we stroll down the street I'm repeatedly assaulted by plastic bags that tumble and frolic in the channel breezes. These capering non-biodegradable flocks are supported by their cohorts, the foil chips bag and the sparkly candy wrapper. They tickle my legs, wrap themselves around my knees. While sipping a coffee outside a restaurant, I'm mugged by a pack of bags whipped into a frenzy by the wind.

To stop my mind from worrying over the car insurance calamity, I focus my intellectual faculties on litter. I attribute much of it to economic doldrums, which are real despite the tourist trade. And there's that distinct lack of trash receptacles, evidence not of disregard but of constrained budgets. Placing myself in a local's shoes, it strikes me as unreasonable to expect people to carry their trash home. More to the point, I'm all for focusing what modest public funds are available on major social issues such as education and health care, which already are strapped and which now face competing demands from the beavers. Yes, those. What started as fifty beavers imported in 1946 to start a fur trade has boomed to a quarter million flat-tailed furry rodents, who find themselves in the equivalent of beaver heaven: miles of rivers and no natural predators. The threat to forests, cattle pasturage, and water flow is real. So what are a few thousand bits of tinfoil and plastic detritus compared to economic devastation?

Aside from introducing me to what I eventually learn is Argentina's ubiquitous garbage trouble, Ushuaia also unveils Argentina's rampant stray dog problem. Combine the fact that a dog can go into heat and therefore breed up to three times a year, with the idea that spaying or neutering stabs at the very heart of Latin machismo, and you have a recipe for a dog population explosion. The homeless dog situation here is of recent enough vintage that all the hybrids are still distinct from each other. We see everything from a groomed and well-nourished German Shepherd, to a pack of what look like basset–Giant Schnauzer crosses, a cartoon dog with four-inch-long legs, wiry coat, big body, and floppy ears. It'll take many generations of unsupervised street copulation before these mutts are blended down to the doggie blandness seen in more sophisticated homeless-dog countries like India, where they've been at it for centuries and where the pariah dogs of the street have been reduced to a common denominator of slim well-proportioned body, long legs, satiny beige coat, whip-like tail, and pointed nose.

Tired of dodging street trash, we return to our hotel to unpack. A sour temper has replaced the sturdy chuckle that saw me through the past week. Bernard asks me which side of the bureau I'm going to use for my things, an innocent question that is standard protocol when we invade a new room. On our long road trips, changing hotels every night, we approach each new room like conquering generals, taking the measure of our spoils. Is there a bureau for T-shirts and socks, perhaps a closet (though hangers aren't a given), a towel larger than hand size, enough outlets to recharge both his gadgets and mine? It's our way of ensuring that each gets a chance at the better drawers and that we take turns returning to the reception desk to ask for whatever's missing. Now I snap an unhelpful reply: "Take whatever side you want. I couldn't care less!"

Throughout the P2P my irritability had risen in proportion to my depths of exhaustion and strain. The further I fell, the quicker I was with a sharp, dismissive comment, each a mirror of my character. It showed an unappealing travel companion, someone unable to collect herself, unfit to manage adversity, in short everything I didn't want to be and not someone I liked. On this trip I'd vowed not to let myself be transformed into passenger-seat hellion by my personal djinn of doubt and dread. Yet here I was, snapping out a rude response. The silence that greeted me made it clear Bernard was chagrined. So was I, in particular to learn that my recent cheerfulness has been more of a temporary lapse than a permanent transformation.

Bernard does his best to lighten the leaden mood in the room. "Let's eat," he says. Eating is our ibuprofen, what we resort to when one of us is bruised, sore, unable to cope, when we need soothing of the most profound sort. For Bernard, the act of chewing seems to release positive endorphins, something a scientist, preferably a French one, should study. For me, restaurants provide weapons of distraction, in particular a menu, which I can place in front of my face like a cop with a riot shield. Behind the menu I can avoid conversation and reorganize in peace, emerging not just knowing that I want ceviche, but more tranquil as well. It's worked before, and it works now.

Bernard steers me up the road to a small elegant restaurant atop an Ushuaia hillside. We're at an altitude too high for plastic bags to reach. The Beagle Channel sparkles far below, the setting sun sending an orange blaze across the choppy, deep blue bay where a multitude of mammoth white cruise ships bob like toys in a bathtub.

In the quiet dining area where we are kept company by a handful of empty, white-clothed tables, all the ugliness of Ushuaia falls away. Cars aside, good fortune has stayed with us, at least on the culinary front. It's *centolla* season. This relative of the Alaskan king crab is the most prized seafood in Ushuaia and we are determined to eat our fill. Each ten-inch diameter crustacean requires the focus of a watchmaker to deconstruct. The crabs are as immense as our insurance problems, but infinitely more satisfying. There's something elemental about breaking open a cracked shell with my fists, gouging out succulent flesh, feeling a warm runnel of buttery juice drip down my chin. It clears my mind, reduces me to my inner child and as such infuses me with feelings of contentment. The copious amount of icy white wine with which we wash down that crab doesn't hurt either. After a silent half hour, I discover that my ability to multitask has returned. I am able to apologize to Bernard for my foul mood even as I lick my fingers.

Finding Dereka

AXUM, ETHIOPIA, 2011

Cars can be hospitable conveyances. A back seat normally home to camera bags, cracker crumbs, jackets, and two Tilley hats can be swiftly transformed into just the right size bench for an unexpected passenger. Passengers are a world unto themselves, a walking incarnation of the whole story of life through which we are driving. I have noticed that no passenger is unaccompanied. Every one of them brings two things with him: bundles and body odor. The former are just lumpy, unobtrusive extras, stashed at the feet or held on the lap like a small child, though less wriggly and quieter. The latter is a stealthier presence, making itself known only after the car door has been slammed shut, as the passenger leans forward, extends his arm over the glove box to shake hands and exhales a heartfelt thanks.

None of these passengers has the money for bus fare—if there even were a bus going their way—or they wouldn't be walking down the long, empty dirt road on which we're driving. As I take the extended hand, feel the dry, leathery palm in mine, I know their thanks are genuine. But that displacement of air, slight though it is, changes the conditions in our car radically. It's like an autobiography in elemental form. I'm not talking about the locker room essence with which any Westerner who's gone to high school is familiar. This is something far more fundamental, a slow, steady accumulation of life on the body of the person sitting behind me that snuck into the car just before the door closed and now slowly fills all available space, most particularly my nostrils.

We have given a lift to mother and daughter, farmer, village entrepreneur, salesman, locals in sandals or dusty black lace-ups, ethnic attire or an old-fashioned faded blue suit over a shirt washed to frailty. One has a weary briefcase, another a small case with a torn zipper, a third just the hand raised, palm forward, to ask us to share our wheels. The odor that joins us is old and new, speaking of small, shared spaces where everything in life takes place. I sniff. There's that greasy smokiness that hints of a bit of meat with the vegetables in the pot last night. Or an odor of that omnipresent cook fire mingled with Ivory soap, still the cheapest bar in this part of the world. Or maybe it's Dove. There's a soupçon of goat, a garnish of loamy soil, and over it all, the icing of old sweat from work, from the pervasive heat, from water being so precious that it's always used first for cooking, drinking, keeping goats and cows alive. Whatever they're wearing is likely to be their best, because they're going somewhere, cause enough to dress up.

In the month we've been in Ethiopia I've become hyper-aware that a bucket bath is a luxury most villagers rarely get. Since we are choosing our own route through the country, taking the dirt roads that track through villages rather than the swift pavement connecting tourist centers, I have ample opportunity to see how locals live. We stop when we wish, drive at our own pace, our only goal to see what's around us, and hopefully to reach our planned shelter at the end of each day. Even when I was young, traveling with a backpack through Europe and Israel for five months after college, I took more pleasure in just looking at what was around me than in spending a day in a museum or traipsing through a monument or ruin. The opportunity to be part of a country's "here and now" has always held infinitely more appeal to me than perusing that country's history. In Ethiopia I would have had to be blind not to glean from even one day on the road that access to water severely circumscribes the life of most Ethiopians. Water is carried by donkeys or on women's backs, from a seep or an area standpipe that can be miles away. Children may spend much of their day in pursuit of water, one plunging up and down on a hydrant handle to keep water trickling into the five-gallon jug that once held peanut oil, another striding purposefully home, the forty-pound jug balanced on their head. When so much time and effort go into securing water just for basic survival, it is no surprise to me that our passengers are ripe. It is also cause for me to cherish the hot water spilling out of a hotel bathroom at day's end, a shower which I curtail to a few minutes while acknowledging to myself the immense luxury that is indoor plumbing.

Not far from Axum in the northern Tigray region of Ethiopia, we decided to search out the one rock-hewn monastery in the area: Dereka Abba Meta. These rock-hewn places are exactly what the words themselves mean: church or monastery buildings chiseled down or otherwise into a rock massif, rather than free-standing buildings built of stone blocks from the ground up. They're not much to look at from the outside, just a low wood door, or a square hole for a window. But inside are rooms sculpted from the cliffside, complete with columns, arches, frescoed walls, and ceilings soaring thirty feet. In other words, something worth driving far out of the way to see.

We start down a road and might just as well have been driving on Mars for all that the landmarks resemble what my guidebook describes. Unlike most travelers, I tend not to frequent a guidebook for trip planning other than to get a general sense of what our route may be through the country where we're heading. Apart from that, we like to decide what to do when we get there, "there" being any place on the road as well as what's around the place where we sleep for the night.

This last-minute aspect of travel can have unexpected consequences. It means that at times we miss something that in retrospect we wish we'd seen. It also means that, absent a plan, many days can have too much of little consequence in them. This being said, the nature of travel is that it's transitory, which means there'll always be someplace else to see, time that feels frittered away instead of meaningful, something that's missed while another opportunity is taken. Being open to opportunity is what defines our days.

Tossing the guidebook onto the cluttered back seat, we stop whenever we see someone on the road. "Dereka?" I ask three women in my best Tigrayan accent. They point us northward. In five minutes we dead-end in a schoolyard full of sulking students. "Abba Meta?" I ask the kids, whose directions soon reward us with an up-close inspection of a weedy lot, the sort of place even a rat wouldn't find hospitable. When, all on our own, we chance on a road into the open countryside, we take it without even discussing other options. Even if it's not the right way at least it promises a pretty drive. After less than a mile, the good dirt lane we are on dissolves into a sand track, one vehicle wide, so littered with pointy gravel it's as if a civic improvement project to fortify the road base got started, but never finished. Allowing us to share the road are small groups of people strolling back from market, the men sauntering with sticks over their shoulders, the women laden as heavily as donkeys. The donkeys, apparently, were given the day off. After another stretch we reach what looks like a cobbled street, not neatly laid like the central square in Brussels, but with blocks flung helter-skelter, creating a torturous bed of sharp ends over which we bump and rattle at two miles an hour. It would have been nice to give up and go back, but the road was too narrow to turn around.

Ahead we spy two priests, paused in a holy moment of impromptu blessing for a young couple, their three children, and assorted friends and relations. It's divine intervention. Even I, who haven't spent more than five minutes in my life chatting with the priestly kind, know that when it comes to finding a monastery, a priest is your man. Adding to my relief is the assumption that, if they don't know the way, they can always call on that guy up above, the one who doesn't need a GPS to know where everything is in this world.

As soon as we stop the car, the two tall, elderly clerics leave their blessing business, trot around to the passenger door and, without us even having the chance to say anything, jump spryly into the back seat. Apparently, we are the answer to their prayers, too. They raise their crosses at us in a general blessing and smile ear to ear, one of them displaying a full set of rotting brown teeth, the other displaying tiny yellowed nubs worn down by decades of *qat* chewing. They set their crosses on their laps, put their sun umbrellas and sticks between their knees, wriggle their bony fannies into place, and graciously motion us to proceed. Though they speak no English, from their enthusiastic nod when I say Dereka Abba Meta, we figure they live there.

We bump further and further into the hills, passing small farms walled with dry laid pink and gold rocks. Inside each enclosure is a square stone house with four-sided tin roof, topped by a silvery finial that looks like a snowflake with little tin bells dangling from it. There's always a thatched rondavel for livestock, and next to that a further enclosure guarding ten-foot-high puffs of bleached yellow hay. Fields are already tilled, clumps of bronze earth turned over, ready for planting. Sometimes the way narrows, wedging us between a stone wall on one side and a thorny cattle corral across from it. It's not a place to drape one's arm languidly out the window, unless you like petting prickly pears.

Finally we must stop, to the dismay of our passengers, who keep urging us to continue. Perhaps they'd imagined we would be chauffeuring them right to the hand-hewn doorstep of their rock dwelling. But the track is no longer a track, just a collection of red boulders skirting the edge of a low brown cliff, where driving is impossible. We all get out and start walking through the red sandstone rubble, the two priests in front, white shawls flapping, caps which look like a three-layer cake with coconut frosting, pulled down over their foreheads. Though we're miles from the nearest homestead, a swarm of children appear, gamboling over the stones, shouting at the priests, laughing and pointing at us. The priests shoo them away like so many flies, but they tag along behind, motioning, I feel sure, at my own decidedly *not* boney fanny.

After a couple hundred yards the priests point across the forested gorge below us, to a cliff tinged honey and coral in the late afternoon light. Near the base of that cliff we see two wood doors inset in the rock face. Their turquoise color flashes through the trees like a diving kingfisher. For a moment, a ray of sun pierces the patchy clouds, illuminating the door and its red and white frame, a celestial floodlight making sure we understand that we have arrived.

To reach the monastery we have to descend a steep boulder slope, cross the densely forested floor alive with birds and monkeys, then climb a narrow path part way up that intriguing cliff face. It's fantastically isolated and hidden. Bernard and I confer and I offer to wait while he enters the hallowed doors of this remote monastery. I'm not being generous. The remainder of the trek does not concern me as I'd get no further than the entrance doorstep. I'm female and as such forbidden from entering the monastery anyway.

We have a problem though, and it's not one of gender. In our absorption with the priests, along with the distraction of dodging thorny things on our way, we've lost track of time. Staring into the west, the sun blinds me as it dabbles playfully with the horizon. It's already low and the twilight that follows its setting won't linger long. To retrace our drive, we'll need light to distinguish the right rocky road from tempting rocky ditches and rocky footpaths. The priests motion us to follow. "Come on," they seem to urge. "It's past tea time." We bow and shake our heads. They bow and nod their heads. We shake and nod at each other until they turn and go. The last we see of the priests they're hopping down the boulders like long-limbed frogs, sticks, umbrellas, and crosses bobbing as they go.

As we drive back to Axum where we're staying the night, our quest feels incomplete. Seeing a monastery door doesn't seem to qualify as seeing the monastery itself. It's like saying "I read about Fashion Week" and expecting that to sound as titillating as, "I was front row at Michael Kors." What we yearn for is a full-on monastery experience, not just an exterior.

The next day we walk through the outskirts of Axum town, along quiet lanes where chickens scratch, and goats help themselves to the free thistle buffet sprouting from rock walls. A faint path draws us up a hill dotted with flowering euphorbia trees, which look like upturned leggy broccoli florets brushed with red nail polish. After half an hour, we reach Pantaleon Monastery, at fifteen hundred years old, one of the elders in the monastery population. The royal blue steel gates are open, and even though I doubt I'll be allowed far, I resolve to walk until somebody stops me.

Entering a dry, sandy courtyard, we are greeted by two immense trees. Their smooth bark is a pallid, silvery skin slicked to trunks that bulge like a body builder's heavily muscled arms, rippling with sinews and twisted veins. The air is still, except for blue-green starlings trilling, and doves hoo-hooing in the broad span of leafy branches above us.

Within minutes a small priest in a beige robe of rough muslin hurries over to greet us, his flip-flops slapping down the stone steps. Instead of pointing sternly at the gate to shoo me out, he leads us to a low stone building. Inside, pillars of light blaze through openings in the wall, striking a woven grass mat on the stone floor and throwing everything else into deep shadow. Using the sort of key you'd think was made for a Harry Potter movie, the priest opens a door behind which I can see burlap sacks of grain, some with their contents leaking onto the floor. We hear soft rustling and shuffling as he putters about, then reemerges cradling several items in his hands with infinite tenderness, as if, should he walk too fast, they'd disappear in a puff of dust. He hands Bernard two tarnished silver crowns, gently places in my hands two exquisitely filigreed Coptic crosses. As we stare at the antiques, too stunned to move, he disappears once more into the side room, rummaging further among the sacks from which he extracts two religious tomes, each as thick as a loaf of bread. Opening the illuminated manuscripts with tenderness, his chapped fingers lovingly caress page after page of the most richly detailed scripture paintings I have ever seen. He traces out a "6" on the mat, to explain this trove has been with the monastery since 600 CE. I watch his fingers swing back and forth over the goatskin pages, exposing dense calligraphy and delicate illustrations lavishly painted with gold leaf, vermilion, and indigo.

That's it for me. I've done as much as a woman can be allowed to do. The priest escorts me to a bench under one of the Mr. Universe trees and indicates it would please him if I would stay right there while he and Bernard adjourn to more manly endeavors. They depart for a steep path improved by crumpled sections of stone steps, up which they clamber a good few hundred yards to crest out on a modest nob where squats a simple buff stone structure, perhaps sixty feet square, where St. Pantaleon lived out his days.

I refuse to complain or in any way taint my religious experience, super-ficial though it may be. Besides, I soon have company of my own. Three school-age disciples begin going through their lessons. A droning *ennhhhnnnaaaa, zhuuuuyiiiiii, pehhhhhtzohhhh* as they sound out the Ge'ez alphabet competes with the birds for thrilling sound of the moment. There are two hundred twenty-four Ge'ez symbols to master along with all their combinations, which means these youngsters have a lot to learn. They sit on the steps of a small storeroom, fourteen, twelve, and nine years old, heads shaved, dressed in shorts with broken-zipper flies and short-sleeve shirts missing most buttons. Their voices ring out from behind a nearby building, a nasal hum of letters and hymns. Every once in a while, however, they're consumed by the mischief that grabs boys that age. They ditch their books, giving themselves over to fits of wrestling, giggling, and pebble-flinging. Then, their energy temporarily spent, they eye me as if confirming a tacit understanding that I won't report them and, of their own accord, return to their books. The monotone chanting and repetition resumes, the doves *hoo-hooooo*, the dry leaves overhead swish in the breeze.

A small flock of brown and white sheep leave through the main gate, and a lone cow wanders in. Outside, young voices sing out behind the hill, children shepherding their goats. A wizened woman robed in homespun white cotton peers around the blue steel doors, then enters. Her brown face is a mass of wrinkles and deep indigo tattoos. She clomps into the court-yard, raising one hip high at each step to swing a lame leg. A bow before the church and she pulls her white shawl over her head, making the motions of the cross. She's so tiny that when she kneels in devotion she's hidden by the rock in front of her. She disappears, gone, like a churchyard ghost.

Getting Down with the Locals

CABO VIRGENES, ARGENTINA, 2008

Dirt is relative. There's the dirt that's avoidable and there's the dirt that you become one with.

I don't go out of my way to seek dirt when at home, but then, mine is no longer an office job. After twelve years in the software industry, preceded by six years in various aspects of public relations, I now live on a ranch, where much of my time is spent out of doors. Between riding horses and ranch work it's a given that I will end most days digging dirt from under my nails. This is not a bad thing, as the dirt speaks of everything I love: nature, animals, and being physically tired at cocktail hour. Still, words like bedraggled, unwashed, and unkempt do not apply when I'm at home. I accept that they're conditions that might occur during the day, but I'm confident they will be banished by night. Being dirty at home is a temporary state, mitigated by the simple fact that I can relegate it to the laundry bin or the shower in time to pour myself a glass of wine at day's end.

My view of dirt changes radically on the road. It's just not worth fighting the dirt of the world. There's too much of it and only one of me. Better to loosen up, breathe easy, and let grit and grime do their worst. Take, for example, the onslaught of earthen elements that blows through an open car window. Drive down dirt roads and the road material will find its way onto and into you. Sometimes it's helped along by a large truck belting down the road toward us, spitting gravel and belching black diesel smoke. Bernard will jerk me out of whatever daydream I've sunk into with a sharp, "Look out! Roll up the windows!" But the devious dust plume behind the truck seeps into the car anyway. It sneaks in through the air vents, creeps through gaps in the door seals, ambushes me with a dust puff in the face when I open the hatchback to extract a bag. Even though we take preventive measures, we still wind up coated with the stuff within a few hours of departure each day.

I've learned to relax about unavoidable dirt. It's like giving myself over to the percussive clangor of a rock band. Rather than fight it, it all becomes more enjoyable if I let myself sink into an altered state. So I've made peace with my dirty condition. I could say that dirt is sometimes as close to me as a second skin, and as with any friendship, I have to put up with it, despite those times when it becomes unbearable.

Then there's the avoidable sort of dirt, the kind you encounter after making a distinct choice. Thus, one day in the eastern reaches of Patagonia, a full day's drive from Ushuaia, we find ourselves crawling on our bellies, military-style, through thick patches of penguin guano. Bernard and I are alone in the shoreline expanse of Cabo Virgenes—that is, if you discount the presence of one hundred thousand curious Magellanic penguins with nothing to do but waddle, primp, and poop. Penguin fluff drifts around our heads, little white down feathers released by the molting chicks standing in droves around us. Barely reaching fourteen inches in a proud moment, the young birds are temporarily stranded, unable to cavort in the frigid Atlantic like their parents, because they don't have water-proof feathers. They're reduced to loitering around scrappy shrubs and nest burrows, trading gossip for days on end until their new feathers grow in.

The chicks are so obliging, so fearless, that we can't help but take advantage of their good nature. The guano-speckled gravel beckons. Bernard doesn't hesitate. "You know, the best way to see them is from the ground," he says. I'm astounded to see my normally fastidious husband, a man for whom "fresh white shirt" is a life philosophy, suddenly drop on his belly, camera snugged to his face, and then inch his way forward on his elbows. Now he is at beak level with the chicks, who stare at him for a second in mild alarm. However, the typical chick predator comes from the sky, so, after a brief confab, they deem it safe to ignore him.

Bernard wriggles closer, snapping away, while I hang back, reluctant to smear guano on my recently cleaned T-shirt. "What's it like down there?" I inquire, just to stall. "Shhhhh!" Bernard hisses at me. He's five feet away from a chick and doesn't want to scare it. As I watch him, the attraction of getting nose to beak with a penguin overwhelms me too. I plop onto my stomach, feeling only momentary revulsion as the small blobs of dung squash onto my clothing. Immediately I have attracted my own coterie of penguin admirers, who preen their mangy-looking bodies, peer at the sky, cluck to each other, and saunter about. Now I, too, am in my element, as there is little that gives me as much pleasure as being in the midst of wildlife.

Within a few minutes I am engrossed in the penguin life around me and become oblivious to the ordure in which I am lying. Bernard and I spend an hour on our bellies before reluctantly pulling ourselves away from the penguin's-eye view of life. By then, having guano on us is nothing to wrinkle our noses at. Which is what makes any contemplation of, or attempt to categorize, things as dirty or not dirty so interesting.

Whether in the pristine wilds of the Carretera Austral or the windswept expanses of the Gobi on the P2P, the impact of dirt on my life or my sense of well-being is altered simply by the fact that I'm away from home. Gone is the expectation that I should be clean at the end of the day. Replacing it is the sense that my clothing now has two purposes only. The first is protection from the law, which enforces certain societal expectations of routine modesty. It simply would not do to get out at a gas station buck naked. The second is protection from discomfort. My clothing has to be comfortable to sit in for hours on end and to keep me from getting scraped, sunburned, and scratched. If my shirt and slacks can also be reasonably flattering, I'm happy.

As we wander through the penguin colony toward the beach, I feel a perverse pride when I survey the guano bits drying on my shirt. The dirt on me is a badge of honor, a sign that we're really on the road, living the itinerant life, being flexible about things that we're rigid about at home, accommodating uncertainties in a way I never could on the P2P. Each stain proclaims I'm succeeding in altering things about me which years ago I would have said are as firmly a part of me as my ten fingers and ten toes. It says here's a person who's not afraid to shed the veneer of polite society and get down with the locals, even if the locals are penguins.

ETIQUETTE

PREAMBLE

Six months passed after completing the P2P in July 2007 before we took to the road again. While our first road trip choice, Patagonia, sprang from my desire to see the mountains of Fitz Roy and Torres del Paine about which my mountaineering father had raved, it quickly grew to encompass the chance to drive one of the great roads of the world, the Carretera Austral. That it was in the Southern Hemisphere was a major draw, driven by Bernard's desire to reduce the number of winter months he spent plowing and shoveling at the ranch, and constrained by my desire to be at the ranch during the prime summer months of horseback riding. And since these were driving trips, it behooved us to select a destination where the weather was conducive to seeing something out the window other than snowflakes. That it would be summer in Patagonia to our depths of frigid white winter in the Rockies was all to the good.

The problem is, once you become addicted to something, as we have to road trips, you start to see opportunities everywhere. Since 2008, our time away has crept incrementally upward, swayed by geopolitical shifts allowing us into formerly inaccessible places and the occasional can't-turn-this-down invitation to join others on a drive after we've already planned a specific drive of our own.

Before we leave for a long road trip, my friends relieve themselves of the burden of their worries and pile them on me, like so many lead-weighted quilts. They think they're being helpful. I know they're just laying the groundwork so they can mouth "I told you so" when I get home. I would be able to empathize with their concern if they questioned me about diseases I might catch, like dengue fever; personal wisdom on how to get rid of head lice since my bout with same in Kolkata; or whether I like spicy curries, injera, or corn mush and if I don't, what will I eat for two months. But no. Their concern is more focused than that. Isn't driving in India the equivalent of being inside a pinball machine with fifty balls on the loose and the flippers stuck on overdrive? Are we mad or just naive to consider driving through the Ethiopian desert, which some say is melt-your-tires hot, not to mention the dunes that can stop forward motion better than the Denver Boot? And the emptiness of Peru's altiplano ... isn't that a recipe for a long, cold wait without coffee if we break down with nothing but alpacas around for help? If anything confirms to me that I have become a traveler with tremendous experience, it's that what my friends perceive as discomforts or threats are, at worst, the least of my worries, and at best, aspects of travel I've come to particularly enjoy.

There's a world of difference between what you read about a country and its reality. India is a good case in point. It is correct that, should a Hindu die encased in a fiery tangle of metal, that would be karma, time for him or her to start a new life, and therefore nothing to get upset about. If the same happened to me, it would be a lawsuit. When considering the charms of driving in India, those who've never experienced it think there are no rules, that it would be like riding a bucking bronco through the streets of Tombstone while being shot at by the Earp brothers: regardless of which way you turn, you're in trouble. Not true. What's happening on Indian roads is rational and normal by local definitions.

Yes, being a foreigner trying to meld with local customs becomes ever more complex the farther we go, but also ever more satisfying as I weave uncertainties into a new coherent whole. There *are* rules. The difficulty, and therefore the charm, lies in figuring them out.

Carma

ORCHHA, INDIA, 2009

Now that we are several days into our first drive through India, I am focusing my not inconsiderable powers of observation and deduction on understanding Indian road etiquette. I'm like a newly hatched chick, cracking open my egg to emerge into barnyard chaos. During this stage, I am a wreck. What I see outside Sexy Beast's non-window is enough to unleash a chain reaction of twitches. Three-wheel mototaxis—affectionately called *tuk-tuks* because of the stuttering sound of their tiny engines—maneuver within seven inches of Beast's non-door, allowing for the rearview mirror. Since that means mere millimeters from my left knee, then the answer to your raised eyebrow is yes, I'm measuring. They navigate through traffic as shifting and unpredictable as rubble in a landslide. Every other vehicle on the road is larger, able with a distracted twist of the driver's wrist to squash them and their paying passenger into a metallic smudge on the melting, garbage-choked pavement. Yet this rarely happens, at least not within my line of sight.

So chaotic is the traffic that it's mesmerizing and horrifying at the same time. A bus whose chassis has never experienced the blessings of shock absorbers lurches ahead, listing at an angle to make the Tower of Pisa jealous, intent on getting around us so it can jerk to a stop, blocking our path to disgorge a hundred or so passengers. Motorbikes swarm around a seething mass of bullock carts and bicycle rickshaws, like flies buzzing a carcass. That they cannot see around the tractor they're about to pass, a homemade one hauling a ten-foot-high load of hay on which perch six villagers, is irrelevant.

The guys on top are all laughing, probably because they know they're about to meet a better life in the hereafter than this one in which they have dry grass tickling their buttocks. Trucks bulging like a middle-aged spread list across two lanes, hauling freshly threshed wheat in burlap sacks closed with Frankenstein seams, grain dribbling onto the pavement. Tempted by this free meal, sacred cows merge with the cars, affectionately licking up the spillage, sacred calves at their side learning the tricks of the trade. It's all I can do to point out to Bernard where we should be going.

Several days of this and, patting myself down to verify that indeed I am still alive and unhurt, I start to discern a method to the apparent madness. I'd like to attribute our lack of accidents to the presence of a benevolent travel god, called upon by those blessed limes placed in front of our tires in the parking lot puja. But given Beast's deteriorating mechanical condition I know the only thing they were good for was lime juice and I rue the day I left my bottle of tequila at home. The truth is, our safety has little to do with gods and everything to do with sound. To be specific, a horn. American cars each have one, but we never use it. In India, they do, like a mobile P. D. Q. Bach orchestra on overdrive.

Whichever engineer picked the sound for Beast's horn must have been a jazz fan. It's brash and insistent, the trumpet in a New Orleans second-line, a soulful accompaniment to my prayers. The Toyota luggage van in which we drive next has a horn that makes a choked squeak, part dying mouse, part fierce politeness in that oriental way which lulls you into believing you're not about to be conquered. Buses sound like a submerging submarine blaring *ah-ooooohh-gah*. Each time I hear one I think of *Red October* and Sean Connery trying to evade Russian pursuit in his quest to hand over his submarine to Alec Baldwin.

The biggest trucks have horns that twitter like Stallone speaking with the voice of Betty Boop. Trucks don't need horns, though. They're so obviously unable to stop within half a mile of hitting the brakes that people cede the road to them anyway. Which leaves us with human-powered rickshaws and bicycles, whose frantic *brrrriiiinnnggg* speaks of outrage and desperation. No one pays them any mind either, which is nearly our undoing.

Traffic moves according to who honks when. If you're coming up behind someone and intend to move into their space, you honk. If you're going to go by them, you honk. If you want someone to move over, you honk. The vehicle in front will ignore you completely, continuing its bothersome, blocking behavior as long as you'll let it. If they think allowing you to pass is going to damage them, only then will they honk back. And also make a motion with their hand that is explicit. Once you've honked, timing is everything. Hesitate a split second and the opening you could have darted through closes. Or the truck creeping along at half a kilometer per hour has pulled right into your lane. Or a phalanx of rickshaws is now scattered across the causeway like buckshot. Our mantra becomes "No guts, no glory." It is our only hope of ever arriving at our hotel before dark.

I can divide road obstacles into categories, which I soon begin to consider as adversaries. That's what it's come to: an us versus everyone else on the road proposition. Each category is worth its own level of reaction, starting with ennui, rising through wincing, past white-knuckle clutching of the oh-shit handle, all the way to breaking my pledge and issuing Bernard a stern warning, or mewling plea, to watch out.

The most vulnerable adversaries initially seem to be animals. However, dogs and cows know that none dare hit them, so they don't move. That is, they know this if they haven't already been squashed by a car during infancy. There's nothing I can add to the copious reports on India's sacred cows. We all know they're sacred and that no one will touch them on pain of creating such extraordinarily bad karma that one's next reincarnation would likely be as a sewage-feeding insect. The only injured dogs I see are the ones that actually try to run across a high-traffic road. Those that blithely sleep in the gutter with their toes sticking into the roadway, or that call a palaver with the neighborhood pariah dogs in the middle of the street where they mingle and howl, have no worries.

Pedestrians, bicyclists, and rickshaw pullers belong to the second most vulnerable category, because they have no armor to shield them, neither sacred nor metallic. It stuns me that they rarely move out of the way either. They must consider themselves in the protected dog/cow category. That, or they're so deafened by the incessant honking that they don't hear us bearing down. At one point we muse that this must be a display of the fatalism inherent in Hindu beliefs, but then we notice that Muslims are as imperturbable as Hindus. Neither flinches when a car—okay, our car—whizzes within centimeters of their behinds at 45 mph.

Truck drivers, for the most part, impress us with their driving skills and joie de vivre. They chauffeur the most colorfully decorated rigs we've seen anywhere. It seems obligatory that every square inch of a commercial transport truck be painted with designs and illustrations. This is driving in ha-ha-ha mode. Jolly blue hearts and green diamonds festoon the wheels. Alluring beach scenes, palm trees and all, decorate rear axles. Gas tanks have a happy diesel djinn painted on them. Windshields are obscured to half their size by frames of scalloped tin. Gods and goddesses dance and wink from the hood, and bulls' heads brandishing horns of mythic proportions adorn the front grille.

Every single truck, bar none, has PLEASE HONK or BLOW HORN emblazoned in decorative multi-colored script on its tailgate. They are dead serious about this honking business. To prove it, they remove their outside mirrors so they can't possibly see behind them, as if to say, "Your call if you want to pass me. But you better make yourself heard, because, bro, I can't see nothin' behind." More than any unwritten rule of the road, this inability to see behind puts the entire burden of safe passing on the driver who wants to get by. If you are ever hit by a truck there can be no dispute about whose fault it is, unless that truck is behind you.

I know this for a fact. One afternoon, as we drive toward Orchha, we inch across a long bridge snarled with traffic as slow moving and sluggish as the sewage clogging the river below. All four lanes are clogged with vehicles. Suddenly, we're unceremoniously booted forward. I swivel my whole body around and see the enormous, heavily painted snout of a cargo truck nuzzling our van's rear end. "We've been hit," I yell to Bernard. "I'm getting out to see if there's any damage." Before he can stop me, I do the most foolish, life-threatening thing I've ever done. I jump into the middle of Indian traffic which at that moment starts swerving around me, likely because the policeman who was directing it has awoken from his nap.

As I move to the back of the van, Bernard starts driving it forward and I wind up jogging in the middle of swirling traffic trying to keep up with him. With amazing forethought, I place myself between the van and the offending truck, so that he cannot pass us, managing to erase from my mind how any truck that could smash into the van's rear once could do so again, turning my legs into a condiment. Thankfully, the policeman resumes his snooze and traffic stops once more. I use this lull to clamber up the steps of the truck cab where I stare down the hapless driver. He eyes me back, embarrassed. Terrified. "You hit our car," I shout, not because I'm angry, nor even because I imagine he'll understand English if I speak loudly, but because the honking around me is deafening. "Please pull over after the bridge." He nods so fast it's like a Parkinson's tremor.

By then, Bernard has gained another hundred yards, so I leap back down to the pavement and trot after him. I'm not a runner, and the amount of exercise I'm now getting in the heat and accumulated exhaust could be enough to kill me. "Stop!" I wail after Bernard, in between gasps. Much too far away, Bernard finally pulls over at a roundabout protecting the policeman from the surge of vehicles to which I am fully exposed. A brief explanation, plus pointing out the fresh dent in the van's rear, is enough for the official, dressed in a white uniform heavily weighted with gold braid, to signal the offending truck to stop. The driver steps out, papers in hand. He's scrawny. I see instantly that his cotton shirt is so worn the tinge of his dark skin shows through. His shorts are tattered too, held up by rope. He looks exhausted.

"So," the policeman turns to us. "This driver says the truck does not carry insurance. And his papers are expired. This is a serious matter. I advise you to press charges. Then we can make this driver pay you right now. Or, we can take the driver to the station, where matters will be settled." His tone is practical and briefly I believe that he's just being pragmatic, avoiding the exchange of many small-denomination bills in full view of the crowd that now surrounds us. The driver peers into his wallet for salvation, his hands on bony wrists fiddling with the cracked and ripped leather. He holds it open to show us just how empty it is. Totally. It's dawning on me I've made a terrible mistake. There's nothing this poor man can do about the dent. The truck isn't even his.

"What do you mean, 'matters will be settled?' Do we have to go to court? Or sue the truck owner?" Clearly the driver has only enough rupees to buy himself an occasional chai and chapati, which means about fifty cents. This is getting worse by the minute.

"No madam. At the station, you can have us settle this matter for you." He places more emphasis on each word than it deserves. The crowd tightens in. Their mass feels vaguely threatening and I have no idea whether they're there to applaud or lynch us. Nothing even remotely alarming has ever happened to me in India, despite the disparity between haves (us) and have nots (them). It's as manifest as a naked man in a fashion show, and as pervasive as mosquitos on an Alaska summer night. If they can take me at face value, who am I to typecast those around me by their personal possessions? I have come to love the country in large part for the unquestioning warmth with which we are greeted by everyone everywhere. That is, until now. Whether it's the mere presence of a crowd, or that the crowd is getting louder, my inner safety-ometer begins to swing from the benign blue zone of cold feet, up past the yellow of nervousness into the orange zone of apprehension, wavering at the red zone of panic.

"Bernard, come over here so we can talk this over," I say, pulling him away from the officer to a street corner as private as one can be with an audience of hundreds. A man I noticed lurking on the periphery of the crowd comes over to us. He's short, unimposing, but his rumpled white shirt and wool slacks define him as a mid-level Indian professional, as does his command of English.

"Excuse me," he says. "I have noticed that you were hit by that truck. That is most unfortunate. I am terribly sorry for this matter." He pauses. We wait. "There is something the police are not saying to you." He pauses again. We wait some more. "Perhaps you do not understand?"

"I don't know. What is it that I wouldn't understand?"

"If you allow the police officer to take this driver, they will beat him. Severely. Very severely." So that's what "settling" means. We shake the driver's hand, shake the policeman's hand, tell everyone we will not be pressing charges. The policeman is crestfallen. He shrugs and returns to his traffic perch, checking each finger of his white gloves as he walks away. If we can no longer provide the possibility of an interesting, quasi-violent afternoon beating a hapless driver in front of his pals, then we ourselves are of no further use. Meanwhile, the driver scampers to his truck, slams the door, and the engine roars to life. In minutes he's easing his way back into traffic, relieved to escape in case we change our minds. The crowd? Well it wasn't threatening after all. It was just a collection of bored people who saw the possibility of something interesting happening. Once the show is over it does as all such crowds do. It melts away. As for us, we both are breathing shallow as we walk back to the van. It's one of those unspoken moments that long-married couples with similar values sometimes experience. This one is that we've narrowly escaped our own type of dismal fate: being complicit in making an already difficult life more miserable. We remain silent, occupied by our private thoughts, as we drive off.

For the remainder of our road trip, Bernard honks at whatever's in our way—animal or vegetable, stationary or motorized. His technique is surgical, easing us through traffic like a scalpel through soft flesh. All that's left is for me to stare steadfastly ahead, memorizing whatever may be the last scene I see before I die. I have shrieked only once or twice.

Bush Spa

DIMEKA, ETHIOPIA, 2011

It's hot in the Omo Valley, 110 degrees at times. That's not as hot as Ethiopia's Danakil Depression of volcano fame, but it is a water-starved region, with parched sandy ground baked brick hard, yielding reluctantly to acacia thorn and razor-edged, spiky plants that only a starving cow could love. Whenever I turn on a tap, I apologize. To anyone. When I find shade, I sit, panting, distressed by thoughts of the crisp, icy winter air of the Rocky Mountain winter back home as well as by the shirt pasted to my back like an over-licked stamp. Despite a label to the contrary it has veered sharply from drip-dry into purely drip territory, thanks to the sweat coursing down my back and from my armpits, all evidence that I have once again lost the climate battle. I struggle to come to terms with a region where the thickly leafed interlocking branches of towering ficus along the edge of the Omo River are so useless for cooling. It's as hot and muggy in the shade as anywhere else and the only beasts not fazed by this are the colobus monkeys chattering above. They spring through the topmost branches in playful frenzy, white mantles fluttering like Casanova's opera cape, setting the leaves a-rustle. I sweat just listening to them. From a high sandy bank, I scan the languid café-au-lait Omo River, which flows like liquid dust, easily spotting the nostrils of crocs drifting mid-channel. There's nothing lovely about a crocodile, but I wish to be one so I, too, can lurk for hours in the water without fear.

We drive to the northern Omo, where the small village of Dimeka hosts a spirited market every Saturday morning. Our plan is to arrive early, so we can see everything that's on offer before it sells out, but our American timing is out of sync with local reality. This is not the neighborhood grocer, open at 8:00 a.m. for your shopping convenience. With everyone walking from miles away, the Dimeka market doesn't get started till midday, or whenever the vendors stride out of the bush toting their sacks and baskets of wares.

We pass the time lounging on wobbly chairs at a juice bar, whose enterprising owner has lashed banana-leaf panels to poles, stringing a blue and white striped tarp over the top to create a shady patio. It's crude, but it works, offering quiet and respite from the heat. Behind a low concrete wall, the owner squeezes citrus on a handheld plastic juicer or whirls thicker produce in a blender whose surface is smeared with the accumulation of past orders. Used glasses and pitchers from the morning rush soak in a tub of what looks to me like watery vichyssoise. If the owner wishes to wash and rinse his barware in bilge, who am I to spoil his fun. I just hope the glass in which my tasty beverage arrives won't spoil mine. We each have a fresh mango-avocado juice, raising our glasses in a silent "cheers" to the locals sitting across from us, and buying a glass for a street boy who's tagged along behind us. The mix is tropical and unctuous, its layers of orange and green making such a fine complementary parfait that I can feel the thud of Martha Stewart kicking herself for not thinking of it first.

The Dimeka market field is flat and open, its red dirt barren but for a handful of thorn trees. Like every local market it has a system to help shoppers find what they've come for. In the case of Dimeka, the system is those thorn trees, under which women cluster according to what they're selling. Each tree hosts its own particular offering. There's the poultry tree, where one can buy small beige eggs the size of a fresh date. If you'd rather have the glossy black and red chicken which laid those orbs, you are asked to pay $1.50, but that's before the bargaining starts. There's the by-products tree, with acacia honey and sour-smelling homemade butter sweating in coiled clay pots. And there's the health tree, with vendors proffering small bunches of herbs and packets of brown tobacco leaves bound with water reeds. Out in the open are tarps with small mounds of savage green and red peppers; just looking at them sets my tongue ablaze.

On the field's periphery are bundles of hay. We put up over a thousand tons of hay each summer on our ranch. When I say "we" I mean it literally. Many summers I've helped our hay crew, driving a tractor pulling a big circular rake or a hay baler out of whose rear portal plop seventy-five-pound, three-string bales of premium horse hay. It's a job that sounds tedious but in truth is wondrous, starting always in mid-afternoon when the freshly cut meadow has had a chance to dry in the summer sun and breeze. For hours I sit on the slow bouncing tractor, squinting from under my broad-brimmed hat at the long rows of hay striping one three-hundred-acre meadow. In the peak of summer, it stays light late and I keep chugging along, swigging ice water from my thermos, staving off dinner pangs with an energy bar. As the sun sinks a coyote trots out from the willows and hawks swoop down to perch on finished bales, both hoping to snatch the mice which recently were snuggly hidden under a lofty swath of sweet-smelling dry grass. Here at the Dimeka market, we each heft a local bale and agree they weigh about fifty pounds, about the weight of one of the sacks of oats I heft into our horses' feed room. It's light by our standards, incredibly heavy if you have to carry it through the bush. If you're skeptical, put six gallon-jugs of water in a pack and go for a twelve-mile walk in your neighborhood park. Then come talk to me.

The market has drawn from villages of Hamar, Karo, Bena, Arbore. Though loathe to be judgmental, my personal vote on attractiveness goes to the Hamar, a good-looking people, with coppery skin, sharp noses, full lips. They're easy to identify, what with their signature glistening ochre bangs and ringlets, strands of chunky yellow, green, blue, and white beads ringing their necks, steel and copper bangles tight around wrists and biceps, a supple goatskin decorated with cowry shells and beads draped from their waist.

There is lots of inspecting going on and not just by me. A girl, glowing with what I imagine is the first flush of married life, hefts one glossy black and bronze chicken after another. Elsewhere, a woman with an infant suspended in a cozy back sling eyes a pot of honey, then strides on to sniff the neighbor's butter. A waft of sweet herbalness drifts from a tarp, where an elderly woman is offering a smoky example of her bush potpourri. A shrewd cattle baron pokes a bale of hay. We buy twenty thumb-sized bananas for twenty cents. Our purchase wipes out the seller's supply. She appears stunned, not sure whether to sit out the day in front of her empty tarp or start walking home.

From the market we move on to visit the Mursi tribe, who live within the boundaries of Mago National Park near Jinka in the Omo's northern sector. The dirt road to their village is rough and unimproved, with sharp rocks that I fear might be the end of our Land Rover's abused tires. Two park guards, foisted on us at the park entrance as protection, perch cross-legged on the Landie's roof, loaded rifle on lap. Their comradely laughter and shouts drift into my open window along with cigarette smoke and the sour smell of sweat-soaked uniforms. At a fork in the road, one of them leans over the windshield and slashes his hand to the left to tell us where to go. There's nothing for them to shoot at. They say there's wildlife some-where in the park, lions, elephants, giraffes, zebras, but I have my doubts. More reliable word has it that wildlife in these parts has been poached to extinction.

Each Omo Valley tribe has its particular type of beautification, created to enhance female appeal and also to indicate that a girl is ready for marriage. For the Mursi it's a lip plate, which transforms the lower lip into a small platter. The Mursi women have their lip plates off when we arrive, as we're the first foreigners of the day. It's like we've surprised an old showgirl in her dressing room before she's put on her curly wig and penciled in her eyebrows, and it's not a pretty sight. A flaccid loop of skin hangs down to their chin, looking like a thin, wrinkly brown sausage. Developing this lip loop is a rite of passage that begins when a girl is nine. To make it, a slit is cut at the base of the lower lip and a small plug inserted. Over time, the opening is stretched by inserting progressively larger plugs, until it can accommodate a clay disk that is four inches in diameter and a half-inch thick.

Everyone is happy to see us because we represent money. The Mursi, like all the other Omo tribes, have learned they can charge for their photo. And they do. They're not shy about this, as I would be, nor are they fierce. They present themselves like so much cabbage or boxes of cereal. We pay for every photo taken and to every person in that photo. Children are discounted 50 percent, an indication that in Mursi society children aren't worth much. I can understand that; who can be certain which children will survive to become photogenic, procreating adults? Still, if they asked me to be their financial adviser I'd suggest an inverted scale, charging more the younger they get. Top scale would go to the babies. They're the cutest.

Many Mursi women have had their front teeth pulled out, top and bottom. I puzzle through whether this is done for extra allure. Then those same women pop their lip plates in, hoping to create a photo op, and I can see that the largest plates intrude into the mouth, where those front teeth otherwise would be. Women aren't the only ones going through painful procedures in pursuit of comeliness. Men have intricate scarification patterns on their chest, twin rows of welts starting on their pectorals, curling around their nipples, and running down the center of their chest to the navel. The welts are raised by rubbing a butter-charcoal mix into the incision. Next time I squeeze my feet into too-tight high heels, I'll pause to remember what real pain is all about.

Mursi existence is even more mobile than that of an air force family. They move every half-year, following the river as it slowly dries. The huts in this village, made of thatch and river reed culled from the surrounding bush, are the smallest and lowest we've seen. The river is their Home Depot, with ample new building materials available 24–7 whenever they need it. They don't seem to invest much in making their huts into a home. Nor are they concerned about taking those huts with them, as the old materials wear out quickly. When I was six, I made shelters this size out of blankets and chairs, in which to play with my dolls. Now I'd have to crawl in on my knees to get through the three-foot-high portal, if anyone were to invite me to enter. No one does.

The Mursi have made clear by their posturing that we and our money are welcome. Still, the welcome feels exclusionary, as the Mursi have learned to protect themselves from repeated intrusions by displaying only a select few picturesque aspects of their life. More than anywhere else I've been I sense that our being here is wrong, that our presence has created a living diorama as artificial as any stuffed animal display in a museum. Squatting down in front of one hut, I see a young girl inside holding a tiny baby on her lap. She smiles up at me, not yet sporting even the smallest of lip plates, which means she is not yet of child-bearing age. From the way she gestures to the right, I gather the baby's mother is the one near me outside the hut, grinding millet; it's the same stone, same grinder as used by the Arbore wife, despite no connection between the tribes. The babysitter uses five fingers of one hand and two of the other to tell me the baby is seven months old. If I were to judge age solely by his size—and I know he's a he, not a she, because he is naked—he'd be no more than half that. I don't say this to imply the Mursi are malnourished. Far from it. Besides millet, the Mursi have cows for meat and milk, which is a veritable banquet compared to what other tribes have. Everyone looks robust and healthy, unless it's only the healthy ones who are still alive. I can't find out whether the baby was born premature, as no Mursi wants to interact with us apart from posing for photos.

The more we wander around this cluster of ten huts, the sadder I feel and the more I sense we have wronged these people by our intense curiosity about their customs and lives. Looking for something, anything, I can connect with, I focus on what the women are doing. Everywhere I've traveled, it's the women who have been willing to open their circle so I can step inside and sit with the local sisterhood. So when I notice a woman lying on her side, very still, her head nestled in an old woman's lap, I stop. The old woman seems to be doctoring her eye. Several other women squat in front, silently observing the operation. As always, I have packed my medical kit full of controlled substances left over from various joint operations and one bout with doggy bone cancer. If there's pain somewhere, I can lessen it with one judiciously chosen pill. I look around for signs that I am in a Mursi medical clinic, but no one seems hurt or sick. It's puzzling and I don't want to stare, because my mother taught me how rude that is and Bernard always reminds me so. But I do want to stare, because I want to know what's going on. And when I realize what's being done on the ground, I also realize why I didn't get it. It's because there's no incense, no bowl of polished apples, no whispery New Age music to define where I am: the Mursi spa. The old one is the beautician, the young the client. And the treatment? Having her eyelashes plucked out. I don't know whether to wince or applaud. I do know not to make an appointment. And so it's with more than ordinary relief that I climb back into our car, relieved to depart from where I now feel I should never have been in the first place.

If It Floats

PUERTO MONTT, CHILE, 2008

With a coastline of 2,653 miles, Chile's length is over three times that of California. If we're to gain a remotely rounded idea of the country, it behooves us to take to the sea. Cars, of course, do not do well in water. Sometimes being on a road trip means being willing to get out of the car and continue on your way by other means entirely. I'm talking boats, one of which awaits us in Puerto Montt, the Chilean port midway down that svelte coastline and gateway to the Patagonian south.

The ferry *Evangelistas*, plyer of coastal waters, sits placidly at dock, painted like someone gone mad with a Crayola crayon box. She's not what I expect. I had pictured a ship of modest, but pleasing proportions, elegant like a private yacht, but of course larger. And like a yacht, painted white or else a handsome midnight blue. What I see instead is a small tanker. Thanks to someone's madcap idea, or else the local painter's limited selection, she is painted an incongruous cherry red, lemon yellow, and navy blue. The effect is like garish makeup on an old lady, a vain attempt to bestow cheeriness on an otherwise lumpen exterior. In her present incarnation, this former fuel transport ship can carry two hundred forty passengers in more or less comfort, depending on what level of accommodation one purchases. The ship is utilitarian, designed to carry a cargo of trucks, goods, and fuel, with the crew tower retrofitted to hold those paying passengers who aren't chickens, horses, or cows.

Parking our rental Suzuki amid the hulking big rigs below deck, we feel a momentary sensation of betrayal. After all, this is supposed to be a driving trip, not a sailing trip. There's a fleeting thought that we're breaking faith with the definition of our journey. Even when we put Roxanne on a truck during the P2P, we did so only because she had broken down, or was about to. And we stayed with her. Apart from that, Bernard drove us every inch of the 7,800 miles between Beijing and Paris. This flicker of P2P rigidity dismays me but doesn't surprise me. The P2P race ended barely six months ago and, being my first ever extended road trip, has permeated my views of what a road trip should be. I swallow daily reminders to remain casual as if they're multivitamins during cold season. Just like a scratchy throat can inspire me to up my regimen of homeopathies, so the occasional relapse into regimented standards of procedure is a prod for the kinder, milder me to reassert herself. On this trip, happily, we're free to do what we want. If I could have kicked up my heels while mounting the steep stairs to the upper deck, without crashing ignominiously to the cargo deck below, I would have.

For the three-day journey to Puerto Natales, we treat ourselves to one of ten AAA cabins, the best the *Evangelistas* has to offer. This entitles us to a narrow, private room containing one set of bunk beds, a small desk, a locker, a three-foot-long porthole seat dressed up in green vinyl, and a private bathroom with shower, all in the space of a cell at the Colorado State Penitentiary and probably painted a similar dingy oatmeal color.

Our cabin status entitles us to three squares a day. Unlike someone in the slammer, though, we are fed in the captain's mess. This is royal treatment indeed, and a perk for which I am earnestly grateful, as otherwise we would have had to eat in the cafeteria with the other two hundred passengers. I don't dislike other people. It's just that I don't manage well when they are in front of me. Sadly, the one aspect of my character that was impervious to the otherwise fully destructive effects of the P2P was my impatience. It's still in full force, causing me to fidget uncontrollably, as ill-humored as a polar bear in Hawaii, whenever I have to wait for anything. I can't fault Bernard when he doesn't hesitate to remind me that whatever line we're currently in surely is not the last one we will ever stand in, and if I can't find some semblance of patience in me I should just go home. This is why standing for an hour in line holding an empty tray, waiting for someone to spoon some sludge into its various depressions, was too Oliver Twist to contemplate. I could feel the barbs of hostile glares that would rain down on me in the days to come, after I had cut in front, flushed with my overwhelming inability to wait as others are fed before me.

On the first evening of our three-day journey I realize just how lucky we are, when I wander into the cafeteria looking for one of the crew members just before dinner. The large, open lounge, bound on one side by a long wall of windows, is a madcap scene of hungry travelers whom I learn from later conversations include kids on their gap year, a carpenter using his earnings to see the world, and a forty-ish woman who's financing her travels by teaching English as a Second Language in whatever city she finds herself when she needs funds to continue her journey. The scene reminds me immediately of cattle in a feed lot when the evening grain is put out, only here it's people jostling and shuffling. The line snakes between banks of six-foot-long Formica tables bolted securely to the floor to withstand the buffeting of high waves. Instead of the bawling of hungry cattle, there are shouts as people wave their friends to the spot they've saved in line, and bursts of shrieking laughter from those who have imbibed several too many pisco sours. As we tend to stay to ourselves when on the road, the sheer number of people as well as their uniformity of age threatens to crash over me like Niagara, and I scuttle back through the door to avoid the torrent.

The captain's mess is cordial and quiet if cramped, with three tables draped in white linen, surrounded by simple wood chairs. In one of those odd coincidences of travel, our dining companions are four French couples, traveling through Chile on vacation. We crowd around two tables and I impress myself by switching between French to Bernard's compatriots and Spanish to the waitstaff. Only occasionally does my mouth mix up the two, uttering something that receives a blank stare. The portholes rapidly fog over as we laugh and exchange travel notes with our dinner mates. The stout captain, who's sailed these waters for many of his seventy-six years, comes over to welcome us before our first dinner, then squeezes himself into a chair at his own table where several other people are already seated.

Curious to know exactly who's along, I turn around, introduce myself, stick out my hand and ask him if this is his family with him. "Si," he says. "Mi esposa, mi hija, y sus niños."

His plump wife looks stuffed like a chile relleno, cinched tight in a black dress that's a size too small, yet her face beams with the happiness of someone who is delighted to have these few days with a husband she adores but rarely sees, thanks to a sailing schedule that keeps him at sea instead of at home. His daughter strikes me at first as overly made up for such a simple ship, but then I recognize the important position her father holds and realize the makeup is her way of participating in that grandeur, relatively modest though it may be. I also feel amicable toward her because her son and daughter are eating their meal quietly, a display of good behavior the lack of which among my own compatriots irks me no end. The captain neglects to introduce the remaining woman at his table, who is young and dark skinned. From the way she tenderly chides the boy not to pick at his salad with his fingers, while their mother flirts with a waiter, I assume she is the nanny. After this brief burst of conversation, the captain turns his back and politely ignores us for the rest of the voyage. Still, I'm glad for the captain, happy that he has his family with him. I'm sure he longs for the day when he had this tiny dining saloon to himself, a privacy destroyed by some land-based COO who decided that ship finances required the addition of paying passengers to the otherwise mute or inanimate cargo.

I soon understand why the captain fills his uniform to bursting. The chef feeds us copious amounts of nourishing food, including, much to our surprise, fresh fruit and salad, excellent mashed potatoes, and as much Chilean Carménère and merlot as we care to drink. I take it easy on the alcohol. Bernard picks up the slack, but I'm the only one I'm worried about. Aware I've traded the possibility of carsickness for the probability of seasickness, I've snagged the bottom bunk in our cabin for myself, figuring if a storm tosses us about, it'll be a short lunge to the bathroom. No sense tempting Poseidon to have his way with me by having heavy red wine slosh in my belly like untethered ballast.

Three days didn't seem long when we decided to take the ferry south, but the time drags. Life onboard is constrained to three things: walking the deck, sitting in the common area, and clambering the short flight of stairs in between the two. It feels like we're in one of those plastic snow globes you shake to get the fake flakes swirling, though ours is filled with wispy fog. We're the couple inside designed to mimic "having fun" but who never move and around whom the scenery never changes. It's claustrophobic and antithetical to the freedom of the road that inspires us. To combat the tedium, the crew do their best to provide entertainment options, as the threat of going crazy or drinking to excess is severe. Bartenders have their cocktail shakers in action by ten in the morning. Other than watching badly dubbed Hollywood B movies, all we can do is walk up and down the stairs numerous times, circumnavigate the deck in both directions, and squint through mist and drizzle at the veiled islands. Well before cocktail hour, I find Bernard in the lounge, feet up on a blue cushion, cheerfully nursing a pisco sour.

After dinner, we play bingo with hundreds of others. It's Bernard's first time at this favorite of small-town church fundraisers. We each get one bingo card. Thankfully they're the US sort: a five-by-five grid, the letters B, I, N, G, and O each heading a column of numbers. I'm relieved to recognize the card set-up, since the last time I played bingo I was twelve years old. "What do I do?" Bernard asks me. It's not often in our life together that Bernard asks me to teach him something, or, to put this another way, that Bernard doesn't know something he wants to know. I point to the transparent tumbler up front, inside of which forced air is sending seventy-five ping-pong balls into a frenzied, leaping dance. "See those balls? Each one has a letter, a B or an I for instance, as well as a number stamped on it. One ball will pop out at a time and the caller will yell out what's on it. As soon as you hear the letter, you look in that column for the number." Bernard stares at me, completely uncomprehending. "What's the point?" he asks.

"It's just a game!" I sigh with exasperation, as this is a sore point between us. I love games. Family nights when I was a kid might have included a round of Clue, in which I was always Col. Mustard, or better still a round of Scrabble, which is how I learned the difference between "sergeant" and "surgeon," two words which, when spoken in my father's Austrian accent, sounded identical. On vacations we packed cards, Yahtzee dice, and Mad Libs. When my sister and I weren't playing dodge ball, hopscotch, or badminton, riding our bikes or trying to jump onto the top of the mailbox at the corner, we were sprawled on the floor playing Parcheesi, Life, pick-up sticks. My scant knowledge of geography, and the main reason I know the location of Irkutsk, stems from the hours we spent playing the board game Pirate and Traveler. In college, grad school, and later, I whiled away too many nights playing hearts, canasta, and cribbage, and have the modest grades to prove it.

Bernard can't stand games, considers them a waste of time. But we're on the *Evangelistas* and this is a time of change and renewal for both of us. I ignore that he's shifting uncomfortably in his chair, getting his feet under him as if preparing to flee. I don't give him a chance to utter a protest. "Here's what's going to happen," I continue. "The caller will tell you what pattern you have to fill in, like all the numbers under the letter 'N,' or a diagonal from the top left corner to the bottom right one. Listen to each number called out. Look for it on your card. Cover it with a chip if you find it. You'll see. It's fun!"

"G47," the hostess calls out.

"What did she say? What do I do?" Bernard asks me, panicked. Here's a man who can deconstruct a complex engine in his sleep, yet he's relying on me to get him through the simplest of board games. I'm in heaven.

"B8. O65." The engine's hum and the buzz of two hundred Bingo players is making it difficult to hear.

"What? What is she saying?" He's flummoxed by this most elementary of pastimes, a reaction I find totally endearing. But he's competitive and this is a game where someone wins. By game two Bernard comes into his own, and I'm beside myself with pride when in game three he jumps to his feet shouting, "I've got it!"

"No, no. You're supposed to yell BINGO."

"Bean-go. Bean-go," he shouts, flushing happily.

The caller checks his card and escorts us to the front where she hands him his prize: a bottle of Chilean red. Then the crew start stamping and clapping, making clear we're now expected to sing for our supper. Or, more accurately, to dance for our wine. A *huaso cueca*, the music of Chile's cowboys, blares over the loudspeakers. "Bernard," I shout, "it's like country swing!" This singer is no Willie Nelson, however. Feeling a bit like a scene cut from *Pulp Fiction*, we slip off our shoes and begin twirling, sashaying, and two-stepping as if our lives, not just our national pride, depended on it. I look to see if the judges are holding up a "10" for our performance but have to be satisfied with a bow to rousing applause from the raucous crowd of sloshed revelers. Our table is particularly happy to claim us as their own, especially when we open our winnings and pour wine all around.

At lunch on the second day, the captain announces that we'll enter the notorious Golfo de Penas that evening. This is what I've been dreading, the one point at which we have to forsake our sheltered passage for the heaving swells of the open Pacific. In my experience, big waves and a rolling ship are a recipe for one thing only: being sick as a dog. I devote myself to ransacking my baggage for my Dramamine. An hour of frantic flinging of personal belongings later and I accept I've left it at home. I do still have one option to avoid spending hours heaving into the head: take a sleeping pill.

It's antithetical to everything about me that I would resort to drugs in such situations. I live a healthy life with lots of physical activity and fresh air of the purest high altitude Rocky Mountain sort. We don't suffer when it comes to freshly prepared meals either, despite no good restaurants within seventy miles of our ranch. With two refrigerators and three freezers, I've become exceptionally creative in managing a week's worth of shopping and daily leftovers, to always have something tasty on the table, all of which I cook myself as my Mediterranean-inspired mother taught me.

When it comes to jetlag, however, I have long relied on the kindness of drugs. For someone whose medicine cabinet is so rarely opened that the medications in it are from the last century, there's one simple reason for this:

I want to enjoy my time abroad as quickly and with as much consciousness as possible. What I don't want is to be the only one ready to party at 2:00 a.m. nor do I wish to sleep through the chance to taste the local breakfast. When I'm traveling I make it a point to be on the same rhythm as everyone around me.

I've done this for years, reading the travel columns, trying each new therapy as soon as it's trending enough to warrant a review. During the P2P, when my mind raced with anxiety and fatigue like an engine revving in overdrive, I alternated between Benadryl and a half tab of Ambien at bedtime to quiet my mind enough to let me sleep. Each worked its charms, helping me maintain a civil, if not consistently cheerful, attitude for at least the first few hours of the day.

Since then, I'm all for doing what's needed to keep myself comfortable and agreeable. If on occasion that means invoking pharmaceutical charms so that I sleep the sleep of the happily benumbed, I'm all for it. Now, breaking one tiny rectangular pill in half, I gulp it down with a sip of warm bottled water and crawl between the stiff white sheets of my berth, reaching my arm up to wish Bernard goodnight. When I awake the following morning, we've traversed the infamous gulf without incident.

The 930-mile inside passage from Puerto Montt, which is about midway down Chile's long coastline, to Puerto Natales which is far to the south, is a revelation, at least when the view isn't obscured by fog or rain. The region, known as the Chilean fjords, is a jigsaw puzzle of rocky islets, covered summit to shore with dense vegetation. From a distance they seem like a tropical paradise. As we glide through this lacy archipelago, we are sometimes only a hundred yards from shore and thus can see they are devoid of human or animal life. At one point, the captain steers the boat into a large hidden bay. The air turns sharply icy, as if we've entered some shoreline deep freezer. The fog lifts slightly off the surface of the water, just enough to reveal the source of the frigid air. It's the tongue of an immense blue-white glacier, a sector of the Southern Patagonian Ice Field below which we've been sailing. The islands and the shore itself have risen so steeply that until now it's been hidden from us. As the boat turns broadside to the ice, the glacier groans, as if in pain. Then a mighty turquoise blue ice floe calves off the base, collapsing into the water like a fat man into an easy chair. A series of waves ripples slowly outward, big enough to rock our small tanker like a plastic duck in a tub.

The three-and-a-half-day journey has an otherworldly feeling to it, as if we are slipping past phantom islands on a ghost ship. What with continually fogged windows, obscuring mists, and a bone-chilling dampness from the constant drizzle, I can't keep my thoughts from turning to my dry, sunny Colorado home. This is not good. One of the reasons I devote so much brain space to my fantasies about an upcoming trip is because it's hard for me to leave home. My daydreams steel me to be away from my bed, my pillow, my food, my view, my routine, all things which, in their bland material way, comfort me. Finding the fun in sleeping on a bed of concrete with a pillow that smells of someone else's hair problems takes energy, as does enthusing over a plate of spicy gristle, or spending the day lost, sweating, and increasingly coated with muck. Yet I love our strange, unpredictable travels all the more for how they bring into sharp relief exactly what home means to me. Not just my home's material comforts, but that ineffable sense of calm belonging, of splendid rightness when I cross the invisible boundary and re-enter my native space. A space whose every aspect and angle defines what I am in this world, a space which fits me as tightly and naturally as my skin. My home nurtures me as surely as do my home-cooked meals; to the extent I can leave it and then return with some new ingredients to add to my world, I keep enriching the broth of my life.

One benefit of a long road trip is that the perpetual change keeps me engaged as well as distracted. If something is too terrible one day, I know I can be somewhere else the next. On the *Evangelistas*, I've been in one place too long. The taciturn captain shows me evidence on a nautical chart that we are moving, but I can't feel it. Worse yet, I can't see it. Apart from the occasional petrel and a pod of Peale's dolphins that briefly swim with the boat, the archipelago we glide through is uninhabited. Bernard's much more present-minded than I am. He rarely gets entangled with "what ifs" when we travel, dealing with each new situation as it comes, without inferring future calamity because of it. Not me. While Bernard's perky because he can get a pisco sour whenever he wants, my thoughts turn morbidly philosophical, like, "If there's no one around to see us, do we really exist?" accompanied by its corresponding mood-lifter of, "If we disappeared right now, would anyone know?"

When the *Evangelistas* ties up at the Puerto Natales docks it's a profound relief to retrieve our spry Suzuki, dump our bags in her trunk, and get back on the road. Any longer on board and I suspect we might have vanished into the mist altogether.

Kindness of Strangers

GHALAT, IRAN, 2016

Shahpur is trapped in one of life's eddies, swirling down an ever tighter, lonelier, more desperate spiral. This puzzles me. Given how dire his circumstances are, how can he be so full of joy? And how is it that chickpeas can both sustain and utterly ruin him?

These questions enter later, though. When we meet Shahpur, chickpeas, mashed or otherwise, are the farthest thing from my mind, which instead is occupied with thoughts of worm-eaten apples and the stubborn perseverance of the elderly. To be precise, that of a woman whose every step speaks more clearly of what it takes to move forward with dignity than any globe-travelling diplomat could ever achieve, 747s and bespoke suits notwithstanding.

It's late fall and we are near Shiraz, partway through a group road trip from Istanbul, Turkey on the Bosporus Strait which divides the Sea of Marmara from the Black Sea, to Bandar Abbas, Iran on the Strait of Hormuz which divides the Gulf of Oman from the Persian Gulf. The drive has been more arduous than we expected, with long days in the car to cover the thousands of miles before us, something we're willing to accept because we'd longed to return to Iran since crossing the country from west to east in 2011. To embark on this trip requires us to ignore the potential perils following Turkey's near-coup some months earlier. I remind myself that machine gun fire at roadblocks is something that happens to others, not me. I also extract a promise from Bernard that he will not diverge from our route to where the PKK (Kurdistan Workers' Party) has street fighters, no matter how tempting the photo op may be. And we do see roadblocks and armored personnel carriers aplenty through Turkey, on one day being told not to proceed on pain of having our tires shot out.

While five years ago I entered Iran from Turkey with trepidation, on this trip crossing the border feels like a reprieve, entering what right then seems a haven of orderly calm: the Islamic Republic run by Supreme Leader Grand Ayatollah Ali Khamenei. Khamenei has sat atop the power structure in Iran since 1989, so the country's mode of government is forcefully stable. In a certain way it's a relief that the ever-present issues defining America's relationship with Iran are so entrenched they've hardly changed since I last was here. Five years ago this felt oppressive, but today, in comparison to the seismic upheavals in Turkey, it feels profoundly reassuring, despite how emphatically I disagree with the way Iran is run. Which just goes to show you that, when traveling, a sense of security is remarkably relative.

Today we're in the old village of Ghalat. The distance we've driven intensifies my exuberance at being footloose. It's just like the airy glee I felt on an elementary school snow day, a sense that without me doing anything to earn it, loads of fun await. Why? Because we'll spend most of today indulging one of my favorite activities: meandering on foot. And that brings with it the potential for untold meetings, as unexpected and full of pleasure as that magical drift of snow outside my childhood bedroom when I awoke on a wintery Tuesday morning.

These wanderings are unpredictable. Nothing's planned and nothing's expected, not our path, not whether or where we'll eat, not how long we'll stay. I won't know what will happen in this particular old village until it happens. If anything even does. We might not do more than wave at people, or we might encounter someone who changes my worldview forever.

The air here in southwestern Iran is smoky, the sun mild and warming. When we peer over a wall from the lane above we see a woman swathed in black. She's poking with her walking stick at hand-scraped canals weaving through her garden, among fruit trees half-clothed in dying leaves, a fond remembrance of a lush summer. Her black scarf has slid half off, revealing thick steel-gray hair, more a tossed-on protection from possible chill than a strictly correct garment of Sharia law. The problem she faces is obvious from the black stain of water dribbling down the cobbled alley outside her garden wall: her shallow ditches are choked with lazily drifting yellow leaves and the water that should be sustaining her orchard is dampening the street dust instead.

She's eighty-five, she tells us, belying her barely lined face with its clear skin and bright eyes. She reaches for low-lying tree branches, apologizing that she is too poor to invite us in. The hem of her black dress drags through an ochre leaf carpet as she picks four small apples and hands them up to us over the high wall. She apologizes further, for the worms that have gotten to them first. Her children, a doctor, an engineer, come sometimes, she explains. They prefer the city, though, while she prefers the quiet of this, her family village. She sighs. She pokes the ground. She resumes her slow clearing of leaves, one modest scratch at a time.

But back to chickpeas—as ubiquitous in Iranian cuisine as potatoes are to middle-American stockpots. Like potatoes they pack more in the way of minerals than any sand-colored, pointy-bottomed orb has any right to do. And just like a celebrity glimpsed without makeup or styling before the Oscars, they transform nicely when the occasion warrants. Cooked slow they become soft and as soothing as my mother's cool hand on my forehead when I had a fever during grade school (after that I was an irascible teenager and wouldn't let her touch me), adding substance to a lean meal and in so doing perhaps to a lean life as well.

As I nibble around the wormholes in my apple I have no idea I'm about to learn that chickpeas have a mission in life wholly unrelated to eating, which is this: chickpeas also serve as unit of weight and measure. People the world over use what's handy and inarguably replicable to confirm the agreed portion of what they're selling. In the Kalewa market along Myanmar's Chindwin River they use a D cell battery to weigh a portion of fish; in Ethiopia repurposed plastic bottles of Fanta line roadside fuel stands, as uniform as soldiers on parade, confirming an exact liter of petrol for the 150cc motorbikes that buzz the roads like a fresh hatch of mosquitos. In Iran, it's the chickpea, which long has led a secret double life as unit of measure. This is because there are a lot of them in the country, the seventh largest producer of chickpeas in the world. These little beige orbs with the nutty flavor and buttery texture pack a huge punch when it comes to nutrition, especially in things like antioxidants and fiber. They make their way into much of Persian cuisine with the added bonus that they help you feel full even though you haven't eaten much. Just like any other pulse or legume, one chickpea is indistinguishable from another. A lentil is a lentil is a lentil. So is a chickpea. Their very sameness makes them the ideal measure for another popular substance: opium.

As I learn later, the similarities between me and a chickpea of raw opium are disconcerting. For instance, both of us have undertaken quite a journey to get to Ghalat. For me, it meant more than sixty hours of driving from Iran's northwest juncture with Turkey, Armenia, and Azerbaijan, through mountains so desiccated and rugged that for millennia they guarded themselves. Now, in the age of drones, it requires soldiers at key passages to keep Iranians in and Iraqis out, soldiers with big guns and aggressive struts, who prefer to point rather than palaver. In the past week of driving we've traversed mountains so forbidding, plains so dry, drought-broken riverbeds so devoid of even the tiniest ripple of water, that I had to wonder why anyone would bother trying to conquer such a place, let alone expend manpower to hold onto it for centuries as the Safavid and Sassanid kings did. Perhaps they recognized it for what it was: a great place to grow chickpeas.

To reach where I'm standing, that chickpea of opium would have come from the opposite direction, most likely starting in Helmand Province in southern Afghanistan, twin to neighboring Kandahar Province in terms of opium-producing stature, but closer to Iran. It could have entered anywhere along Iran's 1,923-kilometer-long eastern border with Afghanistan, a national boundary so porous it would shame a sieve.

Like me, it would have moved by vehicle. While that might sound disturbing, I'm relieved not to have to compare myself to an opium chickpea arriving in the northeast, which could have travelled in the stomach of a donkey or a camel. Regardless of mode of transport, to reach Ghalat our sample chickpea would have jounced across 1,200 kilometers of terrain so rough even Genghis Khan and Tamerlane complained about it.

While I had to be satisfied with lamb heart kebabs from roadside grills, the transiting opium provided the equivalent of an endless Sunday brunch for Iran's military and government, reputedly heavily involved in its trade. We're talking profits from 540-plus tons of raw opium consumed within Iran each year, a quantity that awards Iran the silver medal (second to Afghanistan) for most addicted country in the world.

A chickpea of opium is enough to send a novice smoker into a haze for twenty-four hours. For an addict, smoking one chickpea would be like Usain Bolt saying he's going to jog around the block for exercise. Why bother? Three opium nubs are what you'll need to get you started on the day. This will cost you fifty cents. To maintain a high-quality stupor, you'll smoke three times a day. Despite my C+ in high school algebra, even I can calculate how quickly the gluey black opium paste will not only stain your lips brown and rot your teeth but gnaw away at what little income you have.

Continuing our walk, we amble up a cobbled lane of beige stone, past a tree whose slender branches droop heavy with the blood red globes of ripe pomegranate, through a low arched tunnel funky with sheep droppings, emerging into sunlight dappled by orange persimmon trees, then into a narrow alley, ducking under a low doorway where stands Shahpur, blue shorts exposing his bony knees, his concave chest heaving with an occasional cough. He peers at us, red-rimmed eyes crinkling in his long stubbly face, hair sticking up in tufts as if, though it's 11:00 a.m., he's just risen from a wild night of restless dreams. His smile is immediate, and so I see that his upper teeth are gone, rotted, fallen out. One lone long one remains, stained as brown as bark, clear testimony that Shahpur has made friends with opium in a big way.

I've met many unusual people on the road, though never where or when I anticipated. During our driving days I always feel a bit like I'm going rogue without really wanting to. Often my cell phone won't work and I become creepily aware of the literal truth that no one knows where I am. So it's as yin seeks yang, that I seek the secure predictability—and connectivity, and hot shower—of a nice hotel at day's end. If we can find one. Regardless, I long to shake hands with the next day's unpredictability, because that's how I've had some of my most memorable encounters, from the ex–Black Panther who invited us for barley beer on his farm near Lake Tana, Ethiopia, to the vodka-swilling Kyrgyz who pulled me into a dance circle at his reunion in Naryn, on the road to Kashgar in China. And I've been around men like Shahpur before, too, in 2009 when I was in Nagaland, the foothills of eastern India, steps away from the Myanmar border— which I stepped over, just to make the point that I could. There, in the headhunter village of the Konyak people, a cluster of addicts occupied the back room of the thatch hut of our hosts. Everyone treated them with affectionate nonchalance. Now and then one would wander into the surrounding bamboo forest toting a homemade black powder rifle, in search of bush meat for the pot, whose contents were freely shared with them at each meal. Mainly, though, they stayed close to their pipe.

For those three days and three nights I tried to convince myself to smoke opium. "This is your chance. Don't pass it up," the adventurous side of me said. "Yes, but remember what happened when you tried to drink barley beer. And that was just barley beer," the easily cowed side of me answered. "If they felt like sharing they would have," I countered. "You're a woman. A foreigner. They wouldn't dare suggest it," I replied. And so it went until the last night passed and it was too late. I was filled with regret as well as disgust at having missed a perfect opportunity. After many more years that saw me traveling through countries like Myanmar and China, both of which hold elite status in the world of opium production and use, I figured my days of bumping into opium addicts were long gone. Wrong.

Shahpur covers his heart with his right hand in the Iranian gesture of grateful welcome, then sweeps it round to present his café with its several small tables, assorted wood benches, and a decor of nomad weavings, artistically twisted branches, and old farm implements. The place is empty but expectant, breathless as a high school senior awaiting her prom date. Right now, the quiet fairly roars in my ears, as if I'm the only one who's noticed the date should have been here hours ago and just may not show. Even the neighbors must be away. The rusty pink child's bike leaning against a gray-washed stone wall speaks of abandonment instead of the life-giving force of childhood laughter.

Come up these stairs to my home, Shahpur gestures. Have tea with me. And so we do, leaving our shoes on the threshold. With windows and doors open, Shahpur's small rooftop living quarters are cool and fresh. Red Persian rugs cover the floor and hard rectangular cushions line the walls around a brick fireplace where lounges a plush toy leopard. A few wedding photos adorn the mantel piece, along with one large silver-framed photo of a black-haired toddler. I peer into Shahpur's bedroom, bare except for a floral fleece blanket on the floor. It's in the bedding equivalent of fetal position, rumpled and discarded when Shahpur moved onto his body-sized terrace amid pots of dying herbs, perhaps to cool off a night sweat.

Shahpur wishes us to sit against the wall cushions as honored guests, but we've not only seen the portable gas burner on the floor in front of the kitchen, but noticed there's a tin stew pot simmering on it. Wisps of spicy lamb perfume curl from under the lid. I cannot resist local foods and that rich, meaty odor is tempting to me. Sit politely against the wall when we can all inhale delicious steam? How absurd would that be?

We ignore Shahpur's entreaties and join him cross-legged on the floor, except Bernard whose legs can't pretzel like the rest of us. We're circling the wagons, in a manner of speaking, around what turns out to be *abgoosht*, colloquially called *dizi*, an Iranian stew of lamb, potatoes, tomato, chickpeas, turmeric, and dried lime. Pointing backward on his watch, Shahpur confides it's been simmering now for twelve hours. Lifting the lid as only I can do when I'm shamelessly hungry, I see a rich red-gold broth spiked with all the requirements. But no chickpeas.

Shahpur pours us glasses of tea, puts some crude blonde tobacco—more branch than leaf—in his *qalyan*, and settles himself on the floor for a smoke. Closing his eyes, he draws deeply, the soft bubbling of water in the hookah like an old aunt muttering about her nephew's bad habits. He takes several drags, then opens his eyes and breaks into song. It's a village ode to a local man, Shahpur's strong tenor ringing out in the small house. From the way he wags his head with his eyes twinkling, the lyrics are raunchy. And then, surprise, he belts out "Ay Berrrrrnarrd!" launching into a four-line refrain with three repetitions, at each mention of Berrrnarrd, his winks and smile getting bigger and broader. He draws out the last note, spreading his arms wide to encompass Bernard, me, the *dizi*, life in general, perhaps opium in particular, his one stained tooth prominently displayed as he bursts into proud laughter.

When Shahpur inspects his stew, the smell is so intoxicating we are determined to linger over our tea until lunch is the only possible next step. But he needs no prompting, expressing deep gladness at the unexpected company now filling an empty day. He scrounges two more potatoes for the stew, my cue to offer my services for KP duty. Peeling, dicing, then tossing them in the pot, we return to our floor positions as they soften in the bubbling broth, all of us companionably attentive to the Arctic segment of *Planet Earth* playing on the flatscreen TV. Once, the TV might have been evidence of flush times in the teahouse below, but now it's the only item of value in the house, holding pride of place on a scratched wood bureau facing the kitchen. Though the Iranian station broadcasts the show in an endless loop, we ooh and point over and over again as a polar bear tumbles with her cubs, orcas team up to kill a whale, and a wolf pack drags down a caribou calf.

All of this would be charming if it weren't becoming apparent from what I see around me, and from the melancholy into which Shahpur seems to sink when he's not "on," that he's smoked his way into a downward spiral of loss and solitude. Our companion tells us Shahpur's wife has left and taken their boy to Shiraz, ostensibly for school, but likely also to get the boy away from his father's habit. Now there's little to spare even for a handful of chickpeas for his stew. Despite that opium smoking is a sociable endeavor, the house sighs with emptiness and loss.

Shahpur smokes until it's stew time, which begins with us taking a small portion each in order to leave enough for Shahpur's evening meal. Appalled at our meager helpings, he mines deep in the pot, ladling a more generous heap of neck bones, potatoes, and broth into each of our bowls. Our spoons make poor work of extracting the delicate meat clinging around their boney harbors. Shahpur shakes a vertebra at me with his hands, shreds of meat clinging to its angles and orifices, then, despite his lack of teeth, brings it to his mouth to illustrate I should eat with my fingers. But this is Iran and it's been difficult enough not turning my headscarf into a food catcher at a fork-and-knife sort of meal. It would be impossible to acquit myself with dignity when slurping a dripping bone from a stewpot. I stab my spoon at the neck bones with renewed intensity, determined not to waste a scrap.

Having shared food, we're now proven friends, inspiring Shahpur to offer his *qalyan* to Bernard, man to man. I'm interested in the *qalyan* myself, hoping maybe there's a little something-something left in the bowl. But a woman's lips on a man's pipe? No doubt there's a page or two on that in the Koran, but in plain English it's this: not going to happen.

Bernard fails to coax even a teaspoon of smoke from the pipe, transforming Shahpur into an imitation beetle, on his back, legs kicking, hacking with laughter. He squats by Bernard's side to illustrate with pursed brown lips the slow, steady drag of a dedicated professional. Bernard mimics, then explodes in a vigorous coughing fit, the cloud of cool smoke around his head evidence he got a double lungful.

As Bernard politely puffs I secretly hope for one of those opium chickpeas to make an appearance. Given the chance this time, I'd definitely try it. Instead Shahpur succumbs to a new bout of emotion, this one inspiring him to recite the poetry of Shamseddin Mohammed Hafez, beloved fourteenth-century poet from Shiraz. He selects one of the over five hundred *ghazal* Hafez wrote, his tone evoking all the melancholy, love, and longing of this complex poetic form so ideally suited to being declaimed in Farsi:

Where is the touch of breeze and rain?
Where now the beaming of the sun?
This was a noble lovers' town,
This soil the country of kind men.

Inspired by the poem's lyrics he repeats them, eyes closed, head lifted in rapture. At the end he folds his arms around Bernard, resting his head on Bernard's shoulder, stained mouth wide with the joys of poetry and friendship. He pours us two small glasses of cloudy amber liquid, home-fermented from his own grapes, some of which float in the bottom of my share. I swallow a mouthful. It is sweet and musty yet it burns going down, a fiery forbidden Iranian essence filled with Shahpur's passion.

AFFLICTION

PREAMBLE

I am not a hypochondriac, though my capacious travel first aid kit might imply otherwise. It takes up the entire right-hand corner of my suitcase. So vast is it that I have a three-page list to remind me what each item is for and how to use it.

On the prescription side are four antibiotics, including one in both pill and eye drop form, to treat any bacterium intrepid enough to infect me outside or in. There's atropine to petrify even the remotest hint of diarrhea, relaxants for when muscles become violently disarranged, painkillers that would get most doctors arrested, even the morphine tablets prescribed for my dog when he was dying of bone cancer. I've made a note to myself not to mix the morphine with the muscle relaxant, as the two drugs are like ex-lovers at a cocktail party . . . happier separated and not mixed with alcohol. Why arouse conflict when peace is so much more, well, peaceful.

Then there are my sacks of over-the-counter remedies: one for colds containing the comforts of Robitussin and Theraflu, a bottle of every analgesic in existence, antihistamine tablets, stomach upset tablets like Alka Seltzer and Ex-Lax, clove oil (watch *Marathon Man* to understand this), plus throat lozenges and nasal spray. And a digital thermometer to tell me exactly how sick I am before I get better.

My minor wounds bag contains two types of antibiotic cream, anti-itch unguent, rubbing alcohol, hydrogen peroxide, and mercurochrome for disinfecting any bit of abraded skin, plus an assortment of coverings from Band-Aids and butterfly closures to moleskin, gauze pads in three sizes, second skin, burn coverings, tape, vet wrap, and ace bandages. After a recent bout with two types of fungus that took up residence in my left little toe while I was around Myanmar, I now also have a tube of anti-fungal cream so expensive that it took my insurance company a month to approve. To manage the minor surgery these materials imply I have a small toolkit containing hemostats, tiny sharp scissors, and a pair of vicious tweezers. I used to have a suture kit as well, but I donated that to a clinic in Jinka, Ethiopia which needed it more than I did.

I've gotten all these drugs legally, mainly by being just ill enough for a doctor to prescribe a remedy of which I only need to avail myself for a day or two. Some people can't bear to throw away old newspapers, junk mail, or empty egg cartons. Me? I'm a travel drug hoarder, especially when it comes to painkillers. When Bernard or I have surgery, we fill the prescriptions for post-op pain immediately, and toss those sturdy brown plastic bottles with the aggravatingly secure white tops directly into our travel stash. Though I study maps and skim guide books before each trip, nothing convinces me better that I'm well prepared than the bulge and heft of my dark blue medicine bag, with its laminated cheat sheet of what to use when. It's like a stuffed Thanksgiving turkey, holding only goodness within.

It seems easier to add to the kit than to take out. Yet in my nearly ten years on the road it seems I've swallowed maybe five pills from the stash. This could be because of my reluctance to self-diagnose, or because I never sicken or injure in the way I've anticipated. The sack goes out, comes back, is stored in a sink-side drawer till the next trip, and like a prized sourdough, improves via the unguents and capsules added to it each time something needs treating back home.

So why bother? I'm not sickish, nor do I spend time before a trip worrying about getting ill. I have too much else to be anxious about. In truth there is a strong element of contradiction in me. Though I am someone who believes fiercely in creating my own destiny, at the same time I have no doubt that my tarot reader is the most powerful woman I know when it comes to communicating with the cards. I can just as easily sob when I hear Chopin as I can rock out to the Grateful Dead, exulting at the magical music of both. I love dressing up for the opera as much as I love putting the same clothes on day after day, knowing that I won't meet anyone I know and those I do meet will not care how I'm dressed.

Despite being the pragmatic atheist, I travel by the mantra scribbled somewhere in my subconscious travel guide: "Go forth prepared for the worst so that only the best will happen." So often has my blue first aid kit traveled that it deserves its own passport. I have said to myself, "I could fit a lot of clothing in place of all those meds I never use." But I know the moment I depart home without it, the djinns of medical misfortune will descend upon me. Being prepared means not just having enough white shirts, it means that without a doubt my medical kit is the only thing standing between me and misery.

Toes

PUCÓN, CHILE, 2008

My new doctor friend enters the antiseptic operating room. His white coat blends so seamlessly with the white floor tiles, cupboards, and sterilized mat on which nestle the diabolical tools of his trade that his head seems to float. A nurse briskly clatters the rolling tool tray toward the foot of the operating table, keeping up a peppy banter that's supposed to put me, the patient, at ease. But I am not at ease. I see through her ruse and stay committed to letting my mounting nervousness escalate. Bernard paces, then stands shifting his weight from foot to foot, unsure where to place himself. Should he stand by my head holding my hand and in other ways distracting me with his French version of chitchat, inserting a "ma cherie" here, a "tout va bien" there, to assure me I am well cared for? Or can he proceed immediately to what he'd prefer, which is standing at the gurney's foot to see exactly how this doctor is going to separate my bruised big toenail from the nail bed to which it's defiantly clinging?

Bernard is never at ease when I'm sick or in pain. I learned this during my ten-day tussle with flu during our first year together. As I lay sweating in bed with my eyes closed he became fussy, self-soothing by plying me with so many questions about what I needed or what he should do, that I felt both loved and annoyed. Still, I know I am a lucky woman to have a husband of over thirty years whose concern for me is a constant. It's because of that love that his desire to do something meaningful for me is sorely tried when my only request is an extra ice cube in my ginger ale. On the other hand, his unhappiness when I'm under the weather is one of the intangibles that helps me heal faster.

At this moment, though, I don't much care where Bernard stands, as long as the upcoming procedure is over as quickly and painlessly as possible. It's cocktail hour in Pucón, one of Chile's magnificent lake resorts, and what I want more than anything is a nicely chilled and shaken pisco sour.

It's testimony to the positive aura of our Anti-Rally road trip through Patagonia, that even when things start to go bad they're still good. It was two days ago that we decided to stop in Talca, which borders Reserva Nacional Altos de Lircay (also called Protected Area Vilches), one of Chile's many national parks. The Sendero de Chile winds through Vilches, which means I can hike up high and see the snowcapped peaks of the Andes for myself, not from a plane window. To me these peaks are mythic, as they were the place my father went with his best friend and mountaineering partner when I was eight years old.

At the time it seemed he'd disappeared, and I missed him in the egocentric way of a child, his absence disrupting my world while not spurring me to investigate where he was. Squeezing the red wax rind of gouda cheese into doll-sized dice and marking the numbers with an after-dinner toothpick was not as much fun if I couldn't watch his elegant engineer's fingers shaping the wax, or compare my clumsy dumplings to his precise cubes. We lived in a lovely, leafy suburb of New York City, and I missed bike riding with him and my visit to the tiny farm of Mr. Buccharelli, an Italian immigrant, where I played with wild kittens and picked heavy purple fruit from the immigrant fig tree. The half-built houses we explored on neighborhood rambles, standing in each room to guess how it would be used, were fast getting finished without my father to help me muse about what they'd become.

What seemed a lifetime later he returned, happy and sunburned, and we resumed our father–daughter explorations. Though my father continued to travel to wild places throughout my adulthood, trips we talked about sometimes at length, somehow I never thought to ask him about the Andes. So it is that since the 1960s the Andes have a held a large yet vague status in my mind, remaining a place of intrigue, a place I knew about, that was part of my being, yet knew nothing of. By the time he returned to the southern Andes in the late 1990s, specifically for the peaks of Torres del Paine and Fitz Roy, I was old enough to be enraptured by his photographs and to listen attentively to his tales. Finally, myth melded with memory and I knew I had to see for myself the places of which he spoke.

This is why, on waking up in Talca, I'm beyond excited, but I'm also a bag of jitters. Making a pronouncement on the significance of seeing the Andes that has no rationale beyond "I want to," I've convinced Bernard that we need to do this hike, need to glimpse the real Andes, and that I'm physically able to do it despite severe tendinitis in each ankle and a ruptured ACL in my right knee. The tendinitis, a lingering (okay, chronic) malady that took possession of my Achilles tendons on the P2P, prevents me from walking normally uphill. The ACL injury, a result of an unfortunate ski fall two weeks before our departure, makes walking on anything but smooth, level ground an exercise in diligent attention to tiny, tripping obstacles. That morning, my only deference to my injuries has been to pull on an awkward neoprene knee brace. It makes my knee sweat and I hate its interfering ways the moment I cinch it into place, but Bernard will not tolerate my going without.

Once onto the rubbly, steep trail, I have to walk several miles uphill, which I do on tiptoes to keep from aggravating my squeaky inflamed tendons. Hampered by my precarious mincing step, I struggle to avoid twisting my knee on the uneven terrain. For this I should rely on the brace. But I have no faith in it, so I just clench the knee joint and don't bend it. Once I get high enough to actually see the far peaks, I tell Bernard I've gone as far as I can. It's not the end of the trail, but I'm not disappointed. To the contrary, it's unexpectedly emotional to be there, a generalized feeling of accomplishment coupled with relief that leaves me both exhilarated and drained. Though I advance like a stump-legged pirate on the way down, I complete the long, hot hike without whining. That alone is bracing in a way the knee contraption hasn't been, and it's helped along by the icy Coke I gulp down at a roadside stand when we finally reach our car.

On the drive back, with nothing to distract me but daydreams of the puddle-sized pool at our guesthouse, I notice there's a tiny drummer in my foot, a mild but persistent percussion emanating from my big toe. My toes don't normally emit insistent rhythmic clamors for attention. As a rule I would normally bring up the throbbing beat, but as it happens I'm trying on a new me, an I-don't-always-have-to-complain persona which I'm finding quite refreshing. I say nothing.

When my left foot emerges from its sweaty sock cocoon back in our room, the nail on my big toe is revealed in all its bluish-purple glory. I know what this portends but choose to ignore it, making up a fantasy for myself about how this nail color is just temporary, something that'll subside on its own by the next morning. I peel off the offending knee brace, wriggle into my bathing suit and head out to the pool. As soon as I step in, the warm water acts like a stage amp at a Madonna concert, with my toe the electric bass belting out a throb so insistent in its pulse that I feel sure everyone can hear the beat. I prop my leg up on an extra chair, avoiding Bernard's inquiring gaze.

That night, the sheet is like a lead slab whose full weight is pressing on what's ordinarily a modest piece of body real estate. The next day, a driving day, I do my navigating with foot propped on dash board, hoping gravity will drain the pooling blood away from the toe. I have plenty more out-of-car excursions in mind for us through Patagonia that involve having ten good toes on my feet. It is unacceptable that one out of ten would become such a showstopper.

Things don't improve once we reach our Pucón hotel, though that's not the fault of the hotel, a strikingly modern Frank Lloyd Wright imitation whose gardens of magenta and orange bougainvillea slope down to the electric blue waters of Lago Villarica. Not only is there a steam-powered boat chugging along the shore, there's an immense white-capped volcano on the near horizon. It's so Shangri-la that we decide to stay for a couple of days. On a short exploration around the grounds, I inadvertently bump my toe. It's a light tap, really nothing more than a grazing of the stair step, but it sends me cursing and hopping about like a demented chicken. I go to dinner in sandals into which I slide my foot at the slow careful pace of the spider inching along our windowsill. Regardless, even the caress of limpid warm lakeside air is too much. The continuous pounding in my toe accompanies dinner like a morbid tango.

To say I awake the next morning would be to imply I actually slept. It takes only a cursory glance to confirm that the offending nail is now trying to levitate off the nail bed. "Bernard," I gulp, scared to reveal the obvious, thinking to do so is only going to make it worse. "It's not getting better." I am so forlorn about having to forfeit all my boot-related activities that I'm nearly in tears when I add, "I think a doctor needs to look at it."

Up until now, Bernard's been willing to buy into my stoicism. Hearing the catch in my voice, he realizes the new, improved me has gone as far as she can. Action is needed. He leaps to my suitcase in search of the blue medical kit, in which surely there'll be something to fix me. Cradling it like a fragile baby he starts plying me with questions in a hopeful tone. "Dina, there's a pill that can help you, no?" I shake my head. Next, he tries a smidge of empathy, "Pauvre cherie, tell me which medication you want and I will get it for you." I shake my head harder. With rising uncertainty whether he'll be able to do anything for me at all he starts to panic, issuing rapid fire options: "A painkiller? Anti-inflammatory? Compress? Something else?" The more he's wrong the more irritated I get until finally I shake my head in annoyance and mutter, "*Noooo*. Nothing! I want a doctor!"

From there, things move into fast-forward. Yes, the front desk knows a doctor who will make hotel calls. Yes, they'll phone him to come in. Yes, he will respond to the call even though it's Valentine's Day and he's taken the day off to spend it with his wife down at the shore. Within an hour the doctor has arrived, a dark-haired, handsome man in his late thirties. He enters the lobby with a swagger, oozing charisma, his eyes flashing a come-hither look that surely wants to see more than my big toe. Or so I imagine.

Back in the room, I lay on the bed. Bernard sits on a chair. The doctor hovers close enough that I can marvel enviously at his long black lashes and inhale his musky scent of solicitous machismo. When he turns his eyes on me, deep-set and dark as espresso, I feel like swooning. But I'm no

Scarlett O'Hara in crinoline. I have no glossy curls and large plantation to offer, only the ugliness of my big toe. I wave my foot, then work at calming my fluttering heart. "Yes," the doctor tells me, after inspecting the toe. "The toenail is a problem." I'm relieved he thinks so, as I don't have the Spanish vocabulary for "This son-of-a-bitch is killing me." And anyway, his Spanish-flavored English and mellifluous tone calm me like a valium downed with vodka. I want him to keep speaking, to say anything at all, just so I can listen to his voice and not have to think about the implications of what he's saying.

"So. I can offer you two options," he continues, professional words tinged with vowels of sympathy. "It is okay for you to stay as you are. In a few weeks, the nail will come off on its own. So you don't have to do anything today if you do not want to. Of course, it will be very painful that whole time. And it can easily get infected." Well, this I already know. I was hoping he'd have something more inspiring to offer. "Or," and here he pauses like a good game show host, letting the tension build, "I can take the toenail off right now."

"What? You mean here?"

"No," he says with a laugh. "Oh, no, no, no, no. I will take you to my hospital and we will do it there."

This doctor owns a hospital? And where might that be? Detecting I'm perplexed, he says, "It's just five minutes from here. I will drive you there myself."

"And if I have the nail removed, then what?"

"In a few days you will be able to wear shoes, no problem."

I like the sound of that. Besides, the math is evident: three weeks without shoes versus three days without shoes. It's a no-brainer and I don't waste a second considering the hospital I'm about to visit nor what it'll be like to have a large toenail taken off before its time. I do not ordinarily seek out hospitals at home. I don't like their smell, their sense of uneasy mystery nor what they portend in terms of pain and illness. So it's a surprise even to me that I'm quite peppy at the thought of what I'm about to see. The toe calamity has become my ticket to a great adventure which I will be the only traveler to experience, namely, an insider's tour of a Chilean hospital, in a state alert enough to appreciate it.

Unlike hermetically sealed American hospitals, the one in Pucón is a low, airy affair. It's run by Catholic nuns who skim along the hallways in floor-whisking robes. As we walk in, a few waft by in their efficient, prayerful way, bestowing on me a smile filled with kindness and silent blessings. An affable breeze moves gently through open windows, bringing in the perfume of flower beds and trimmed lawns. It rustles papers at the intake desk and flirts with the hems of the nuns' white habits. "My charge nurse," the doctor says, grabbing one of the passing nuns by the elbow. He whispers conspiratorially to her, then slips away so discreetly I wonder whether he's decided to abnegate on his surgical responsibilities. "He goes to change," she tells us. "Into sterile garments, and his doctor coat." I hadn't thought about that. What a relief that he has one of those white jackets with his name embroidered on it. It's proof either he is what he says he is or a fabulously clever priest. Now she takes me by *my* elbow. "Please, follow me," and she ushers me down a short hallway into the operating room.

Waiting for the doctor to reappear, I make myself comfortable on the gurney, which is so high I need a stepping stool to mount up. Lolling fully and happily conscious I inspect the surgical arena. It looks like a kitchen, except the glass-fronted cabinets hold surgical supplies instead of dishes. The chevron pattern of the white-on-white floor tiles gleams from an intensity of scrubbing that I'm aware exists in this world but have never witnessed until now. Lace curtains framing tall windows are straight out of *Masterpiece Theatre*. Perhaps if I stay long enough, someone will arrive with a tray of crumpets and tea.

The doctor bustles in, bends his handsome head to his nurse for a brief *sotto voce* conference, then turns to us and says, "There's been a bad car accident. The victims are being brought here." The sort of sulk that clouded my not-very-sunny disposition when I was a child now threatens to emerge. I can see that my toenail no longer holds much interest. No more chatting, no more commiseration, no more suave stroking of my ankle. I have been reduced to nothing more than a purple keratin impediment to the messily intriguing surgeries currently being ambulanced over.

"Okay, let's begin," he says, with a snap of sterile latex gloves that the nurse has obligingly held open for him to wriggle onto his hands. "We will shortly need to use this room again." He nods to the nurse, who rips open sterile packets as if they were cookie wrappers, laying glistening surgical implements and a small mountain of gauze onto a tray. There seem to be more of these items than a simple toe procedure would warrant. I lie back and stare at the ceiling, invoking the two lessons in biofeedback I took during my freshman year in college. Breathe. Clear your mind. I breathe. My mind does not clear.

Bernard squeezes my hand as the doctor injects Lidocaine around the tip of my toe to numb it. "Hey! Yow!!" I chide him, in the universal language of outrage. There is pain involved in this procedure after all, and although it lasts only a few seconds it seriously disrupts my barely functioning biofeedback skills. Pinching, or for all I know stabbing, my now numb toe, the doctor asks me if I can feel anything. I've never really trusted anesthetics, and now that breathing and mind-clearing are no longer working, I'm uneasy. "A little," I choke out, to buy more time. Bernard seems to sense that I'm stalling and, not wanting to miss a slash, he drops my hand and sidles to the foot of the gurney, where he and the doctor discuss the merits and strategies of various nail removal tools. I refrain from shouting, "Hey, I see you down there instead of up here. I'm not knocked out by anesthesia you know." My fingers, left to dangle, start fretting.

"Would you like to watch your matrixectomy?" the doctor asks me.

Matrix-what? My final shred of desire for new experiences expires on the operating room floor. "Actually, I'm finding endless amusement in staring at the ceiling. So, thank you, no." I wait for him to warn me he's ready to start, imagining the searing burn of ripped skin parting from tightly bound nail if he begins before the Lidocaine has worked its magic.

"It's done," he says, forceps held high, clamping the equivalent of a piece of uncooked macaroni for me to look at.

"Really?" I prop myself on my elbows to assess my foot. If you've never seen one, a nail bed is nowhere near as pretty to look at as a toenail. And this one, having received the pounding of its life, looks like an inch-square cube steak. The nail, which had loomed so large over my life, now lies curled, pale, and innocuous, on the tray.

But this is no time to tarry on a hospital gurney, dreaming of hikes that might have been. My toenail has been unceremoniously dumped in the trash and the nurse is flapping new sheets at me, shooing me off as if I were a bee on an anaphylactic arm, eager to prep the room for the enticingly injured victims to come. More importantly, it's Valentine's Day, and awaiting us at the hotel is a six-course dinner. For this elegant *soiree*, however, I must resign myself to reality: the allure of my outfit will not be complemented by my bloody bandaged toe.

Despite my fashion crisis, I have to give my toe credit. It immediately proves its value when it scores us a front-row table from which to watch the evening's tango entertainment. Face filled with concern, perhaps more for the distaste of the other guests than my toe swaddled in its bulging white cartoon bandage, the maître d' presents me with a stool upon which to rest my foot, then discreetly thrusts it, along with my leg, under our pink tablecloth. Happily settled for the evening, I let my mind turn to the future—like what I'll do the next time I want a pedicure. I can only hope they'll give me a discount for painting nine nails instead of ten.

Shoulders

Mysore sounds like a word that has special meaning for me: *masseur*. Within a few days of starting any road trip, I feel like I have been crammed into the clothes dryer and pummeled. When my mind isn't occupied with where we are and where we need to go, I am thinking about massages, in particular how much I need one and whether I can get one at our next hotel. Though we do strive mightily to reach somewhere with a hotel each night, not often is it a place where a massage would be offered, let alone a place where I'd indulge such a hands-on experience if it were. After all, a bad massage can be even more distressing than no massage at all. For me, there's a pure and objective measure of whether it's time to prostrate myself on the table: can I turn my entire torso rearward when Bernard asks me to guide him into a tight parking spot.

I'm no stranger to the massage table. At home, I have cultivated a relationship with a massage therapist who applies ancient Japanese arts in nigh miraculous ways, practicing what I consider the body equivalent of shuttle diplomacy. After an hour and a half on her table, the war zone that was my sore back, stressed-out nerves, and glued fascia once again agree to friendly terms of coexistence.

Sadly, she is now thousands of miles away, leaving me with only two options: live with my discomfort knowing it will get worse, or put myself in the hands of a stranger knowing there's a good probability I'll still get worse, but also a possibility I could get better. I remember one of our drives through India. A week in and we enter the mid-continent city of Mysore, pulling into the security-guarded portico of a hotel that yesterday's research confirms has a spa. I am so uncomfortable my lips are downturned, eyes ringed with dark circles, my face in general pinched with despair. Dumping my suitcase in our room and bidding a cursory adieu to Bernard, I head for the promised land.

Sweet incense as I enter the spa immediately calms me, as does the polite, "Yes madam, we can do a massage right now." Sangita is assigned as my savior, a middle-aged woman with a sumptuous black braid, strong-looking hands, and kind eyes. She leads me to a room that's a cross between an operating arena and the J. Peterman catalog. It's warmly clinical, with teakwood and brass appurtenances surrounding a surgical-looking massage table standing on ivory tile. Checking to be sure there are no trays of scalpels or sutures nearby, no IV stands or beeping monitors, I arrange myself facedown on the table and Sangita starts her massaging.

Right from the beginning I notice she's inordinately fond of oil. No moderate skin lubrication for her, no timidity about unguents. She's splashing so much oil onto my back and legs that I imagine her squirting great gulps of it onto her palm from a fifty-gallon drum. After rotating me onto my back and repeating the oil bath on my flip side, she asks if I'd like the head and face massage too. Already as slick as a newly caught trout, I become almost faint at the thought of what that might mean.

Ever since landing at Indira Gandhi Airport in Delhi, I have been captivated by Indian women's hair. It is the most beautiful, the most lustrous, the thickest hair I have seen. Most of the time it's worn long and braided. I too have long hair, but mine is somewhat fine, though there's lots of it. Throughout our trip I've been weaving it into one long plait, reveling in the thought that I'm aligning myself just a little closer with the local women. But who am I kidding? My hair doesn't come close to theirs. I ache to know the secret that makes theirs so lush.

I have read that head massage, called *champi*, reduces mental and emotional stress, and relieves headaches, depression, and insomnia. I'm not bothered by any of these maladies and have ground my teeth ever since I had any without any latent side effects. But I am fascinated with claims that *champi* activates hair follicles and stimulates proper hair growth. Legends say it was developed thousands of years ago as a grooming technique by women who used it to strengthen and improve the fullness of their hair by massaging pressure points on the scalp. Some even says that the word *champi* is the root from which our word shampoo is derived.

My current smothering in oil should have been a hint at what lay in store, though perhaps my oil-suffocated pores are preventing oxygen from reaching my brain. Regardless, I am oblivious to the clues, swayed instead by a desire to have pressure points on my scalp, wherever they might be, massaged.

"Yes," I tell Sangita, "a head massage sounds great."

"With oil or without oil?"

I ignore the red flag. "With."

Sangita encourages me to slide closer to the top of the table. Turning my head left and right and then lifting it up, she manages to scoop all of my hair out from under me so she has full access to every strand. Then, silence. I have no idea what's in store for me. I fight the urge to rise on my elbows to see if she might be stealthily wheeling her fifty-gallon oil drum closer. The more seconds tick away the more nervous I get.

Suddenly, I hear a chair scrape behind my head and I realize she's back. Sangita settles herself in. Without so much as a "Hold on, here it comes," she sections off a goodly portion of hair at my forehead and pours what feels like a cup of coconut oil onto it.

Simultaneous to the pouring, she starts gently but firmly massaging the oozing, unctuous thickness of it into my scalp and through the long strands of my hair.

My first thought: Ah, oil overdosing is the secret of the beautiful hair of Indian women. And then: Oh god, this is going to make me gag. Finally: How can I keep from launching myself from prone to vertical and throwing up?

This is where experience with carsickness comes in handy. I give myself a stern talking to about traveling for the novelty of experience. I practice a few moments of meditation to calm myself, remembering Confucius's dictum—"Wherever you go, go with all your heart"—and talking my heart rate and blood pressure off the ledge. I let out the deep breath I hadn't realized till then I'd been holding. In a Zen-like moment that I have to say I'm proud of, I accept the situation for what it is and decide to go with the flow.

What's flowing is a truly limitless quantity of oil. Over the course of fifteen minutes, Sangita repeats the pour/massage series six times. A quick calculation (I'm not so Zen-like that I'm above keeping track) shows she's used at least three cups of oil and massaged every drop into every strand of hair attached to my scalp. But with so much oil on everything, Sangita can barely get purchase on her turf, let alone dig in. Abandoning my scalp, her oil-slicked fingers wend their unwelcome way inside my ears, pressing and tugging my lobes. Oil from her cupped palms drenches my face, where more pressure points are pressed to make my body relax.

The experience is so slimy I become tense. The tension leaves me flustered. The more flustered I feel the more miffed I get. Confucius's wisdom vanishes along with any benefits of the earlier massage. I can't wait for this to be over.

When Sangita finally declares herself finished, I mumble thank you and stumble toward the locker room, leaving splotches of oil in my wake like one of those ancient cars on the P2P. My head does not feel good. I suspect I look like Medusa, with heavy ropes of oily hair hanging from my head like serpents. I know that spa treatments can only do so much for me, of course. Dirty or clean, scowling or smiling, patient or frustrated, I am who I am. After this one, I am also as slick as ice melting on a hot day. I head for the showers, turn the tap to hot, and step under the forceful jet of water. Lifting my face to the steaming water, I close my eyes and empty a full bottle of shampoo on my head, letting the heat and soap and water work the oil out of my scalp, my ears, my face. When I emerge, it's a relief that not only can I now turn my head, but when I look in the clouded mirror I can see I'm still me.

Knees

EL CHALTÉN, ARGENTINA, 2008

I t's the Patagonian Anti-Rally, and I have dabbled my toes in Argentina's Atlantic waters, proof to myself that I have made it as far as I can go, and that penguins really are robust if they can enjoy swimming in such frigid water. Our Nissan jalopy has benefited from a sorely needed tune up and now is deemed ready to carry us westward from the penguin heaven of Río Gallegos. It's time to head back to the lower Andean chain.

As soon as we merge onto the highway out of Río Gallegos, we're suffused with that good feeling of driving again, speaking as it does of obstacles surmounted and new places awaiting us. We're fast approaching Parque Nacional Los Glaciares, which is home to a mountain—no a basalt spire—so unique in form and so devilishly difficult to climb that, like Prince or Bono, it's known the world over by its unadorned name, Fitz Roy, needing no embellishment of "summit," "peak," or "mountain" for people to know what you're talking about. Named after Captain Robert FitzRoy of Darwin's *HMS Beagle,* it was only climbed for the first time in 1952, just a year before Mount Everest. Though it's less than half the size of Himalayan giants, its sheer granite face is often obscured by violent storms, making it a treacherous peak to summit. In mountaineering annals, it's fabled for such long stretches of arduous technical climbing that only the most experienced climbers attempt it; the first to make it to the top were the Frenchmen Lionel Terray and Guido Magnone. It looks like a thin, elliptical spaceship that's crash-landed nose first into a series of spiky gray teeth. In this era when a hundred people may summit Everest in a single day, it's a successful year on Fitz Roy when one alpinist makes it to the top.

My strange connection to Fitz Roy has everything to do with my father, a refugee from the Holocaust, who, in fleeing his home in Vienna in 1938, took to the Austrian Alps as an escape route. Even after my sister and I were born, and despite building his own engineering design firm and working hard during the year, he always took time off to regenerate his spirit in the mountains. Once his company was successful and stable, he allowed himself the luxury of extended mountaineering trips through Uganda's Ruwenzoris, Nepal's Himalayas, Peru's Andes, and of course the beloved Austrian and Italian Alps of his youth. My mother supported these endeavors by staying home with us two girls. I was still young then and admittedly oblivious to what my father was doing when he wasn't at home.

In some ways, I was the son my father did not have, a moderately fearless tomboy who loved to make my father proud. On summer weekends he taught me how to balance on unstable rocks, to cross a river on a slippery log, to find my way back through the woods by checking what the view looked like behind me. He enrolled me in rock climbing courses on the white cliffs of the Shawangunk Mountains in upstate New York, encouraged me to learn ice climbing with a famous mountaineer in Switzerland, sent me on a five-week wilderness expedition in Wyoming's Wind River Range with the National Outdoor Leadership School. He showed me how to form my new leather hiking boots to my feet by making them wet and wearing them till they dried, and he trained me to carry a heavy pack by filling it with four gallon-jugs of water, which I slung over my shoulders every time I went up or down our staircase at home. My father was innovative in his thinking of what girls could and should do, at a time when junior high school still had a dress code stipulating that girls could wear pants only if the temperature were 10 degrees or lower. I don't want to sound like I'm Laura Ingalls Wilder in *Little House on the Prairie*. I was growing up outside New York City in the late 1960s, a time for gender bending if ever there was one. Even so, what seems like nothing now was a big deal then, especially since at that time Roe v. Wade was visible on the horizon, but not yet law.

Though I knew little about his mountaineering escapades during my youth, his trip to Patagonia took place when I was an adult, so I was well aware how Fitz Roy utterly mesmerized him. By that time, he was in his seventies and able only to walk to Fitz Roy's base. Still, when he talked about it, showed me photographs he'd taken, his voice took on a different tone, one of awe, of respect—of love. Its pull seemed magnetic, and at first incomprehensible, given the gorgeous landscapes he'd seen. Yet there was no escaping that he adored this peak, was smitten by its even gray pallor, its wild winds, its uncompromising thrust to the heavens. I had long thought that if a mountain could hold an experienced mountaineer and traveler like my father so entirely in its thrall, I needed to see it for myself. Despite attempting to schedule a trip here several times over the past fifteen years, I'd never been able to manage it. Now, I had a plan.

As we drive toward El Chaltén, what I survey from my car window makes it abundantly clear that Parque Nacional Los Glaciares is home not only to Fitz Roy, but to all that is sparkling and beautiful in the world of glaciated peaks. The entire landscape lives and breathes glaciers, interspersed with jeweled turquoise and green lakes. It is easily the most magnificent scenery Bernard and I have ever seen. Now that we're back in hiking country after two weeks along the Patagonian coast, and with my dream of standing at Fitz Roy's base about to become reality, it's time to assess The Toe. I've babied Biggie for weeks now, obediently swallowed antibiotics, applied antiseptic salves, rebandaged it morning and evening. It's improved enough that I can sleep through the night without it waking me up. And if anything were guaranteed to banish negative thoughts, it's my first view of Fitz Roy. We round a corner on the highway and there it is, its great gray slab face silhouetted unmistakably against an immaculate blue sky. I've imagined for so many years what it would be like to see it, that when it finally is visible on the horizon, majestic and stunning, I'm overwhelmed.

I can't come up with anything eloquent with which to commemorate the moment. "There it is," I say to Bernard. "Fitz Roy." Tears spring to my eyes as I accept that, since my father died four years ago, it is too late to let him know I'm finally here.

We set out for Fitz Roy the very next morning, and immediately get lost. We know the peak is there. We know we are stumbling along trails that should lead to it. But we can't get there. Still, I refuse to let go of my good mood. After all, I'm hiking for the first time in weeks and my magical mountain is nearby. Somewhere.

After several hours of tripping and slipping over lichen-covered roots, we stop to pore over the map together. We're in a moss-hung forest that obscures all landmarks, whereas we should be traversing open meadows and seeing scree fields. After some head scratching we decide we're on a trail taking us opposite of where we should be going. But where's the right trail? And why is this a question that someone who's navigated over 7,800 miles even needs to ask?

We turn around, Bernard striding in front, me falling further behind. Having refused on principal to wear my knee brace and having left my walking sticks in the car for the same reason that has everything to do with stubborn pride and nothing to do with logic, I walk gingerly, intent on not bashing my toe against any rocks, and nursing my unstable knee over uneven terrain. Already my quest to the base of Fitz Roy, to see what my father saw, has taken on outsized importance. This is never a good thing with me, as in such situations I lose all grasp of reason and stick to my original idea long past the time when anyone could find stubbornness attractive. Or useful.

After an hour or so of backtracking, modified by some creative bush-whacking related to where we *think* the proper trail should be, we find ourselves in a treacherous field of monstrous boulders, tossed there like marbles by a playful giant during some distant glacial ice age. They're almost close enough to each other to hop from one to the next, if one were well-balanced and strong, which I'm not. "I think this'll get us to the right place," Bernard says, and is off like the mountain goat I used to be, springing blithely from one to the next.

"But wait, wait," I yell into the wind. "I can't do this." Abandoned, I slide down a boulder on my backside, stumble across the loose scree, and clamber up the next. And so we go, Bernard sprightly, me on hands, knees, and butt, until I'm too aggravated to continue.

"Dina, stay where you are," I hear from somewhere far ahead. Not that at that point I am even moving. I see Bernard bounding back in my direction. "I've found it. There's a huge river up ahead," he tells me. "It's raging. It looks like the trail's on the other side," he finishes brightly. He is so pleased with himself that I want to slap him.

"Well, can we get across?"

He hems and haws. "I don't think so. Maybe you want to come see?" Bernard surely can make the decision of whether we can cross on his own. But he seems to want me by his side, which is something I try hard never to refuse. Pushing myself up from my rock perch, we set off. Now Bernard stays with me, giving me a hand from one slick boulder to the next, till we come to an abrupt halt in front of frigid silver rapids rushing headlong from glaciers cleverly hidden above the placid green lakes we passed on our drive to what we thought was the trailhead.

"Bernard, there's no way we can cross this. It's too wild. Did you see a bridge anywhere?"

"No. Sorry."

I survey left and right, hoping I might see a crossing, even one of those slippery trunks that in days of yore I was able to cross like a circus acrobat. There's no bridge in sight.

I slump on the grass by the river's edge. "Here I am, Little Miss Navigator who's guided you halfway around the world, and I can't even tell what direction we should be going." My voice cracks; I hate admitting defeat. Bernard peers at me sorrowfully. My profound disappointment is upsetting both of us. This won't do. Aside from not finding my special peak, it's a glorious day, with sun, a breeze, tiny yellow flowers growing around me, and close by enough cold water to slake even the most outrageous thirst.

I peel a tangerine and offer some sections to Bernard, wiping a sly tear from the corner of one eye, which I pretend is a spurt of tangerine acid. I put on a weak grin as I chew. This is a trick I learned from a gruff professor in college who offered me some sage advice: Even if you're angry or unhappy, when you smile it changes your tone of voice and you come across as cheerful. And pretty soon you feel cheerful, too. "So," I continue, looking for a way to turn the situation around. "We are not going to get to Fitz Roy today." Bernard chews and nods. "For one thing, I can't leap about on these rocks anymore. Not without my brace," I confess, though it bruises my ego to admit it. "But, there's a bright side," I say, and now my smile is genuine. "We're here for three days, so we have time to come back for another try. Which is great! No?"

The way Bernard gapes it's as if he's suddenly noticed Yoda sitting next to me. I know what he must be thinking: *Who is she kidding? For three hours she's barely been able to walk for stumbling.* He opens his mouth to voice his doubts, then decides against it. Though I'm trying to present a cheery exterior, Bernard knows me too well. He can tell from my eyes that I am crestfallen. He puts his arms around me and I sag into his chest, choking back a sob. "Come on," he says, rubbing my back gently. "Let's head for the car and we'll figure out what to do next." What I'd like to do next is cry, if only to indulge for a good long moment my setbacks on this trip, to give due recognition to the disappointments and to how I've braved them, even if only in my modest way. But since I've never fully revealed to Bernard how long I'd wanted to see Fitz Roy, he can't know that years' worth of planning is on the verge of being shattered. My disappointment is my own, and that's how I'll have to bear it.

Instead of returning the next day to Fitz Roy, we decide to heal our wounded map-reading egos with some ice climbing on Viedma Glacier, one of forty-eight outlet glaciers flowing from the colossal Southern Patagonian Ice Field, its crumpled white tongue breaking off in mammoth chunks into Lago Viedma. The rugged rock cliffs at the glacier's edge have been worn to rounded heaps of deep umber, met at their base by the lake's midnight blue waters. It's spectacular, breathtaking, everything I yearn for. We are part of a small group that has signed up to go with a guide on the glacier. I'm feeling pretty cocky about the day ahead, because I have some experience with ice climbing. Banging an ice axe into sheer blue ice walls is just what I need to vent my aggravation at the previous day's fiasco. That my experience has been gathering cobwebs for thirty years doesn't worry me in the slightest. A boat carries us across the immense glacial Lago Viedma to an outcropping from which we can access some good ice walls within half an hour of the shore. Our guide distributes a pair of crampons to each of us, which I now buckle onto my sneakers. They're as unsuitable for the enterprise as possible, as loose and goofy as clown shoes, but the only footwear that doesn't press on my big toe. I cinch the crampon straps another notch tighter, wiggle my shoes, cinch some more.

I do know that my sneakers, which aren't even adequate for hiking, are far from ideal for crampons. To perform well, crampons need to be attached to a rigid surface; my sneakers are squishy soft and a size too big. Still, I elect to ignore this, in part because I refuse to accept that another day's plan may go awry. There's no way I'm going to tell Bernard my crampons are too loose. What would happen then is he'd turn all his attention to me, devising an entirely new, undoubtedly brilliant, system of crampon attachment. The inner woody core of me is a person who generally does not want to be anyone's focus and who definitely wants to be left alone right now. I just want to climb an ice wall, go back to the hotel, and consider how I'm going to get up to Fitz Roy tomorrow. So I stump over the crevasse-ridden ice, crampons clanging. At the thirty-foot-high wall that will be our first climb I throw my arms up and inhale deeply, hoping to distract Bernard and the guide from what's obvious to me: that my crampons, missing the support of stiff hiking boots, are wobbling about. After the guide ties me onto the safety rope I head up the wall, eager to illustrate competency for a change, in this case that I haven't forgotten the ice-climbing technique I learned a generation ago. I slam the front points of each crampon into the ice, whack the ice axe in overhead, and step by vertical step slam-whack my way to the top. It's exhilarating, a mix of physicality and pure fun, banishing jittery nerves. "This is just what the doctor ordered!"

Leaning back, I rappel down and for good measure brashly swing across the base of the wall to try another route. I'm having a hell of a good time, ready to scale another pinnacle, when the front points of my right crampon hook into the ice while my sneaker continues traveling. I feel as well as hear the telltale pop from my knee, a sound as familiar to me as my best friend's voice but decidedly less welcome. When I'm released from belay, I cast a rueful glance back at Bernard. "I think something's happened," is the best I can say. Now I really do want him to focus his attention on me, because I know I can't walk back to the glacier's base without help. Then I bend over, standing gingerly on my weakened knee, determined not to crumple to the ground.

En route to the El Chaltén medical clinic, I decide that since my precarious knee joint was a fait accompli, I am not going to worry further about it. Surgery can wait. "We could go home now," Bernard offers, tentative and solicitous. "We *should* go home now."

"No. No! Absolutely not. Look around. We're in a climbing mecca. People have knee accidents here all the time. What better place to be with a hurt knee than where a doctor routinely tends to them." At the medical office, waiting for a doctor to arrive, we have a good laugh about how this voyage has turned into a personal sampling of health services. "Maybe I should write a guidebook on clinics and hospitals in picturesque settings," I say. "You know, come to think of it, I find it bizarre that on the P2P, we never had any such problems." It seems to me that on that drive we were doing far more hazardous things, as our fifteen-pound medical kit complete with stitching thread and oxygen mask would attest.

The reason hits us both at the same time and as we start laughing harder, remembering our unrelenting problems with our car's suspension system throughout the P2P's thirty-five days, we squeak out, "Of course not. We never got out of the car!" Which I follow with, "Except to fix ..." and Bernard finishes with, "Shock absorbers!"

Looking around, I go over to a wall where a tattered poster advertising dental treatments is displayed. I translate it for Bernard. Tooth extraction: $1.50. Cavity filled: $3.00. Cracked tooth repair: $7.00. Root canal with crown: $15.00. "We're on a roll with these clinics," Bernard says. "Maybe I should have that old crown replaced while we're here." I'm not enthusiastic at the thought of dealing with Bernard under the influence of any ailment. He doesn't do sick well.

The timely arrival of my pale, slender doctor saves the moment from degenerating into the sort of petty disagreement that can lead one of us to

Our Land Rover, Brunhilde, has carried us from the depths of the upper Rift Valley, to the highs of Peru's Andes. Danakil, Ethiopia.

In some places, just having a cot to sleep on is a luxury. Hamed Ela, Ethiopia

Plucking eyelashes for beauty's sake, in a Mursi village near Jinka, Omo River Valley, Ethiopia.

The road to Alaungdaw Kathapa National Park sometimes disappeared. Sagaing Region, Myanmar.

Tea for unexpected visitors is a hallmark of village hospitality, en route to Pinyaung, Myanmar.

Me, sitting on an anchor, a sign I was tired of driving. Puerto Montt, Chile.

Molting Magellanic penguin chicks, ready for their moment of fame. Cabo Virgenes, Argentina.

Unsure about local customs, I took this photo with my camera at my hip as we walked by. Ishkashim, Afghanistan.

Below Torugart Pass nomadic herders leave summer pastures for lower altitudes. Naryn, Kyrgyzstan.

Even sky-blue highway railings can't dispel the dense smog from coal-fired power plants. Taklamakan Desert, China.

The rocking lull of a camel cart is a rhythm perfectly suited to village life. Kesroli, India.

The Zagros Mountains define Iran's western border with Iraq. I like that the highest point is Mount Dena. Kuh-e Takht, Iran.

A young Brahmin bride goes through hours of rituals on her marriage day. Hampi, India.

Sometimes a wedding seems more like a tragedy. Hampi, India.

Horses, small and hardy, are vital to Tibetan life. Rongbuk Valley, Tibet.

A young couple move house, kettle and all. Ngari Prefecture, Tibet.

harbor hurt feelings for a long time. The doctor's eyes are interested and kind, eyelids smudged with fatigue. His sallow skin and hunched shoulders tell me the glories of the local outdoors are something this man rarely gets to experience.

He escorts me into his small office, where I sit on the exam table and let him gently jerk my lower leg. Bernard lurks behind, eager as always to engage the physician in a detailed review of knee surgery techniques à la Argentina. My knee isn't much swollen and the doctor pats it reassuringly as he confirms that the ACL still is torn, and perhaps a little something else too. He lets out a small sigh and smiles, as if to suggest he's used to seeing much worse than this. Unlike US doctors, this one seems in no hurry to go anywhere. With the diagnosis complete, we spend time chatting with him about medical costs. "The price list outside?" he says. "That's new. With this latest government we have some new policies. And one of them has eliminated free dental care." He and other doctors are dismayed by this, he tells us, because they don't just fix visiting climbers here. They're the *clínica campesina* for the indigenous farmers of the entire valley. That locals have to pay anything for a dentist's help is an insurmountable obstacle to treatment for those who need it most. He shrugs, not with nonchalance but with resignation. "We are a small clinic and very far from the cities. We have tried to protest, but they don't hear our voice in Buenos Aires." For his present diagnosis, the orthopedist now humbly requests $5.00.

Body

Picture me: I stand alone, naked and shivery in a treatment room decorated in Italian faux-barn. The whitewashed walls are adorned with iron pots, wood butter paddles, pitchforks, and scythes, all looking too new and clean to ever have been used for farming. A black cast iron stove squats behind me like a garden elf, still hot from hours spent heating tubs filled with Völs's sweetest, most tender meadow grasses. In front of me, a cot spread with a clean white sheet beckons. But I'm not here in the Italian Dolomites for a nap. I'm here for a hay bath, and right now, goosebumps are the least of my worries.

Our drive into the Dolomites of the Tyrolean Alps is a short one, the sort of shakedown excursion we sometimes do after finishing one long drive—in this case the nine-thousand-mile jaunt from Istanbul to Kolkata—and before starting off on a new one—in this case, a planned tour of the states of Rajasthan and Gujarat in western India the following winter. Even on the best of long road trips a point comes where we both feel the onset of road trip weariness, something I'd sworn after the P2P never to undergo again. Bernard, though by nature willing to do whatever needs to be done, will seem jaded, and dog-tired. He'll get in the car in the morning with an "Okay, here we go again," sigh, followed by a tight, dutiful smile. I'll see him lost in a trance staring at the fuel gauge, hear his muttering as he argues with his seat belt. The jousting with traffic and bad roads that would draw a shout of glee at the start has lost its luster.

Since Bernard has more stamina and commitment than I do, I am amazed how at certain points in our driving we feel exactly the same way. On this road trip Bernard has been relaxed the whole time. That it took only a few hours to get to our hotel, most of it spent on smoothly paved roads so twisty they resemble a nest of fine Italian spaghetti, probably had a little something to do with his good humor. As for me, the road trip's been my ideal of what a driving expedition should be: hardly any time spent in the car, days filled with hiking under the dolomitic spires of Val Gardena and evenings sitting with Bernard over cocktails and dinner, nary a stressed-out muscle in my body. It is unusual that I should be able to utter the words "road trip" without adding the phrase, "I need a massage," immediately after. But there you have it. I feel great and am of sound mind when our innkeeper starts to expound on the glories of hay massages. What he cannot know is that seeking out the unknown local habits on our road trips is my not-so-secret addiction, a guilty pleasure best accomplished behind the curtain of a visa. Being one who cannot say no to a local body treatment I am hooked before I can even say "Achoo!"

This helplessness in the face of something new is why, when I waggled my head side to side at Bernard in a sign of inquiry, he waggled back immediately. This head waggling is an endearing Indian gesture that we had to practice at first, but that we now do almost without thinking. It's an agreeably indeterminate signal, always accompanied by a smile, that says, "I see your lips moving but don't understand a word you're saying" or "I have to think about this, so I'm going to waggle my head to buy myself some time."

In this case, the waggle means, "I'm so glad I'm married to you, that we both feel the same way. See you in the hay!" I am thrilled by his willingness to accompany me into the hay quarters. Bernard doesn't do such treatments at home, let alone in a country where he has to yield his body to unknown hands.

I understood that for reasons having everything to do with long, dark winters, large meadows, and isolation from normal civilized entertainments, Italy's South Tyrolean farmers have long used the hay bath to cure rheumatism, arthritis, and general aching muscles—and as a major social event. However, that was a century ago; in 2012 I am having serious doubts about what I've signed up for.

I have more hay experience than most. At home I'm surrounded by it, as our Colorado ranch produces more than a thousand tons of the stuff, which I've often helped to rake and bale myself. I've walked those fields of waving, waist-high grasses to inspect the coming harvest, and I know those stalks are more likely to induce itchy eyes and a running nose than soothe, as my annual contribution to the profit margin of the firms making Claritin, Zyrtec, and Allergan will attest. I've helped load twenty tons of hay bales on flatbed trucks and stacked them in the barn to feed our horses through the winter, so there's nothing about the unpleasantness of prickly dry grass with which I am unfamiliar.

My hay bath attendant arrives, while a second attendant goes into Bernard's cubicle next door. Each has on red oven mitts to carry the shiny ten-gallon copper cauldron in which hay has been steaming for two hours. She lifts the lid, releasing a fragrant cloud redolent of lady's mantle and mountain arnica, thyme, and cinquefoil. It's grassy, fresh, an alpine meadow in a pot. If I were a cow I'd have stuck my face in the pot immediately. This is no average bovine lunch, though. The hay in the pot is highly regulated fodder, subject to Italian government rules on content, altitude, and minimum distance from roads at which the grass with its forty native herbs can grow.

She hands me a crinkled wad of pale blue tissue paper and I hear Bernard say a laughing, "Thank you," at what I imagine must be a similar little gift. It's a tiny disposable G-string, barely enough to cover that part of the body where I would not want damp hay to intrude. "Put it on," the attendant instructs, in a heavy German accent. (Most residents of Italy's South Tyrol prefer to ignore that they haven't been part of neighboring Austria for nearly a hundred years).

Somewhat embarrassed by attire that would make a Las Vegas showgirl blush, I peer around the corner to inspect Bernard and find him standing awkwardly wearing the same little triangle as me. We both let out a snort and then, trying to stay quiet and respectful, convulse in the sort of giggles that can quickly transform into hiccups. I wait while the attendant spreads a mass of dark green, wet hay on a water bed. "So. Lie down please." Steam rises as I crawl onto my sylvan bower. It's hot, but surprisingly soft. Lying on my back, arms clenched at my sides, I hold my breath while the rest of the hay is spread over my body, including a moist hay pillow under my neck.

"That's it," I think, just before the attendant pulls a flannel blanket over me, yanks the edges tight and then seals me in with a vinyl sheet. "This will keep the heat. I will come back in ten minutes, yah? To see how you are."

All I can think is that if I sneeze—and why wouldn't I, what with hay all over me—I will not be able to wipe my nose. Grateful now that South Tyroleans are so Germanic-ly punctual, my only concern is that the next ten minutes will feel like an hour. I close my eyes, do a full-body inspection searching for itches, detect warmth seeping into my skin. Perspiration dots my forehead. My breathing slows as I inhale a meadowy bouquet with overtones of mint. Swaddled inside my hay blanket bundle, I fall into a reverie, thinking about how the purple-flowered prunella herb, commonly called "heal-all," should soothe the scratch on my calf from our hike that day. I also think this is what it must feel like to be a steeping teabag.

Suddenly a cool cloth is dabbing at the sweat on my forehead. "Yah, so, it is ten minutes now. All is okay?" the attendant asks, more grandmotherly than authoritarian. I nod. "Good! Ten more minutes and I will check again," she tells me. The clack of her spa sandals fades, leaving me to percolate in peace.

My world is now one of hot, aromatic dampness. The heated waterbed keeps the grass mix warm while the soft scratchiness of the hay makes my skin feel alive. If I had rheumatism, I have no doubt this would cure it.

In what seems like too short a time, the cloth is again clearing beads of sweat from my face. My kindly attendant looks searchingly in my eyes. "Twenty-five minutes is the maximum to be in the hay. But if you would like to end the treatment now, it is okay." I shake my head. I have no desire to end the treatment ever.

OUTSIDERS

PREAMBLE

Paul Theroux said it best when musing on the peculiarities of travel: "You're like a wraith, with your face pressed to the window of another culture, staring at other lives." This situation often demoralizes me. I don't want to be the Little Match Girl, nose flattened against that frosty window, able to see the indulgent glories a few feet away, unable to join in. I want to feel I'm standing under the Niagara Falls of sensory experience, drowning in serendipitous personal interaction. On every road trip, after days of driving and no human encounters to speak of other than with gas station attendants, I reach a point where I'm disheartened. My mind grumps, "What am I doing here? Why am I once again putting myself through this numbing routine that's predictable only its continuous uncertainties, something I've never enjoyed?" I don't say this out loud, in part because it's usually too clattery in our car for Bernard to hear me, but also because doing so would inflict my anxieties on him, and I learned long ago he has little understanding and less compassion for my fretting.

I've thought endlessly about my reasons for once again getting back in a car, maps in hand, to see what's out there. For one thing, driving through a country gives me an unparalleled view of ordinary life as led by the locals. We are all cursing at the same potholes, waiting for ages at the same railway crossing, having our flat tire fixed at the same repair stall, buying our fruits from the same street vendor, and drinking from the same kettle of tea. More importantly, at some divine moment during our often tedious, always arduous road trips, the car will place me at just the right place at the very instant someone looks up and locks eyes with me. Before they can even say, or more likely mime, "Would you . . ." and definitely before Bernard can be consumed by French manners that require him to decline all invitations on the premise that "they're just being polite," I am in, ready to participate in whatever they have to offer, regardless of what it is. Does that make me a bit of a Peeping Tom? Sure. But every good traveler has a bit of the voyeur in her. Besides, I'm a hosted Peeper, happiest when inspecting someone's musty rumpled bedroom, seeing what's hanging in their closet, looking at their toiletries, realizing their floor isn't carpeted, it's cardboarded. I thrive on sheer sensory overload. I'm Alice down the rabbit hole, one minute on the sidewalk, the next inside a village compound in the midsection of Turkey, picking herbs from the owner's garden and making a mid-morning salad with him, all because I chose to linger staring at sheered fleeces drying on his whitewashed wall.

The most memorable encounters often begin one way, and then, without me noticing, veer in a different direction, something I discern only after the fact. I'll share one such with you, by way of example.

On a sunny day in February 2011 we were walking through the fifteen-hundred-year-old Muslim citadel of Harar, Ethiopia, a maze of winding cobblestone lanes hemmed inside old stone walls. With the majority of Ethiopians devoutly Coptic Christians for two millennia, Harar is an anomaly: the fourth holiest city of Islam, after Mecca, Medina, and Jerusalem.

As we wandered a narrow lane, pressed by house walls painted lime green and ochre, I noticed a hand reach out from a curtained doorway to wave us in. While I never know when or where such contact will occur, I have learned that world events have nothing to do with the hospitality and warm openness of local people. That I, an anonymous Jew, should be bidden into the home of an anonymous Muslim did not surprise me, but the unexpectedness of it certainly did thrill me.

It was cool inside those thick mud walls, quiet and dusky too, as there were no windows. A shelf filled with books of the Koran lined the back wall of the high-ceilinged room. On a raised seat sat the neighborhood sheik, a small-time patriarch nevertheless essential to the well-being of his community, a genuine multitasker, acting as counselor, mediator, advisor, and religious leader for his community. This small man with smooth, copper-colored skin and a scraggle of beard, bade us sit on one of the carpet-covered benches below him. From his platform he surveyed us frankly, as if taking our measure. Looking up at him made me feel like I was back in kindergarten, seeing in the eyes of my teacher that I had done something naughty though I was unsure what. My dignity reasserted itself when he gestured for coffee to be made for us. We were guests after all, not fractious children.

We sipped sociably, without conversation, while I mused how I was having coffee with a sheik, becoming part of his story, sitting on the same bench whose hard surface had hosted the buttocks of myriad supplicants. I was delirious with happiness to be smelling, touching, tasting a moment in this sheik's life. Everything about him—his clothes, his living quarters, his life—seemed so old-world, as if time had literally passed him by. This calmness, I thought to myself, is what it means to live a life without modern distractions.

Then the sheik pointed to a bucket below him, from which his assistant retrieved some branches of glossy leaves. For an instant, I thought he was displaying his garden prunings. But the street had been devoid of anything growing, so it could only be one thing: *qat* (pronounced "chat"), the coca equivalent used as a stimulant and appetite suppressant throughout the Horn of Africa and the Arabian Peninsula. I was now about to suffer the effects of my unquenchable curiosity. I plucked a handful of leaves, eager to show I knew what I was doing, though in reality I'd only ever nibbled a corner of a leaf prior to that moment. Even Bernard, who normally doesn't indulge in things not found in the *Larousse Gastronomique*, took a few leaves for himself. I suspect it dawned on him, as it did me, that one does not refuse the full hospitality of a sheik, however modest his empire may be. The leaves were tough and, well, leafy, as if I were eating an office ficus plant. I waited to be suffused by a wave of euphoria, but all I felt was embarrassment at all the green bits now stuck in my teeth.

Coffee sipped and *qat* chewed, we rose to take our leave, unsure when the *muezzin* would next issue a call to prayer and not wishing to impose further. The sheik motioned us to be patient, and then mimed taking a photo. "This is odd," I whispered to Bernard. "I hadn't expected he'd let us take a picture of him." I reached for my camera. He swatted at the air for me to put it down. And then he pointed from himself to us. "I'm not sure I get what's up here," Bernard whispered back. "But it looks like he wants to take *our* picture."

"Okay," I thought. "He's the sheik. If rising up and taking the camera from a lady so he can photograph us isn't what he's used to, I can deal with that. I'll bring it to him." He shook his head as I advanced, one arm digging around in his *thobe*, the loose-fitting ankle-length white robe worn by many Muslim men. For a second, I thought he was scratching himself, which struck me as an un-sheik-like thing to do in front of a woman, what with Islam espousing modesty and all. Withdrawing his hand from a pocket hidden within the folds, he displayed a late-model iPhone as matter-of-factly as a baker would hold up a loaf of bread. Then he raised it and snapped our picture. "My brother in Arkansas will like this. We Skype each other weekly," he said in perfect English, as he waved us out.

Camel Carts

KESROLI, INDIA, 2013

One afternoon, arriving early in the village of Kesroli southeast of Delhi, we hire a camel cart to take us to a nearby hamlet. Do not think Conestoga wagon when you imagine a camel cart. Think old back porch of Appalachian shack hoisted up on wheels, becoming a dusty open platform that's ten feet long. It's sized for the hugeness of a camel, as compared to a wheelbarrow-sized cart that would be pulled by that other ubiquitous beast of burden, the donkey. It's also open-air, which suits us fine since we spend so many hours closed in the confines of our car. A wheeled amble down quiet side roads at a convivial pace would bring us closer yet to Tolkien's sentiment that "not all those who wander are lost." For us to be able to sit side-by-side, even to loll staring up at the clouds, is an unparalleled joy. That we will move at stately camel pace, and that said camel will be under the control of a camel wallah who won't need my input to get where he's going, is better still.

Our camel wallah unfolds a pile of thick quilted blankets—or perhaps they are thinly batted mattresses—which he flings with great fanfare across the cart. These are intended to form a good barrier between us and the dust churned up by the wheels. They are flowery and gay, and make me feel so as well. While he's arranging bedding, we inspect our camel, whose ribs are prominent enough for me to count. Since we are in India, our camel is a dromedary, the one-humped camel version, as compared to the Bactrians we saw in China and Mongolia, which are two-humped. "This is not the robust camel of the Sahara, is it?" I whisper to Bernard. The local camels work hard for a living, carrying about five hundred pounds on their back. And even though they're about the same height as LeBron James, Stephen Curry, or any other NBA star, they weigh barely more than a good stout horse. That this camel displays the svelte sides of a model isn't cause for alarm, but does give me twinges of guilt that we will be making this underfed animal work, despite that I know that's exactly what he, or at least his camel wallah, needs if he's ever to get more to eat. In his favor, our dromedary clearly knows what's expected of him, not even batting his third eyelid while quilts flap within a foot of his posterior. Had I been tall enough I would have checked his teeth. But his feet, which are as large as dinner plates, look capable of plodding along at our desired leisurely pace. He also sports some attractive shaved swirls on his haunches, though I feel a flicker of disappointment that he wears no jingle bell cuffs below his knees. Overall, he appears good-natured, unfazed by the large pin stuck through his nose to which the reins are attached.

Declaring ourselves satisfied and with a merry heave-ho, we toss cameras, caps, and sunglasses onto the blankets and hoist ourselves up. Ray Bradbury was correct when he intuited that "half the fun of travel is the aesthetic of lostness." As far as I'm concerned, it's also the aesthetic of lostness being someone else's responsibility. When the wallah gives the reins a sharp flick and issues a practiced kissing "Mwahh!" for our camel to move out, I am elated.

It's mid-afternoon, the sun still hot, the camel's stately pace barely enough to stir up a shy breeze. In five minutes we have cleared Kesroli proper and turned left to skirt a reservoir, heading to a hamlet an hour or so away. Bernard and I dangle our legs over the side, not so much to be able to jump off at a moment's notice, but to appear as though we're old hands at this mode of transportation. I snap a few photos.

A clod of dirt thuds onto my quilt bedding. As I inspect the offending chunk to see if it's dirt or manure, displaying it as if it were Martian, two more clods hit the platform in quick succession. Turning in the direction of the attack, we see seven women sitting on a berm above the road. Next to them is a stockpile of dirt clumps and small stones, which they heave at us with a smile as we pass. We each grab a fold of quilt to shield our heads from the fusillade of dried lake mud.

Having things turn sour so early in what was to be a relaxed outing through the countryside was never in our plans. Our only thought was how nice it would be to move even more slowly through villages, to better smell the fields, to feel the true warmth of the sun on our skin, to just have time to be where we were, instead of thinking about where we next needed to turn. For reasons that I can attribute only to Bernard and I having one of those wonderful moments of married synchronicity, neither of us is bothered. Without a word being said we seem to agree that we are not about to let this unceremonious pelting deter us from our happy outing. We are determined to be, if not quite sitting ducks, then at the least slow-moving ducks. We instruct our wallah to keep his camel at a placid walk. He responds with a glare. I notice he hasn't even flinched under the artillery assault, and wonder whether what to us was a demilitarized zone to him is a known mine field.

As we amble by, we can hear the women's voices rising and falling as if shouting at us. Ever predisposed to feeling personally guilty about my intrusion into local life, I imagine their chat goes something like this: "Don't you dare raise that camera at me! I'm sick of having my photo taken. What do you think we are? Zoo animals?" I have no idea if this is really their reason for welcoming us with dirt projectiles. Perhaps they've been cleaning out the reservoir and just needed some way to get rid of the extra dirt they had on hand. Or in hand.

Our camel driver, who might have translated for us, is concentrating on the swishing tail of the camel and avoiding my gaze. Proving the accuracy of their aim, a few more clods come flying our way, one striking me on the shoulder, another sending squirts of dirt into my eyes. Feeling unjustly tormented, we each breathe a sigh of relief when we are finally out of range. Flushed with surviving the reservoir gauntlet, we get chatty for a few seconds before being lulled into reverie as the cart slowly bumps and lurches onward.

Though our camel wallah is small and young, it makes not a jot of difference to his command of camel-ese. There is utmost respect between beast and driver. While camel seems to know that, as long as he does what's asked, he'll be left in peace, wallah knows that as long as he isn't unreasonable in his requests, camel will obey. Achieving the same, easy level of unspoken understanding does not exist between camel wallah and us. We want nothing more than to prolong our soporific jouncing along the narrow village byways. Wallah has other, apparently more pressing, engagements and wants to keep his camel moving at a ground-eating trot. He sits perched on the front of the cart with his back to us, shoulders hunched, short thin legs swinging over the front. For a good five minutes at a time, he lets the reins hang lax in his hands, head bowed, for all the world asleep as the camel plods up the road. Then, in a fit of pique, he perks up, collects the reins, and, with an authoritative cluck slaps them smartly on the camel's back. The camel, taken by surprise, and somewhat offended at the brusqueness of the exchange, leaps into a trot, jolting us out of our heretofore mentioned reveries, and causing us to cling to whatever scrap of quilt or exposed cross beam we can grab.

"Please, no!" I shout, hoping to convey that we don't want to go that fast. The wallah twists around, fixing me with a baleful stare that insinuates, "What's wrong with you? Who wouldn't want to go faster if they could?" His lack of comprehension forces us to resort to more complex concepts. I toss out short phrases using Valley-girl tones, to make my demands seem more benign. I say, "Slow down?" and "Not so fast?" followed by "No trotting, please? Only walk?" Still failing to produce the desired result, my only remaining option, short of grabbing the reins, is the international hand gesture language. I turn both hands palms down, and slowly lower them. Frowning and exuding all kinds of dismay, the wallah reins in the camel and we all sink back once again into our respective daydreams.

Thus we progress, in the rhythm of an inverted classic quick step—slow, slow, FAST, slow, slow, FAST—past children working in the sugarcane fields, saried women balancing bundles of gnarled branches or plastic water jugs on their head, men meandering along the roadside in plaid cotton shirts and stained dhotis, arms interlocked in comradely twosomes and threesomes. The sun beats down, birds flit over planted fields of rich dark earth, heading to the deep shade of a midfield copse of trees, and occasionally a slow motorcycle buzzes by.

After an hour of bucolic bliss, we reach the end of the road, a hamlet half in ruins, home to a small Hindu temple and perhaps fifty families. Executing a magnificent broken U-turn, the wallah parks the camel in the small village square, an area perhaps thirty yards wide. On our left is a heap of stone rubble from buildings in peaceable decline, their separate construction components forming a serene, if jumbled, pile of rocks and mortar dust. In front of us is the temple, squatting above a flight of eight stone steps, basking in the shadow of a venerable and enormous banyan tree. The remaining sides of the square are bound by a couple of two-story structures, impressive compared to the rest of the village. One is sky blue, housing tiny shops on the ground floor and just as tiny apartments above. The other is mud-colored, home to a refreshment stand at its base and living quarters above. A woman leans over one balustrade, shakes a dishtowel with a smart snap, and hangs it on the blue railing to dry.

In most of the world's small villages, the arrival of a stranger is news. Whether in the vast emptiness of rural western China, the remoteness of Andean Peru, or the density of countryside India, a stranger never goes unnoticed. For one thing, a new face is immediately obvious. Villages are small and everyone knows everyone. For another, there is little travel between villages, as people perforce spend all day every day taking care of their and their families' immediate needs. If someone new is in town, it's cause for curiosity. And then, of course, there's our visible otherness. Who wouldn't pause and question who we are and why we're there?

Barely has camel come to a halt than a small boy in a dark blue, one-button shirt and shorts held up with twine, arrives at a run, rolling an old bicycle wheel in front of him with a stick. He is followed at full tilt by two more boys who seem torn between the desire to steal the wheel and stick from the first boy or to sidle up to us and see what we're about. We win out over the wheel, which is a great boost to my ego. They gather round, laugh and jostle each other, try out a few words of English on us. But the boy with the stick only grunts. He's mute.

A ramble through the hamlet is in order. Proud, wary, excited, the youngsters shepherd us through narrow lanes, dodging into doorways and courtyards to draw our attention to a baby or a cow, displaying us to the mistress of the house, and hanging behind bashfully as we talk in gestures with the grown-ups. I don't mind being the trick pony for a change. Offering the novelty of "me" is a kind of barter for the photos I want to take of them. And it seems only fair that I not be the only one looking intensely around. Okay, the only one staring. The chatter I'd imagined earlier during the reservoir pelting may have been a truth, but it wasn't the whole truth. Because here, women pull us forward to look at their babies, men shake our hands, elders pose, and everyone seems genuinely delighted, beyond politesse, to be photographed and then to see themselves center frame on the camera screen. The only hiccup in the general bonhomie is when, as if by magic, the wheel-spinning boy appears in the center of the viewfinder, miming for the camera, contorting his small, lean body into winsome positions, lifting his wheel and stick over his head to call attention to himself.

At first this is charming. "Oh look, he's mugging for the camera. Cute kid." But soon it becomes irritating when he pops up in every shot. The problem is entirely mine. I'm never completely at ease photographing people. What makes for a good travel photo is the colorful, picturesque shabbiness of rural villages. But shabby isn't comfortable and shabby isn't what people choose to have, should they actually have a choice. Shabby is the best they can do with the means at their disposal.

Although I do want to capture the scene, I feel that I'm intruding into the villagers' daily chores or daily drudgery, or daily doing without. They may not feel that way, but to me there's a sensation that I could be working just as hard to frame a shot of an animal in the Serengeti. Yet I'm not in the wilds of Africa. I'm in someone's home, someone's back street, someone's courtyard. They haven't dressed their toddler or left the undies off their little boy to appeal to my camera. They're just going about their business. I take the photographs quickly, with mixed emotions at best, and a strong sense that I may be missing a stronger human connection by placing my camera between me and what's happening around me.

Though I'm hyperaware that this is someone's everyday life I'm intruding in, I also find it irresistible to turn my camera to a turquoise blue wall framing a yellow door on the stoop of which sits a young woman holding a baby swaddled in a knit onesie, or a slate gray water buffalo munching an emerald green shaft of hay, or the spread of scarlet chili peppers drying on an orange clay tile roof. Add a woman in a violet and yellow sari embroidered with blue-green spirals, and I dissolve into a puddle of photographic desires.

And so, when I frame a great shot of that mother with her baby, only to find the mute boy's head bobbing up in front as he jumps up and down, waving his stick over his head, it strikes an already raw nerve. And when I kneel down to get just the right angle of a placid cow with a red-billed bird on its nose, and the shot is suddenly composed of the cow with the boy's head leering at the camera from the side, his wheel waggling in the air, I do not do the right thing. I do not chuckle and wag my finger at him, admonishing him in friendly fashion for wrecking yet another photo. What I do is yell "Get out!" and shoo him away. It's horribly impolite, especially for a visitor in a poor village. I am reduced to an unappealing caricature of the impatient foreigner, an ugly American.

The villagers exchange knowing glances of forbearance. A few smile, looking at the ground. They know this boy and of course cherish him and his antics. Unlike me, they are far too polite to issue me any remonstrance, like, "Hey, leave the kid alone. Can't you tell you're the better entertainment—more distraction—than he's had in ages?" Then—such is the misplaced egotism of the traveler—it finally occurs to me that I probably am not the first white lady to arrive on a camel cart wanting to photograph their everyday lives. They all are used to this. People coming in, feeling they've discovered something authentic, and photographing the hell out of it. And they all patiently let us snap away, turning somber gazes on us when requested, stopping their endless round of work to accommodate the camera.

The boy looks crestfallen but only momentarily. Recovering his joie de vivre, he jumps out of the shot and grins at me, all liveliness and wheel-spinning vitality. I may have succumbed to boorishness, but he forgives me.

For a minute he's able to restrain himself while I take a photograph without him in it. Then he's back to prancing and cavorting around us. As we stroll back to the square where camel and wallah are waiting, I expect him to tumble off down a side street. He doesn't. He sticks closer to me than the others, as if to say, "I see you. Do you see me?"

Hidden

MASHHAD, IRAN, 2011

Imam Reza, descendant of the Prophet Muhammad and eighth imam of Shiite Muslims, was martyred in Mashhad twelve hundred years ago. It was a time when religious figures of any sort who fell out of favor could expect to pass into the next life via a variety of excruciating deaths, in this case, by poisoning. Reza's shrine is in this city in northeastern Iran, near its border with Turkmenistan.

As Iranian cities go, Mashhad is a lovely one, the shelter of the nearby Binalud and Hezar Masjed mountain ranges blessing it with a kind climate. It's a holy city, too. Thanks to its association with the imam's untimely death, *mashhad* now is the Persian word for "place of martyrdom." Just as those who make the pilgrimage to Mecca receive the title of hajji, those who make the pilgrimage to Mashhad—and especially to the Imam Reza shrine in particular—have a title. They are known as mashtee. For reasons I can't quite grasp, other than that I am here and it is feasible, I want to find out what it's like to be one. Superficially there's no reason for me to feel this way. In fact, there are many reasons not to. First, I've always been a confirmed atheist. Second, if there's a crowd gathering, I make it a point to be far from it. Third, I normally prefer to do whatever everybody else is *not* doing. But here's the beauty of travel: the very act of being far from home and routine seems to open the possibility of being someone other than my usual self. As Marcel Proust is often quoted as saying, "The real voyage of discovery consists not in seeking new landscapes, but in having new eyes." And if ever there's a place where I can indulge my love for seeing another culture from the inside, it's here.

To get into the inner sanctum of this immense marble and mosaic mausoleum, I have to wear a chador, the full-length, shawl-like semicircle of dark fabric worn by some Muslim women in Iran, to conform to the Islamic dress code of hijab. It's not a requirement to wear the chador, but a choice, and unlike in Afghanistan or Arab countries, wearing a chador does not require wearing a veil to cover one's face. However, since it has no hand openings and nothing to fasten it shut, going about one's life in a chador, which is draped over one's head to cover the hair, not one's shoulders, takes practice. When women who choose to wear the chador go out on errands, they hold the fabric closed with their teeth, to keep their hands free. When errands aren't scheduled, they scrunch the open ends from inside with their hands, to keep it from floating away like a lost kite. Although most cosmo-politan women in Iran conform to the laws of hijab by wearing a beautiful French silk scarf, there's no question that inside one of the holiest Muslim shrines in the world, a chador will not be discretionary.

I do not own a chador and therefore have every reason to be concerned that the most I will see of Imam Reza's shrine is the street outside. I need not have worried. The enterprising shrine managers have been faced with improperly clad non-believers like me for eons. They know exactly what to do with us: earn some money. They've opened a rent-a-chador booth, filled with wrinkled lengths of fabric. A small deposit of fifty cents is all that's required and I can have my choice of chadors with which to robe myself appropriately. I consider renting one of the black offerings, but decide, rashly, that it looks too mournful. I point to a crumple of white and blue print cloth. Big mistake, which I will only discover after I've paid my fee and retired to the curb to try chadorizing myself. At first, I find the white and blue pattern flattering. It's fresh and summery. Then I look around. Every woman I see is swathed in black. Instead of blending in, I am imme-diately marked as the interloper I am. Worse, no cosmopolitan Iranian woman would ever wear what I'm wearing. My chador is not meant for the urban sophisticate. It is one a country bumpkin would wear. It's neither long enough nor wide enough to fully envelop me. I've chosen the chador of a child, and a village child at that. Why I thought I'd make a fashion statement, be the Badgley Mischka of chador-dom, I don't know. But this chador is ridiculous. It barely reaches my knees. The worst part is that the fabric is a swath of cheap, slippery polyester, sliding off my hair at the first opportunity. To keep it even remotely in place I have to pull it far forward, giving me a hooded look more appropriate to a Gregorian monk than a Muslim anything. But I am not in a fitting room and this is not Blooming-dale's. I'm in Iran, the chador I've been given has been handed to me by an official Muslim. Who am I to argue?

Bernard is already at the front of the men's security check by the time I join the women's queue. His line moves briskly, but mine is one of those societal contradiction in terms, being both sluggish, with women standing around not moving, and disorderly, with women shoving themselves through the clots of nonmoving believers, tugging their children along with them. My line seethes with properly chador'd women in black, all pushing toward a curtained booth where they are frisked and their bags opened within the privacy of sheltering canvas. Once out of the cubicle they have only to pass through a metal detector under the stern gaze of two female security guards and they're into the immense courtyard of the shrine itself.

I push with the best of them, trained as I was by rush hours at Grand Central Station, but when I make it to the front, I am not allowed to pass. A guard points to the ground. I follow her gaze, look around me and begin to understand. All the women are wearing stockings or socks. My feet are in sandals, toes bare and offensive. I look chagrined, pantomime apologies, point toward the exit while clutching my scrap of cloth under my chin to at least keep my hair covered. The guard asks me if I'm Muslim. What to do? I don't think this is the place to do the big reveal that I'm born Jewish. I keep my mouth shut, wobbling my head in my favorite Indian head waggle, to connote a middling response of maybe yes, maybe no. The female guards stare at each other, arched, perfectly tweezed black eyebrow answering bored uniformed shrug. It seems they do not want their job to be about deciding which feet can stride forward and which must slink back. I learn only later that there was a bombing here fifteen years ago that killed twenty-five people, giving weightier concerns than sacrilegious feet, concerns such as ferreting out cleverly hidden explosives. At the time, though, I'm ignorant and stewing—how Bernard can determine that I'm not one of the chador'd many who've been let in, without, so-to-speak, lifting a flap, and therefore how will he glean that I'm stuck out here while he's in there?—when they wave me through.

I emerge into a vast courtyard tiled with slabs of white marble which gleaming so relentlessly in the sun that I am tempted to pull my chador over my face after all. It's blinding, as if someone had turned on a theater spotlight and shone it five inches from my face. The courtyard teams with men, women, and children come to pay their respects and to pass the rest of the day within the mosaic walls of the holy site. Everyone streams toward what must be the mausoleum. The arch of its lofty entryway is lacquered in gold leaf, as is the minaret above it and the high dome behind. On either side extend two-story arched walls intricately tiled in curlicues, diamonds, and filigrees of greens, blues, turquoise, white, and gold, the patterns mixed with Farsi prayers from the Koran. It is chillingly ostentatious, designed to uplift and humble at the same time.

I remove my offending sandals at the carpeted entry, thinking to mark them by the black shoe nearby. Then I notice all the shoes are identical: black, solid, low-heeled, blunt-toed footwear, as if the Mashhad branch of DSW had one style and one color only. I find consolation in the knowledge that no Iranian would bother taking sandals such as mine, so delicate, so frilly, so unfit for normal wear. It's also consoling that my DSW has more to offer. I walk over the carpet toward a large open door. Within seconds, I'm in a mass of people and like a riptide they catch me up and sweep me onward with them, into the mausoleum, toward the shrine.

I start gulping air like a freshly landed fish, washed by panic that the people around me will discover I don't belong here. How stupid could I be? How could I think that if I dressed like everyone else I'd be one of them? I berate myself, because I learned this lesson in high school, when even on those days when I escaped our house in proper hippie garb, I still never pierced the shield of the "in" kids. Inside, or rather underneath, I'm still me and now that I'm here with the devout every instinct screams that I should be elsewhere. I clutch my chador tighter around my face terrified it will slide down and expose my hair inside Iran's holiest religious site. I am so far out of my comfort zone that the word "zone" can't even apply.

Bodies squeeze and hug close. They move with the fervent blindness of the faithful, pushing around me to get down the stairs and into the mauso-leum, intent on getting close to the imam's tomb. I shuffle forward, carried along by a black current of warm bodies, until the moment I feel silky fabric under my toes. Looking down I spy with horror that I've stepped on the chador of the woman in front of me. It's hard to move my feet anywhere but where they are, as I have ladies on all sides. But the woman ahead continues to drift inch by inch away from me. I fear provoking an interna-tional incident, in which not only do I improperly disrobe one of the faithful, but am disrobed myself, to reveal the lying, sockless, sandal-wearing infidel I am.

In the nick of time a miracle occurs, which I have since titled The Miracle of the Two-Step. A dance lesson from decades ago finds its way to my offensive feet and reminds them of a country western step I learned in the early days of my marriage. Beyond receiving a blessing of which I am definitively unworthy I have no other way to explain why suddenly my feet mince out a tiny two-step, shifting me an iota to the side, enough to release the chador just as the woman inside it finds an opening and disappears into the cavernous room below.

Shortly I, too, am within sight of Imam Reza's tomb, at the rim of a marble ramp leading into a multi-chambered hall swarming with praying, weeping women. They keen, they shout a prayer, they bow and kneel and bow more. The hubbub swells and recedes, wave after wave of voices ascending the stairs to where I stand. If I go down into the maelstrom, I may never make it back up the same day, so I observe the passions from above, the chador'd heads reflected by a million mirrored facets lining the surrounding domes and columns. After a few minutes, I swivel around to go back out, thereby wedging myself more tightly into the crowd. Then a hand is pressed against my back, shoving me insistently forward. I'm fifty feet from the exit to the general courtyard, but it's all black in front of me and I'm only going to get there at the pace of the women around me, many of whom stand transfixed, intoxicated by the experience, their eyes puffy and red from weeping. On each face I see an expression ranging from bereft to ecstasy. With a liquid sigh the women surge gently onward, an ocean swell of religious fervor, until I, too, reach the courtyard.

It seems fitting that it was a clergyman, Henry Ward Beecher, who said "clothes and manners do not make the man," to which I must add "nor the woman." I know this now, as I also know that not all travel experiences result in smiles of pleasure. Despite this, each one is profoundly worthwhile for the way they allow me to see myself, if not necessarily to always change myself. Released from the crowd, my spirit soars, relief floating high. I have been privileged to join with other women in a rite that has moved them deeply. I'm a *mashtee*. And my sandals are waiting right where I left them.

Huaso Initiation

Having reached Puerto Natales, the terminus of our three-day ferry trip from Puerto Montt on the cargo ship *Evangelistas*, it is time to get back in our rental Suzuki.

I live my life very much in the present. This means I keep nostalgia to a minimum, with few sops to sentimentality. A couple of drawers is all I need to hold those albums and old photos I rarely thumb through, though I confess I cart around my baby albums like the treasures they are; I love to admire what a cute infant I was. Despite reading copiously as a child, cherishing my library card more than the aquamarine three-speed bike I got for my eighth birthday, only half a shelf in my library is given to favorite childhood books. I've never returned to gaze at any house I've moved out of. Yet here I am, sighing with happiness to be reunited with a car I've known for only ten days, three of which she sat in a cargo hold with the cattle and fuel tanks while we wandered the fog-shrouded deck and let bartenders tempt us with pisco sours well before cocktail time. Now, as we prepare to return to land once more, all seems right with my world.

The ritual of settling into the car is comforting, and it pleases me no end to gently lay the napkin-wrapped cheese sandwiches, which I'd surreptitiously assembled from our final meal in the captain's mess, on the floor behind my seat. Even Bernard, who likes to pretend everything is status quo, is joyful. As he goes through his now-I'm-preparing-to-drive ritual, he wriggles around in the seat like a puppy released from its crate, smiles to himself as he places his fingerless black leather driving gloves on his lap.

He inspects the glove compartment, patting the sheath holding his long blade knife, shimmies his shoulders as he adjusts his seat forward and then back, as if checking whether the sea legs he acquired during the 1,100 nautical miles (1,260 land miles) between Puerto Montt and Punta Arenas are the same length as the legs he left land with three days ago. Glancing left and right, his good humor is momentarily blackened when he realizes the rear-view mirror is askew. He's like Papa Bear, concerned someone's been sitting in his seat. "I knocked it with my head just now," I tell him. "When I got in the car." Instantly he's relieved, toggling it back into place, flexing his hands into the gloves. We're ready.

Clanking down the *Evangelistas's* gangplank, we head north to Torres del Paine National Park. If I wanted to be purely geological, and if I were able to pronounce obscure terminology, I would tell you that a large swath of the Paine mountains is made of Cretaceous sedimentary rocks intruded by a Miocene-aged laccolith, between five to twenty-three million years before I was born. And that in the case of Las Torres, a thick cloak of sedimentary rock layer has eroded away, leaving behind gleaming obelisks of more resistant granite. These statements would be accurate, but wouldn't convey the jaw-dropping, eye-rolling, hair-grabbing splendor of the place.

Probably only Switzerland's Matterhorn is as iconic an image as the Torres del Paine. The shape and character of these massive, pale gray spires are unmistakable. There's nothing else like them in the world. They erupt straight from the pampas to a level that would equal the rise of Everest from its base camp. The pampas themselves are only a few hundred feet above sea level and there are no gentle foothills here. We're talking granite and we're talking vertical. The immense glaciers Grey, Dickson, and Tyndall have eroded the spires over eons, in the process dropping rock powder into lakes that are now milky aquamarine and teal jewels.

Torres del Paine is a hiker's mecca, a fisherman's dream. I can do neither. Because of my toe, painful and bandaged since the nail was surgically removed at the Catholic hospital in Pucón on Lake Villarrica, I'm not fit for the former, and I know nothing about the latter. What I do know is that pampas mean gauchos. Or to be correct, since we're in Chile, *huasos*.

Where there are huasos there are cows, in this case Herefords, just like at home. And where there are cows and huasos, there must be horses. That's all to the good because at this point, the only thing I can do is ride.

When we reach our hotel, we immediately add it to our secret society, the one we've started calling CASA—Chilean Association of Stunning Architecture. It's vast, airy, and whitewashed, with walls of windows framing perfect views of the Cerro Paine across the aquamarine waters of Lake Pehoé. The bathroom in our room is another wonder, with a cutout in the granite wall so even in the shower we don't have to miss one moment of awe-inspiring beauty. It's so genius it demands to be used immediately. I stand in the shower with my bandaged toe propped on the wall, explaining to Bernard why our trip will end right here, because I will be taking a shower forever.

Now that we're actually in prime hiking country, and I can't hike, some negotiation is needed. It's generally a disaster if I organize Bernard's time for him. He goes along with the plan because he's courteous, but then he doesn't enjoy what we do and we wind up grousing at each other. I don't blame him for being this way. I'm the same. Sometimes I even wonder whether he might not have learned the "polite now, crabby later" thing from me. Still, I've been so unusually chipper and stoic that it could be Bernard thinks I'm healed and is expecting we'll be hiking together to the base of the Torres.

"So, Bernard, what do you want to do?"

"I don't know. Don't really care actually. It's beautiful here. I'm up for anything. What do *you* want to do?" This is the way activity discussions always start between us, with each bowing and scraping in front of the other, firmly expressing how little our own needs matter—which is a big lie.

"All I can do is ride, but that makes me happy. So that's what I'm going to do every day. This is prime horse country you know, so they've got to have good horses."

"Okay, let's go for a ride." This is terrible, not at all what I want to hear. Bernard can ride, but he doesn't enjoy it as I do. He's made a move which he thinks is chivalrous and which I know will make him miserable. And that, in turn, will spoil things for me.

"No, no, you should go on a hike. Get some good photos."

"No, no, no. Of course we'll ride."

"But you have your new hiking boots. Use them."

"No. Riding." End of discussion. Once a knight in shining armor, always a knight in shining armor, though in this case I'd like to rip the armor off and fling it into sparkling Lake Pehoé outside our window.

At the stables we are met by three huasos. I launch into a rundown on our horsiness, to back up my request for two good, responsive mounts. "We have our own. Horses. *Caballos*," I gloat, expecting this to distinguish me from those whose horsemanship extends to reclining in the plush velvet seat of a movie theatre as galloping herds thunder across the screen in the opening sequence of *Tombstone*. The huasos do not respond. "Five Quarter Horses," I say, flashing all the fingers of one hand to support my claim, thinking the size of my herd will impress upon them how competent and savvy I am. One huaso walks away. "They live on our *rancho*. I ride out in the open, like here . . ." to confirm I am not some ditzy dressage doll for whom the word "wood" simply is the material used to fence in her local arena. I am as yet unaware that my definition of riding and theirs is like comparing a backyard swing to a Cirque du Soleil trapeze act.

As soon as I say we'd like good horses, that I'm a good rider, I know I sound like every other pompous tourist. "Yeah, yeah, sure," I can almost hear the remaining huaso mutter as he strides off to tack up their two most placid steeds. "We who are huasos know how to ride. You? You accompany the horse on his back."

The horses they put us on confirm my impression that I've been perceived as clueless and overbearing. They clomp slowly around the easy trail, so inured to carrying one clumsy rider after another that they've turned off their brains completely. The thing is, I wasn't being presumptuous. I really do have a handful of horses at our ranch. I really have spent years training those horses in natural horsemanship, I really have taken a mustang from bucking, snorting territorial stallion to companionable mount for a child, and I really do spend my days riding alone through thousands of acres around our ranch. I have in all ways put in the work to accumulate the knowledge, skill, and experience to proudly call myself a capable horsewoman, and I have the scars to prove it.

The morning's ride is two hours of disappointment, as diminished an experience as chauffeuring a Ford Focus would be for a Formula One driver. The only benefit is that Bernard now agrees that, despite infinite regret, he must allow me to ride alone. However, the stable is beautiful and the horses shiny and fit, so clearly the huasos know their horseflesh. Now all I need to do is get them to trust that I know it, too.

The opportunity comes after we've plodded back to the stable, where Bernard catches an early lift back to the hotel, on the pretext of getting cameras ready to photograph the approaching sunset. "Quiere mate?" the head huaso asks me. Most tourists don't really enjoy this tea-like beverage (pronounced mah-teh) which is practically a national drink in Chile and Argentina. Sipping the bitter liquid from its little gourd is picturesque, but doesn't often appeal to those who haven't grown up with it. I know he's being polite, but I accept because I have an agenda.

"Sí, cómo no," I say, and follow him to the back room, the huasos' private lair. As we sit by a wood-burning stove, surrounded by the tobacco and oily sweat smell of leather saddles and bridles waiting for cleaning, I'm content just to relax and inhale the sweet, rough bouquet of saddle soap and horse. It reminds me of my own century-old barn's smells back home, which soothes me since I'm more nervous waiting for the mate to brew than I was riding.

During much of my life I have accepted lack of attention as a sure sign that I'm not worthy of the person's interest or friendship. This is the introverted side of me, which is actually the whole of me. I'm the one who has to take a nap after engaging in social conversation with more than one person, so worn out am I by the effort to engage. I'm not proud that I so readily subside like a cold soufflé when knocked by someone's cold shoulder.

To those who have worked with me or are old friends, I present an impressive and talented woman. I've achieved great success with Bernard as we built our software localization company. While he ran the company, I headed up sales and marketing. My voice on the phone and my presence at meetings helped seal million-dollar deals with major players in the computer world. I've spoken to large audiences at conferences, gone from not knowing how to halter a horse to being an accomplished rider, traveled all over the world. The truth about me in others' view is well-founded. It's just that in my heart of hearts, I don't feel it.

Part of the allure of being on the road is that I permit myself to become another person, one who sees an opportunity, wants it and works strategically to get it. In the cave of the huaso clan, I am intent on getting mate right. So bent am I on making a good impression, that I determine even before the first sip that I will adore mate, will sit and chat with these huasos till Bernard bursts through the door wearing that frowning look I adore, the one that says he's at once relieved to find I haven't come to a painful end and aggravated that my absence made him worry.

As one of the huasos explains while we wait for the water to boil, mate is as much a ritual as a beverage and therein lies its appeal. It's prepared by placing dried leaves of yerba mate in a small hollow gourd and filling it with hot water to steep. The tawny gourd, shaped like the belly of a happy Buddha, is about three inches in diameter, just the size to nestle comfortably in the palm of the hand. Fancy ones are decorated with engravings and silver filigree, but the one I'm offered is plain, rubbed to a dark oily sheen by countless rough hands. Within the intimacy of huaso circles, certain men are known to have particular finesse with how many leaves to steep and for how long. A head brewer is to mate as Daniel Boulud is to French food, or Gustavo Dudamel to conducting. No one does it better and everyone's happy to leave it, whatever "it" may be, in their capable hands.

Unlike American hot beverages, this brew is meant to be shared, with the mate maker sticking a silver straw into the soggy mass of leaves and passing it to each person in turn to drink. You can suck up all the liquid or you can take just a sip. Then you turn the gourd so the straw faces the mate maker again, and hand it back to him. He refills it with a bit of hot water and hands it, straw facing outward, to the next person. And so it goes, round and round. When the mate maker considers the brew too diluted, he plucks some sodden leaves out and stuffs a pinch of new leaves in. It's the beverage equivalent of sourdough starter.

I'm given a friendly final caution. When you hand the gourd back, never say thank you. Thank you means you're done for the day, so you say it only when you don't want any more. Until then, just look solemn and sip. Now that I know this, I know *gracias* isn't going to exit my lips till the cows come home. I just hope they have some.

As we start circulating the gourd, waiting now and then for it to be replenished and steep, I find that, while mate may be a highly caffeinated drink, the ritual itself is calming. The sipping, sharing, refilling has the rhythm of a dance and soon it feels like we're all gently swaying, even though no one's moving. We talk sparsely, not wanting to break the half-silent spell. An hour passes. Though there are no cows and no Bernard, I hear myself announce gracias, and return the gourd for the last time. I've done what I can. The rest is up to them.

Next morning, I wave goodbye to Bernard, who's off on an early morning hike to the base of Torres del Paine. He'll be gone all day, and so will I, on an all-day ride. This type of separateness never happens to us on a road trip, where by unstated agreement we do everything together except get sick. (The latter is by default, since it's no fun being bedridden unless you have someone to take care of you.) This going our separate ways feels very grown-up to me, something mature people can do because they know they'll be back together again before long.

It's not new for us to happily spend all day, every day, side by side. We've always been a couple whose daily rhythm meshes uncommonly well. That was repeatedly put to the test during the twelve years we worked together building our company. While over the long term the stresses of managing a large company did fray some edges, overall the exercise of making our marriage work along with our business tightened the weave of our relationship rather than shredding it.

Things changed, though, when we moved to the ranch. Bernard was intent on being hands-on with every aspect of rough work and mechanical endeavor that running a ranch could offer. Most of that didn't much interest me. He also indulged a long-held desire to become a helicopter pilot, and was often in the air somewhere, leaving me on the ground clutching my useless Dramamine. My days were filled with horses, riding, and all the activities one can indulge when nature is the preferred playground, as it is for me. Plus, with no restaurants worthy of the name within eighty miles, I cooked every meal we ate.

The upshot of this was that our lives took separate directions, with days in which we'd say goodbye after breakfast, regrouping late in the day for a cocktail and dinner. The notion that we could and would pursue separate interests was new to us. In a way this was refreshing, but we both also felt a bit sad that we weren't seeing each other as much as before. And so it came about that we looked forward to our drives, when by the very nature of our choice of travel, we'd be together again all day long. Kissing Bernard goodbye I feel both delighted and a traitor.

At the stable, a huaso brings me a tall sorrel horse. He's well mannered and lively, prancing and posing like a gymnast on the balance beam, but standing obediently still while he's tacked up. He's also young. I surmise this by the lack of wrinkles above his eyes, a tell-tale sign that horses get when they're up in the twenties, as if they're struggling to hold their eyelids up. We mount up, just us, as no other visitors want to attempt the twenty-five-mile ride we're doing.

Off at a canter across the vast blondness of the short grass pampas, we ride toward Glacier Grey. The basalt cliffs of Cerro Paine shimmer blackly in the distance across the emerald waves of Lake Pehoé. At a hidden glacier overlook, we spread a wool horse blanket on a small patch of rough grass for a picnic of cheese, tomatoes, and hard-boiled eggs. Below is the rumpled tongue of the glacier, which melts into unseen Lago Grey. It's far enough away that the ice looks like crinkled gray-blue silk. The horses graze while a condor hovers high in the blue sky, sailing the thermals with its ten-foot wingspan.

On the way back to the stable we pick our way down along a twisty, narrow dirt trail, ducking to avoid low-hanging branches, before breaking into a ground-covering canter once more as the horses head eagerly to the barn. It feels like we have always ridden this way, in comfortable saddles lined with thick fleece pads, on willing horses light to the touch, under a cloudless sky, in companionable silence. Though I am technically a guest, I put my own horse up, taking off the saddle, currying his sweaty back. I take this as it's meant, not lack of interest but a sign of acceptance. Another hour of mate in the saddle room cements a firm friendship.

The following day I'm offered La Reina—the Queen, as the huasos call her. They tell me all their best horses have the day off after competing in the annual endurance challenge the day before. But she will do, they say, and they think I will like her spirit. I know I've been given an honor. Riding all day with the huasos confirms they are by far the best horsemen I have ever seen. When a horse needs to be moved it is not led by someone walking beside it. It is mounted at the run, bareback. "This horse is like a teenager," the huaso leading the ride tells me, pointing to his mount. "Everything for him is new. Of course he is nervous. This is natural. So I will let him decide what he needs to do. And then he will feel he can listen to me. It is more fair this way, I think." What the young stud apparently needs to do is gallop, disappearing over the hilltop in a matter of seconds. When we crest the hill ten minutes later, they are there, standing calmly, waiting for us. More than any cowboy or trainer, the huasos meld with their horses as if centaurs and communicate with a clarity of intention that I can only admire and envy. Far from being bereft that I've been unable to hike to the famous towers, these days in Torres del Paine have turned into a rare privilege.

Before leaving the park, Bernard and I try our hands at fishing. I don't like to fish and neither does Bernard. My perception is that it involves a lot of standing in one place, getting a sore back, swatting insects, and watching fish swim away. It's like watery chess, and if I wanted to play a board game, I wouldn't do it in uncomfortable, breast-high rubber boots. However, we'd never be able to excuse ourselves to our friends who *do* love to fish if we didn't wield a rod at least once, here in what's acclaimed as the world's best fishing locale. Also hard to ignore are reports of spawning Chinook reaching sixty pounds. If we could hook just one, we'd eat for days. Or offer a free dinner to everyone at our hotel.

The Río Serrano, which channels many of the glacial rivers and lakes to the Última Esperanza Sound, is a short drive from our hotel. On its flat grassy banks, we don our rented waders, grab our rented fishing rods, and enter the water. It's frigid, a barely liquid form of the glacier ice that feeds it. Under a persistent cold drizzle, I head far enough from Bernard that my expected errant cast can't hook him in the poncho. While I still have control of my feet I wade out from shore, stopping fifteen feet away because the current is so strong I'm already struggling to stay upright. Within minutes, my legs are tingling, so cold that the only thing I feel is searing pain as blood flow slowly departs my calves and feet, turning them to unresponsive blocks of ice. Unsure whether commands from my brain will enable my legs to carry me elsewhere, let alone if I even have legs, I decide I have reached the perfect spot to fish.

On my first cast, my line looks like it's trying to tie itself into a knot while airborne. Subsequent ones are no better. In my finer moments, the fly plunks into the water ten feet from me. I could almost pick it up with my hand. Suddenly I see one of the fabled behemoths undulate out of the icy depths. He's so huge he can barely break the surface before flumping back with as resounding a splash as the kid doing cannonballs at the neighborhood pool. These are no ordinary Chinook. They're mutants run amok, escapees from a salmon farming operation some twenty-five years ago. Somehow they found the Río Serrano; perhaps there had been salmon-style conversations between the wild ones on the move and the captive ones inside the cages: "If you ever get outta here, come find me. I've got a little place up the Serrano where you can lay low." Now it's become their spawning ground. My initial eagerness to catch one is replaced by a healthy respect for a fish that, who knows, might get me in his gaping jaws and drag me under.

Blinking back the rain, I glance at Bernard. He's looking like a real fisherman. When he casts, the filament arcs gracefully, tracing lazy silvery curves in the air, his fly landing gently on the water's surface, many yards away. A pod of ducks drifts behind him, while he casts and reels in, casts again and reels. It's mesmerizing to watch, our own little *River Runs Through It* moment. I try a bit longer in hopes of getting into a tussle with one of the genetic anomalies rising from the channel, but they're wily, keeping to the deep water in the middle of the river, far out of range. I can't get close.

Hyena Bait

HARAR, ETHIOPIA, 2011

While every road trip is about the driving, it is also about the end of the day when I get out of the car. My car world is a cocoon. In it Bernard and I incubate together, so close and comfortable in our side-by-sideness that often we don't speak for hours, except for the occasional direction, request from him for a sip of water, or offer by me of a handful of almonds and raisins.

We've been married a long time and if you saw us at a meal you might say, "How sad. They have nothing to say to each other." If you did, you'd be missing the point of what a long relationship can give. In our case we've lived through an entire adulthood together, managing decisions that were literally life-changing. We've been though momentous times: founding a company in the deadline-driven, shape-shifting software industry, building a house, moving, selling the company, buying the ranch, moving, making new friends, learning a new business. Each of those periods was fraught with uncertainties, decisions, and arguments, which we weathered together, learning along the way that we were able to find agreement on most every subject with neither of us feeling ignored or wronged. At least not for long.

Without ever specifically voicing the need to, we've each allowed the other to change with the varying demands of our life together. There have been times, long stretches even, when we were out of sync. But even during those spells it's been understood that we would each get the benefit of the doubt as we struggled to find our footing once more. This sense of "You are what you are. Sometimes that's annoying but I still love you for it . . . and

I still would choose you over everyone else if I had it all to do over again," is not something that has to be said out loud all the time. The reward of sticking it out for more than three decades is that now we no longer have to speak profundities, or even inanities, to prove that we're aware of the other person. It's simply a lovely relief to be side by side with a best mate, someone whose every breath or blink speaks volumes without words.

A friend once told me she longed to spy on the profound and fascinating philosophical discussions we indulged in over those weeks on the road. "You must talk about such interesting things," she said. "Because you're there, together. And there's no interruption. Don't the thoughts just flow?"

"No, not really," I told her, hoping by my three words to make a point. It's not that there's nothing new left to be said. It's more that, even though the long road itself is wearying, and the driving conditions stressful, the inside of the car is the one place where there's sameness from day to day, a meditative interior sheltered from the often-chaotic exterior.

I do sometimes wonder whether a butterfly newly burst from its fiber wrap experiences what I do when I open the car door and emerge. Just as I'm relieved to get in the car in the morning, so I'm expectant when I get out. Nothing makes me happier than downing more shots of vodka than I'd normally drink in a year while standing in the parking lot of a Kyrgyz yurt hotel, having crashed a local family's reunion. That they then break out accordions and sing while I get to dance with the local headman, elbows linked and head thrown back as he whirls me around, is a thrill I will not be denied. That this happens before three in the afternoon is even better. When the car stops, I open the door to a whole new world from the one I left that morning, and I feel that it's been created and is waiting just for me.

Early in our drive through Ethiopia, when we reached the city of Harar, we decided to get out of the car for two full days. That's how we were able to meet our sheik and I was able to accomplish two other firsts for me: chewing *qat* and using my very talented piano-playing fingers to feed wild hyenas. And perhaps I do the latter because of indulging a bit too much of the former.

A little more information on *qat* for those who find such things amusing: *Qat* is to the Ethiopian worker what coca is to the Colombian highlander, a cheap, leafy stimulant that keeps him going in the absence of food and liquid. As my initial modest experience in the sheik's presence showed me, *qat* chewing is about what you'd expect if you ripped a handful of leaves off your neighbor's privet hedge and stuffed it in your mouth: bitter, green, leathery. But I was searching for a reaction so I bought more at the market and chewed it, too, which precipitated a reaction akin to mild hysteria. I felt like a fussy baby, fidgety and in need of distraction. That's why as dusk settled to a densely black night, I was more than willing to kneel by Harar's hyena feeder, take the match-size stick he gave me, let him drape a strip of raw mutton on it and then extend it into a cluster of five hyenas. Why he insisted I hold the stick in my left hand I can't know for sure. I imagine he assumed I was a righty, and if a hyena chomped more than I was technically offering, at least I'd still have my good hand with which to sign off on the lawsuit.

The hyenas of Harar are spotted hyenas, their coarse gold fur covered with ragged black splotches, a thick ruched mane standing permanently upright from head to shoulders. I've been up close, but never personal, with spotted hyenas, having seen them repeatedly while on horseback safaris through the bush of Kenya's Maasai Mara National Reserve and Botswana's Okavango Delta. They're fascinating animals whose bad rap is based on their scruffy coats and a lurching walk reminiscent of Igor in Frankenstein, or the Hunchback of Notre Dame. Like other misunderstood animals—the pig comes to mind—hyenas are not only essential to the bush ecosystem, they have a lot going for them. For one, their voices soar like an opera diva on warm-up, whooping, giggling, groaning, and whining. For another, they groom themselves like cats, which no dog would ever do. For a third, 95 percent of what they eat is what they kill themselves.

All this was the logical reason why I would not forego a chance to be right in the scrum of the hyena pack. There's little related to animals that I will pass up, and while I cannot call myself a dog or horse whisperer, I would be comfortable with the title Horse Mutterer. That is to say, while

I do not put myself on a par with animal handlers of exceptional talent, I do feel I have a preternatural rapport with all animals and that they can sense it. At least that's what I hoped when the hyenas lumbered in, looking like broad-shouldered, small-rumped dogs that had just stuck a paw in an electric socket. As they approached and circled, their eyes glowed green in the headlights of our car. They were big, well fed, standing about the height of a German Shepherd. If it weren't for their round ears and sloping, slouching walk, I could have called them cute, though maybe that was just nerves talking. Or the *qat*.

They all recognized the hyena feeder's voice. To me, his voice sounded like a saw cutting through dry pine. For them, it was a version of their own hyena whoop, a sound as unique to each hyena as my voice is to me. The whoop is used to bring the hyena clan together, and in this case it also promised a meal without any need for hunting. When he called them by name, hoarsely shouting "Ertika!" and "Howah!" they knew dinner was on, loping in through the old town's Fallana Gate. They circled, dipped, and ducked as the largest alpha females took up favored positions, squealing and groaning in greeting as they arrived.

I was prepared to like hyenas, because they have a matriarchal society, which I'm all for. It was only later that I learned hyenas have the most powerful bite of any mammal. They're also one of the world's most accomplished predators for their size. Those are mere statistics and at the time, data was not on my mind. Quite sensibly I figured if they got the urge to hunt, damaging my hand would be the least of my problems. Still, it seemed to come naturally to me to make like a statue when the largest hyena approached within two feet of me and took that bloody bit off the tip of the stick. As I held my breath I calmed myself with the profound understanding that there must be some sort of natural selection at play here. Any hyena foolish enough to disregard proper etiquette when taking raw meat from a visitor's hands would have been dispatched without pity long ago.

At one point, the hyena man took a sheep shank from his bag of tricks. It was dripping with pink fat and gristle. He smiled wide, gripped it in his teeth, and stuck his face toward the hyenas. All of them wanted it, and the clan let out a chorus of shrill shrieking laughs in nervous excitement, as did I, though mine sounded like a strangled cackle while theirs sounded like the yelps of relief when Nik Wallenda stepped onto Canadian ground after crossing Niagara on a high wire. The hyenas dodged and circled closer in a dance of submission, the smaller ones making increasingly quieter groans of distress on realizing the bone would not be theirs. At last the largest female made one final feint then dodged in and grabbed it, having mentally swatted away all competition for that prize.

Unlike other mammals, hyenas are born eyes open and teeth in place. In fact, sisters from the same litter may fight to the death while still babies. Whether it was the *qat* euphoria wearing off or the effects of hyena-feeding adrenaline, I started feeling distinctly exposed. Proximity to animals that will off another female just for her gender does that to me. With the loser hyenas crouching and darting about for a consolation prize, hooting to each other, their green eyes glinting, I began to wonder whether I might not look like the consolation prize. In that moment I knew precisely what Bilbo meant when he said, "It's a dangerous business ... going out of your door." Right now the thing of import to me is finding a door and getting behind it. Spying one on our car, I scuttle that direction and when I pull it shut, leaving furry predators outside, I know I am home.

BORDERS

PREAMBLE

I find borders fascinating. Because we choose the back roads for our journeys, it's inevitable that we wind up at the most remote borders. In these isolated posts, my perception of the differences, and at times the animosity, between countries is the clearest it will ever be. Borders, more than travel itself, confirm for me what Henry Miller said: "One's destination is never a place, but a new way of seeing things."

For most travelers, their first entry into a country tends to be the opposite of mine. They arrive at a modern airport, where the uniformed official in a stiff-billed cap sitting at a computer is all too blasé about foreign passports and entry visas. The land borders I'm talking about are mountains, deserts, and rivers. They are, as Paul Theroux observed, "a contrived and arbitrary dotted line, a political conceit dividing communities and people, creating difference and disharmony." Sometimes the border post is so modest we can't even find it. In other words, these are places that have nothing in common with airport immigration control.

Things rarely go wrong at airport immigration, other than being asked to stop holding up the line as you fill in that immigration card you forgot to deal with before landing, or mistakenly allowing your luggage to bulge with such temptations that a bored customs official can't resist opening it for a little look-see, amusing himself further by scattering your undergarments onto the countertop just because he can. Not so the land crossing, where you'll find an official in name only, whose training is minimal, whose pay is less, and whose desire is to be anywhere but there. His days are filled with emptiness, smoking, keeping warm, keeping cool, and ticking off the weeks and months till his next home leave. Though his job is important to him because it feeds his family, the limitations on his authority are as vast and vague as the empty no-man's-land surrounding his post. This is officialdom with all the responsibilities and none of the perks. The man in charge frets about what he should and shouldn't do, ripe to take out his uncertainties on the next person who appears, assuming it's not his commander on a surprise inspection.

Despite knowing all this, my peace of mind flies out the car window when I have to hand over my passport. I exude an air of flustered agitation, while Bernard sinks into meditative calm punctuated by the occasional guffaw to show that while he may seem like the Brother from Another Planet, he's a comradely brother. Unlike Bernard, I have never been comfortable relying on the kindness of strangers. And while a lone border guard might be happy, indeed relieved, to see a carload of his compatriots pull up, we with our American passports are as strange an apparition as a Benedictine nun at a Madonna concert. It's not that we're not allowed to be there. It's just that our appearance alone raises questions. And if there's one thing you don't want to do when traveling, it's create a situation where a petty official has a question he cannot answer simply by looking at your passport and visa stamp.

This notion of being inconspicuous and going with the flow is totally against my nature. I am a person who is always keen to let others know exactly what they're doing incorrectly, and that I for one am well aware of the proper way to do those things. This does not serve me well. It was on our drive through Peru to Bolivia in 2010 that things—not our car—nearly went south. Despite a much-transited border further north, we chose the village of Desaguadero, on Lake Titicaca's eastern shore, as our crossing point. We were intrigued by its reputation as a black-market and smugglers town and neglected to factor in that smugglers attract police like crows to a carcass. Why I said yes to the potential for making a border crossing even more nervous-making I'll never know.

Wending our way through the packed streets of market day to the border gates, hoping to sight a blackmarketeer, I saw my first test awaiting:

long queues of people whose potential for carrying firearms I figured was high, what with them being smugglers and all. Knowing that flitting from line to line—as I do at the supermarket when I can't stand waiting—would only call attention to us in a negative way, I fingered my passport and heaved sighs while Bernard remained stoic. Fortunately, Peru proved amenable to letting people out of the country easily, with lines moving if not swiftly, at least smoothly, through passport, car, and police checkpoints.

Within an hour we drove under the big WELCOME TO BOLIVIA sign. I always smirk at those signs, because what they really mean is "Good luck getting in here!" Awaiting us was our first encounter with Bolivian military police. These two men in green fatigues were puffed up with self-impor-tance, despite—or, in retrospect, because of—the fact they were just glori-fied parking lot attendants, charged with pointing out where incoming vehicles should wait. As is my job as navigator, I jumped out, papers in hand, and asked them which building I should go to first. Bernard, as is his job, waited in the car for me to come back and tell him where to drive.

Both policemen sucked in their bellies and chins, giving me a long, hot once-over. One scraped his gold teeth assiduously with a toothpick, sucking little bits from between them, which he spit on the ground. At my feet. The other had expressionless black eyes and at my question gave a dismissive wave to include every building in sight. Turning to his comrade with a snarky chuckle he said, "Esta señora no sabe que! Vamos a ver cual errores va hacer." Then both hacked out a "heh, heh, heh." They leaned back, arms crossed, to see what amusement I could offer in the way of flustered scur-rying from one doorway to the next.

Here's where things took a turn for the better, because I understand Spanish. Knowing I'd just been insulted, my knee-jerk reaction was to offer a rejoinder like, "I feel sorry for men doing a job so easily done by any woman." And I almost did. But then something about the dark patches of sweat under their armpits gave me pause. These were men in a situation that made them feel bad enough already. Any lip from me would make them kick back harder, and I had no doubt who would fare worse in that virtual martial arts fest. Thus in the time it took me to figure out how to issue my pithy comment in Spanish, I realized it would be a shame to spend my first nights in Bolivia inspecting the dank walls of a border jail cell.

To buy myself time I walked back to the car as if I'd forgotten something, and that's when I discovered the surefire cure for whatever ails Latin men in general and border guards in particular: candy. So it was that I avoided a grave mishap by offering two policemen free choice from a bag of sweets I'd bought in Puno. Each took a bonbon with pinky raised. They unwrapped the bright foil, chewed, and considered. I saw shoulders relax, because who can stay tough when working a caramel around in your mouth. And then they escorted me personally to the right doorway.

Remote borders represent arbitrary precision in the most mutable of environments, by their very location a place where the human compact of law and nationality is taken purely on faith. It's because of this that they attract people for whom bending the law may be the only form of exercise they know. Here is what I've learned from long experience with such borders: we have no real business showing up at such places. We're passing through and, in such circumstances, anything could happen.

Isolation

PASO ROBALLOS, ARGENTINA TO CHILE, 2008

Chickens are gabbling around my ankles. The turkeys are not far behind, making the chickens more frantic as they sense that the turkeys, on longer legs, are about to overtake them. They scrabble at my feet, huddling close, seeking refuge. A weathered wood door set deep into a lichen-spackled stone wall is all that stands between me—between us—and the border control officer.

I must say that this low, windowless structure is different from any border facility I've seen. Unlike at other posts at midmorning, we are the only vehicle here at Argentina's Paso Roballos border station. We've chosen it to cross from Argentina back to Chile precisely because it is known as the least-used crossing in the country. Most people we questioned about it were suspicious about whether it even existed, let alone manned full-time. But the fact that I can't see any tire tracks on the ground is taking isolation to an extreme.

I'm captivated by such posts. Imagine what life must be like for the officer whose presence defines a separateness between countries that otherwise would be indistinguishable. Silence all day until, suddenly, the sound of an engine coming round the bend. Then it's, "Quick, quick, get into a uniform, slick the hair, straighten the shoulders. There's work to do and I'm just the official, well, the only official, to do it!" Except the car carries occupants who resent having to stop and want only to get away from you, to move on with their journey, to leave you behind. No pleasantries are exchanged. You go about your work, worried faces staring at you as you concentrate on checking documents, entering information in a ledger, waving them on.

It was before dawn when we crept out of our dingy bedroom and left Bajo Caracoles. It had been a chilly, wakeful night curled in scratchy blankets on hard mattresses, stomachs wrestling with the dinner of shredded beets and tough steak prepared for us by the gas station owner's wife. Given the options, which were none, we'd been grateful for it all. We drive into the sunrise, following a winding dirt road upward. Sun gilds the tawny fields with gold. A rare colocolo cat emerges from the grass to glare at us, outraged that we've disturbed his morning hunt. The desolate lowland country gives way to isolated patches of green; a gully has captured some recent rainfall and a creek now babbles downward through the amber hills. As the road climbs higher, these solitary patches segue to bigger ones, where an enterprising farmer has scratched irrigation ditches to water some fields of wheat. Only twisted, gnarled, wind-ravaged trees grow at this high altitude, their wind-ravaged forms a tormented echo of how stately, tall, and straight they would be lower down. The meadows are coarse and bumpy; fences made of crooked branches and barky split trunks separate oddly shaped pastures for grazing. Traversing one isolated estancia we pass creamy merino sheep grazing on clumps of tussock grass, kept company by pink flamingos standing in windswept ponds. Clouds scud across the sky, and when I pull my hand in from testing the air outside the window, it's red with cold.

There's little green at the border post; we're high enough now that we and it are surrounded by tundra. As we pull in I notice a modest white wood cottage, with a dog chained in front, across from what I assume is the office. The cottage sits, lonesome and drooping, amid a small, tattered bed of wilted flowers and tired vegetables. Not much is willing to take root and grow in this austere place. When Bernard cuts the engine, I see a faded curtain flicked aside and catch sight of a face peering at us from behind it. I assume the face belongs to the officer, so I heave myself out of the car to get our papers. We've gone in and out of Chile and Argentina seven times now. I'm an old hand at border crossings. While rummaging for my portfolio of car documents I hear the house door slam shut. But by the time I've found everything and turn around, the official has vanished. "I'll go do the formalities," I tell Bernard. "Hang out here. I'll get you if I need you."

This is when the chickens appear. They are moving like a feathered school of fish toward a coarse stone structure opposite the cottage, running first in one direction, then abruptly and collectively veering in another. Figuring they're used to showing strangers the way, I follow them. Soon I'm swept up in a strange Argentinean poultry tango. When they see me willing to move with them they gather speed and swarm around, clucking happily as we approach the hut door. The appearance of the turkeys turns their clucks to cries of alarm. "Hurry!" they seem to be warning me. "Don't let them get there ahead of us or you'll have to stand in line forever."

I am always slightly nervous at borders. There's an ominous sense, which I can't quite pinpoint, that something in our paperwork will be awry, that we'll be missing an essential signature or an obvious document, and the official won't let us through. While it's not a disaster to be turned back at a border, for me a driving trip means moving forward. I hate the thought of retracing steps. It smacks of failure to get ahead.

So, despite the support of the chicken chorus, it is with a mild sense of trepidation that I grab the leather strap that serves as a handle on the hut door and push. The door creaks, as an old wood door should, and swings open. Inside it is dark, sunlight filtering through cracks in the roof tiles, dust motes floating up light beams that slice through the dimness. There's a musty odor of disuse, coupled with something vaguely sweet-smelling. As I take a step, decades of rodent droppings crunch underfoot. I move gingerly onto the uneven dirt floor tamped down by countless shoes and peer around. Something doesn't feel right.

The chickens, however, are beside themselves with glee. They scurry through the open doorway and begin to romp around the floor, turkeys hot on their heels. I step farther into the deeply shadowed interior. Surely someone should be welcoming me, urging me forward with a practiced flick and swirl of the wrist, and a commanding "Entra, señora." But it is eerily still in this hut.

I pause to let my eyes adjust to the dark and my heart thumps a bit harder while I stand there, waiting. I can see something in the back corner, but I can't distinguish any details other than that it's a large, huddled mass. I move forward just a little more, unwilling to completely let go of the door in case whatever's in the corner moves. And then it all falls into place. The huddled mass is a tumbled pile of grain sacks. No wonder the poultry are happy. Not only have I led them to the promised land, I've flung open the pearly gates and they think I'm going to feed them.

Exiting the feed shed, I see the officer waving at me from the more proper-looking building behind it. Trying not to betray how dopey I feel, I stride up to the customs office, still surrounded by my flock. I believe they would have come right into the customs office with me had they not been turned away for lack of passports. Their clucks of dismay as I disappear inside are distressing.

In the office I find Soldier Cabral, a man of perhaps thirty-five years, the lone resident of this isolated border post. Knowing that I've roused him from his midmorning snack, or nap, I expect to see striped pajama bottoms peeking out from his dark olive regulation-issue army trousers. But no, he is fully pressed, buttoned, polished, and tied, all set to go through the formalities.

I respectfully place myself in front of his desk while he searches through drawers for the necessary books and forms. There's a wedding band on his ring finger, evidence that there's a life for this man away from Paso Roballos. I feel sorry for him, posted here in the middle of nowhere, and so it pleases me to know that he is married. Filled with the desire to make our encounter as memorable and full of human contact as possible, I ask him if his family is here too. "No. Están en la ciudad," he answers. "Es demasiado aislado aquí para ellos."

Cabral seems to have lost the habit of speaking at length, and who can blame him, living as he does in such intense solitude. As if suddenly realizing there's more he can say, he tells me that every few months a relief officer comes up to allow him time off so he can go visit his family. Apart from that it's just him and the chickens. Cabral is manning the border entirely by himself—no compadres, no computer, and, usually, no cars.

Finally, he brings forth the necessary ledgers and places each lovingly on the desktop. To track the infrequent comings and goings, he maintains four journals, one each for vehicles arriving and those departing Argentina and one each for people doing the same, all with meticulous handwritten entries. As he begins flipping the pages, moistening his thumb and carefully lifting the edge of each page to turn it, I can see that the pages offer mute testimony to Cabral's dedication and precision. They are flawless. No errors, no crossed-out or smudged entries are going to take place on his watch.

I can also see that the lack of foot or vehicle traffic through his post means a distinct lack of familiarity with the paperwork. At one point in the laborious proceedings, Cabral reveals that he rarely sees more than five hundred cars a year at this post, most of which come months earlier than we. There are days at a stretch when no car at all comes his way. Nevertheless, Cabral's motto, if he could express it, seems to be, "Better slow and safe than sorry." He is careful and meticulous to a fault. This is not a man you want in the infantry with you, and I begin to understand why his superiors have given him this particular assignment.

Every action Soldier Cabral takes, he takes three times: The first is in preparation: *I am now going to make an entry in this book by looking at the label and opening to the proper page.* The second to double-check himself: *Did I pick up the correct book? Better look at the cover again and check a few pages back to be sure.* And finally, once to make the entry needed: *Yes, this is the proper book and nothing has changed since I checked the cover label two seconds ago.* He does this without self-consciousness, simply going about his business with stern seriousness and, no doubt, some prayers.

At one point, baffled, Soldier Cabral feels the need for written support. Rising from his scarred office chair, he turns to a slender wood cabinet containing two columns of small drawers with filigreed brass handles, each perhaps two inches high. He pulls open the top two simultaneously and peers inside. From my vantage point, I can see that they hold blank forms. No help. He goes down the chest, drawer by drawer, getting increasingly perturbed as he finds them all empty. Although he's the only one who could have filled them, he betrays shock at finding nothing in them. By the time he gets to the last of the twenty drawers in the chest, I can tell by how wearily he pulls them open that he's given up hope of finding answers in any of them. He sits slowly back down in his chair, flexes his arms several times, and is ready to lick the nib of his pen, realizing only at the last moment that it's a ballpoint, not a quill.

Though the proceedings take longer than expected, I have to say that my half hour with Soldier Cabral seems par for the course at such a forsaken crossing. I am inclined to excuse his clumsy lack of fluidity. After all, how can anyone become acquainted with their responsibilities if they have few opportunities to practice them? A hint of melancholy sets in as I return to our car and Bernard starts the engine. Who knows when Cabral will next see a human being?

He raises the bar, a symbolic gesture only, since it's so thin it'd barely stop a bicycle, and waves us into the no-man's-land between Argentina and Chile. I imagine he might feel a certain despair to see us go. We wave as we drive off, feeling fortunate that we are free to leave this solitary spot and equally stricken for Soldier Cabral, alone, far from his family, uncomfortable with his job. On the desolate plateau separating Argentina and Chile, we brace ourselves for what we expect will be an even more distressing entry post for Chile.

Without doubt, border crossings are some of the more intense cultural experiences one can have on a long road trip, especially a trip designed to tempt fate by hopping between Chile and Argentina over and over again. It's at the border that a country's true feelings about its neighbors, as well as foreigners, are brought into the bright light of day.

Relations between Argentina and Chile are sometimes cordial, but often sour. Even though the two countries gained their independence from Spain at nearly the same time two hundred years ago, they haven't been happy neighbors since. This is due primarily to disagreements on who owns what in Patagonia. The countries are like fighting cocks on leashes, strutting and pecking in each other's direction. I think this is a legacy of each country's military juntas, though no one I talk to dares formally agree with me. Take, for example, El Chaltén, where the clatter of helicopters fills the sky. It's almost as if we're in a war zone. Bernard and I wander over to the landing pad, which happens to be just below the little hill on which sits our hotel. "Hey, what are you guys up to?" I say, or something in Spanish to that effect. This is just my opening gambit, since the green drab uniforms with bars and chevrons on the sleeves, and the slouching, leather-rimmed matching berets on each head, give me an inkling this is a military operation. That, and the fact that the soldier barring our access to the landing pad has a rifle firmly held across his chest, which he now puffs in our direction, confronting us with an unwavering, steely gaze. Nevertheless, I persist. "Nice helicopters. Can we offer ourselves as passengers on your next flight?" This last is meant to break the ice, which right now is as vast as the Southern Patagonian Ice Field they're overflying. It succeeds enough that the soldier gives us a two-sentence explanation of why choppers are taking off and landing for eight hours a day. They're establishing GPS points for certain peaks in Parque Nacional Los Glaciares, determined to prove to the inch what belongs to Argentina. This despite the fact that Chile doesn't agree that the border even runs along the highest peaks. In Chile's view, the border is defined by the drainages from those peaks. It's too complicated for me. And apparently too complicated for them also. The two countries signed a treaty about this in 1881, and one hundred twenty-five years later, there's a spat going on that reminds me of five-year-olds on the school playground.

Which is why an Argentine government that wouldn't spring for a three-dollar filling in a campesino's molar, was spending millions to prove exactly which bits of granite, in places no one would ever go, belonged to it, and which it would agree were Chile's. That same government couldn't be bothered to equip many of its border outposts, not just the isolated Paso Roballos post, with a computer and a stipend for family. It's not entirely surprising that, despite formal diplomatic niceties on the subject as recent as 1998, word doesn't seem to have reached the guys manning the actual border. How would it get there? Which is probably why the officials on one side of the border have nothing good to say about the officials across the way. Ask a Chilean how things will go when we reach the Argentine side of the border and we get a dramatic rolling of the eyes. Ask the same thing of the corresponding Argentine official and he clears his throat, indicating he'd spit on the floor if he weren't too polite to do that in front of a lady. Strained is the word I'd use to describe relations. The Chileans disparage their Argentinian counterparts as shabby and ill-equipped. Which is true. The Argentinians can't help but take this personally, caustically describing their Chilean counterparts as babies in cushy jobs. Which is also, almost, true. Here at Paso Roballos, despite living only fifteen minutes apart from each other, as compared to many hours from their own compatriots, these guys are never going to be passing around the mate cup.

Our spirits lift as we cross several miles of gorgeous tundra. The tiny plants struggling to grow form a green-gold velvet blanket through which our road cuts like a silk cord. Around us rise rounded peaks freshly dusted with white. These are not the granite spikes of Fitz Roy, but humble hilltops, nevertheless high enough to capture a sprinkling of snow from an early fall storm. It's wild and desolately beautiful. When the sun breaks through the clouds, I feel I'm moving through a fresco by some alpine Michelangelo.

Soon we're driving past neat expanses of mowed lawn dotted with shade trees. It's another high-altitude farm in a most unexpected location. "Can you believe that there's an estancia up here?" I say to Bernard. Not too far away is a fairytale cluster of red and white cottages, each nestled next to a flamboyant flower gardens. Workers tend a flock of fattened sheep, while others irrigate a thriving vegetable garden and everywhere, happy chickens peck for insects. Everything is upright, spruce, and flourishing, as if someone had waved a magic wand. "Whoever's doing this is a lot more talented than those people whose places we drove through on the way here!"

"But my god, what a long way to get to market," Bernard says, filled with respect for such hard work. "I can't believe anyone can make it up here. These people are amazing."

As we crane necks to get a closer look, a veritable platoon of armed men appears. And the thought that I have, because this place is so incongruous, isolated yet manicured, and because I have men in uniform around me holding automatic weapons, is "Of course, this belongs to a drug lord. How stupid of us to slow down." One waves us forward to a neatly paved and striped parking spot. "Ah ha, drug lord's expecting visitors." Still unable to process what's happening, I catch Bernard's eye and make an imperceptible nod toward the guards that now encircle us. "Lock the car, Bernard," I say. "Because who knows . . ." Now one of them points his rifle to a door in the largest cottage. I'm half-curious, half-scared about what's going to happen next. Inside there's a high counter and behind it are three more uniformed men, one of whom looks at me without much interest and says, "Papers, madam." We're at Chile's border post, and far as I can tell, it's a nonstop party here. There's such a surplus of officials that they begin filling forms for us—directly on their computers. Someone lifts a whistling kettle over a small stove, pours hot water onto tea leaves, and the mate gourd with its silver straw is passed across the counter to us. In a back room, more soldiers casually stroll in and out. Conversation broken by a swift burst of laughter, they smile at us, clack confidently on their keyboards. I feel a certain arrogance from these soldiers, as if they know we know how fortunate they are to be on the Chilean side of things.

"Muy bien, señora. Bienvenidos a Chile." Within ten minutes we are done, descending from Paso Roballos and leaving Soldier Cabral and his woebegone post far behind.

We are close to the Carretera Austral now, separated from that mythic route only by some thirty miles of meandering dirt road. We both feel relieved, our thoughts on the road ahead. But the solitary Soldier Cabral sticks with me. There's no border trickery going on here. Facts are facts. There he is, alone. And here am I. With Bernard. Together.

Gated Community

KARAKUL, TAJIKISTAN TO KYRGYZSTAN, 2011

Snowflakes swirl in a wild Tajik dance as our car approaches Kyzyl-Art Pass. Behind us the road winds through a landscape of jarring potholes, ruts and rocks to the base of the pass, where it splits the Pamir plateau in a line as sharp as a scalpel cut. A five-strand barbed wire fence topped with razor coils shadows the road, placed by some shrewd Soviet who thought it would prevent Chinese from infiltrating this former Soviet republic. (As if the Pamir Mountains couldn't do the job alone.)

Now that Tajikistan rules itself, herders who wander the Pamir plateau have cut through the wire to give their yaks, sheep, and motorbikes ease of travel. The concrete pill boxes in which bored Soviet soldiers once sat for hours have a new life. They bulge obscenely out of the sandy dirt that once cloaked them, sprayed with graffiti, walls smudged black from fires, floor littered with shattered bottles left by herders who took shelter on a day such as this.

At dawn, the Pamir peaks still shone with the white of religious conversion. Here on the pass at fourteen thousand feet, the unseasonable snowstorm has drawn a foggy curtain around the summits, and the road blends too easily into the surroundings. A final hairpin turn and we see it: a gate so shrouded by the gloom that when it emerges we are on the verge of crashing through it.

It's a crude barrier, just a pole with a sack of rocks on one end for ballast, more a gesture than a blockade. But it does the job, signaling we've reached the border station of Tajikistan with Kyrgyzstan. Our car tires crunch on gravel as we halt next to a hut built of wood scraps and tar paper.

"Don't worry," says Bernard from the driver's side, finely attuned to my border nerves from forty thousand miles of husband-wife road trips. He thumbs some dust off our GPS. My foot refuses to be still, tapping on the floorboards for what seems an interminable wait. I crack my window to get a whiff of how cold and windy it is outside. Very.

A soldier steps out of the guard shack. With a raised hand and a shrugging of his rifle he motions me to follow him. I bid Bernard what I hope is a temporary goodbye. He won't be alone in my absence, though. A guard of insufficient status to take refuge indoors is already shambling over to get a closer look at our Land Rover. The synthetic-fur collar of his bulky blue and gray camouflage jacket is turned up, his face and neck are chapped red and raw. Warding off the wind up here is futile.

Opening a dented, creaking steel door, I enter the border office, passports and car papers in hand. Except it's not an office, it's the officer's own spartan boudoir. A shaft of bleak light through a book-sized window makes the dim glow of a bare bulb look bright. The small stove in a corner chuffs and smokes, its heat struggling to reach the middle of the cell-like room, leaving the walls glacial.

I stand in a hot spot while the officer takes the one chair and scrapes it closer to a cluttered card table. When he removes his hat and looks at me I see he's a young man, with a heavy thatch of greasy, dark hair badly in need of a shampoo. He is courteous. "Please," he says, motioning me to sit on the only other furniture in the room: his cot. The bedding is rumpled, a coarse green wool blanket hastily pulled over graying sheets.

I sit, my weight dislodging a fusty smell of sweat, smoke, cooking oil, and diesel from the bed. Standing again is not an option; hovering over a soldier as he does the necessary exit paperwork would be rude, if not vaguely threatening. And then there's my general border caution. I scarcely dare move, so uncertain am I whether what I do might incline him to have a little sport with me and peruse my passport for hours. I dread being the fuel that enlivens the tedium of his morning. Today though, my paranoia is replaced by novelty. Rank smells aside, I have never sat on a man's bed while he decided whether or not to release me from his country.

Remote borders where few travelers cross are the most arbitrary of places. They ooze all the possibilities of proximity while making manifest all the divisions of distance. How can it be that people separated by nothing more than a bridge over a narrow river never mingle? They've lived for centuries just across the way from each other, yet on one side the women tie their floral headscarf pirate-style, have blue eyes, fair skin, and hair that's brown and wavy. They pile harvested wheat in mounds, bake flat bread with dot patterns, and decorate donkeys with flags. On the other side, the scarf is tied under the chin, children have black eyes, swarthy skin, and straight black hair. Harvested wheat stands in pyramids, flat bread is decorated with stars, and the donkeys sport tassels. Even their homemade liquor is different.

I want each border official to like me, under the unproven assumption that he wouldn't unnecessarily inconvenience a friend (would he?). Now, to put myself more at ease while the Tajikistani soldier frowns and thumbs our passports looking for visas, I make innocuous small talk like "Cold here!" at which I rub my shoulders and shiver, and "High!" rolling my eyes heavenward to mime altitude. Each utterance provokes a nod, no more. He reaches for my folder of car papers just as I lift it to give to him, and our hands touch. I laugh awkwardly and so does this young man with the deeply lined face. The implications of the unusual setting are not lost on either of us. I'm sitting in a man's room hoping that the only thing that's going to be scrutinized is my visa. He's sitting with his back to a woman who's on his bed, surely a rare occurrence.

He bends to the serious task of entering passport and visa number, with dates and places of entry and departure. I don't know where to rest my eyes. They watch him, stare at my hands in my lap, glance around. I notice a plastic bowl on a shelf next to the door. In it are perhaps twenty nubbly white orbs, the size of golf balls. This is *irimchik*, made from curdled, pressed yogurt cheese that has been left in the sun for many days to desiccate further, until it is so hard and dry it can last for a year. It's the dairy version of beef jerky, something a yak herder can carry in a saddle bag and gnaw on, or grate into a watery soup.

Yesterday I was given a ball of irimchik by a woman near Karakul Lake. I tried it. Despite my strong, orthodontically corrected, crowned, veneered, and whitened Western teeth, I barely made a dent in the rock-hard surface. What bits I did scrape off tasted like the smell from the seat of a well-used saddle after a hard day's ride. Loving irimchik is an acquired taste.

After having his way with our passports, the young officer hands them back with a look that says "Rules! Regulations! What can one do!" He stands. I stand. And there we are, knee to knee. We both twist away. "Please," he says, pointing outside. The door out, though, proves sticky and unobliging. Edging around me to help, the young man takes one of the petrified cheese balls out of the bowl and gives it to me. Then, thinking himself remiss in his hospitality, he hands me two more. And finally, a fourth.

Lacking even the most rudimentary Tajik, I *ooh* and *aah*, hoping to convey that I appreciate his generosity, recognize the value of his gift. I imagine a wife or other beloved woman he has not seen for months, handing him a sackful as he's leaving for his remote mountain post. Scraping at one of them may be one of his few pleasures. I exclaim a broad, delighted "Thank you," as I wonder whether stuffing the four balls in my pocket will give offense.

"Please," he says, as he shows me the door. Outside, he lights a cigarette behind a cupped hand. I fairly skip back to the car, amazed that we have completed the exit formalities so quickly. Narrowing his eyes from the smoke being blown back at him by the wind, he motions me away from the car, waving me around the gate. Though Bernard and I are cleared to go, our car is not.

Taking our car out of Tajikistan should be a simple matter. It's a country's *entrance* formalities that make driving halfway around the world in your own vehicle an exercise in patience. And those formalities are the responsibility of the official who let us in. All the exit official has to do is stamp the papers to note he's seen us leave in the same car in which the papers say we entered.

However, if the officer on duty hasn't slept well, or is searching for amusement in this bleakest of high-altitude posts, or has been chastised by his superior and needs to vent his frustration on someone, we may have to unpack everything in the car. And it's a big car, with rear seats removed to store all the gear we imagine we'll need for a nine-thousand-mile drive. If we have to remove the car contents, we will be here all day. That would be very bad indeed, because after the Tajikistani border there's twenty kilometers of country only a yak herder could love, before we reach the Kyrgyz border post. Arrive there late and they'd be closed. Stuck in no-man's land, unable to go back yet prevented from going forward, we'd be relegated to a night of upright sleeping in a cold car. As I contemplate these possibilities, I know that, although I long to be Zen-like in the face of officious behavior, I'm unlikely to achieve it here.

Several more soldiers swaddled in camouflage stamp about in the cold gray morning, plumes of icy breath mixing with smoke from hand-rolled cigarettes. They glance at me from under their hoods, keeping their distance. The only one inclined to be friendly is a handsome German Shepherd. I smooch for him to come. As he trots over I recollect that this is no suburb and he's not a local pet. He's a guard dog, trained to sniff, to attack on command, to be fierce-looking as well as simply fierce. Though I know this, the dog does not appear to have been so informed. He wags his tail, happy to be scratched, and leans against me sharing his warmth.

Eager to get the remaining formalities underway, I knock on the door of a white trailer and open it onto what I expect will be a modest office with a proper officer sitting behind a desk. Instead it's again a bedroom, where I see a man frantically shrugging into his jacket. The odd thing about a soldier without his uniform buttoned and tucked is that he seems unmanly, without much authority. This soldier waves in desperation for me to leave.

Back outside, my thin cargo pants flap about my legs and my light fleece jacket surrenders to the wind without a fight. I search for a wind break, but our car's back at the lower gate some fifty yards away and I've been denied entry into the only building around. I'm stuck in a mini no-man's-land, with only a German Shepherd for company. I hug myself to ward off the cold.

Finally, the trailer door opens and the inspector struts over, all spit and polish. He gives the Shepherd a good kick with his shiny, black boot. As the dog yelps and cringes, tail between his legs, the officer snatches away the folder I'm holding. If we want to leave here any time soon I cannot let my dog-lover side show. But I can't help myself. As the official swivels to return to the trailer I shoot him an angry glare. He hesitates a moment, raising one eyebrow, before marching off with nary an invitation to join him.

I stamp my own cold circle outside. Soldiers drift about. Snow swirls. The dog stays away. I try to imagine what it must be like to live out one's assigned posting here, for months on end. The officer returns, papers in hand. He points at them, looks around. "Your car?" he asks in a stiff voice. "Where?"

My stomach sinks as I rue my earlier undisciplined glare. "Here we go," I think. "He's going to search the car." I point to the gate, behind which sits the Land Rover, Bernard snugly warm inside. "Back there," I mumble. "Waiting."

"Bring it," he points to the trailer to show where. Then he shakes the folder at me. "Bring it."

Waving both arms overhead to attract the attention of the gate guards down the road, I signal to raise the bar so Bernard can drive in. When he's parked outside the trailer I rap a tentative knock on the trailer door and step back. I know when I'm not welcome. The officer circles the car, peers inside the door that Bernard graciously holds open in a gesture we've perfected which conveys we have nothing to hide. He retreats to the trailer, letting the aluminum door slam. I shake my head at Bernard. Things don't look good. I now wait in the car, foot again drumming the floorboard, wondering if I can kidnap the German Shepherd and take him with us through Kyrgyzstan, China, Nepal, India, and eventually home.

In too short a time, the officer is back. Holding out the folder, his face cracks in a wry smile as he snaps a salute. "I stamp," he says, issues a desultory wrist flick to the guard at the exit gate, and retreats indoors. We're free.

Checkpoint

KAPIKOY, TURKEY TO IRAN, 2011

I have an extended passport, its extra twenty-six pages already half-filled with visas. Though my nervousness at borders hasn't abated despite so many crossings, the experience is now as much a love relationship as a hate one. From the smarmy officiousness of Bolivian military police at that country's Desaguadero border with Peru, to the polite studiousness, accompanied by tea, of a barely literate Nepalese civil servant at the Friendship Bridge border with China, borders are a perfect microcosm of the remarkable differences between countries. Borders also are the place where my imagined perception of a country meets up with hard reality.

Kapikoy Checkpoint is the newest crossing between Turkey and Iran. Set in a shallow valley beneath modest scrub hills, the entire border post is compact enough to fit in a football field, its surroundings barren enough to discourage anyone moving where they shouldn't. Open only since April 2011, it's an hour and a half by car east of Lake Van on the D300. The Turkish roads are rough, but the going is far worse in Iran, which is probably why Kapikoy sees little traffic. When Bernard and I crossed from Turkey into Iran in our own vehicle, Kapikoy had been checking passports for all of five months.

I was thrilled to be going to Iran, the incarnation of my feeling that the people in a country are not the same as the government. That as sure as policies affect lives, they do not represent them. Paul Theroux's impression, that at a border you may hardly tell one country from the other, was confirmed on the visual end immediately. Both country's facilities are housed in modest trailers so similar it's as if they were ordered from the same catalogue. Cube-shaped huts serve as barracks, the whole encircled by chain-link fence topped with coils of razor wire. Some borders, like Paso Roballos between Chile and Argentina, are separated by kilometers of no-man's-land. Not so Kapikoy, where Iranian and Turkish border guards live in such close proximity they can look in each other's windows.

On the day I cross, it takes me less than thirty minutes to complete Turkey's exit formalities, in which they verify our car is our car, and we each are who our passports say. The formalities for Turkey are so informal the border police sip coffee and barely interrupt their conversation while we're in front of them. Despite such cursory attention, I'm reluctant to move on. Turkey is, after all, nearly Europe. I feel safe there. Even though the Iran entry trailer is only ten yards away it's another world, one in which petty officials make decisions that can provide newspapers with fodder for months. That uncertainty played a big part in my desire to visit the country. Doubt and mystery are powerful emotions, double-edged swords that make me sweat at the same time they heighten vision. It's in those situations that I am most aware that I am no longer at home.

There's more to our interest in Iran than that, though. After several years of road trips, I've been on the lookout for places that most Americans do not want to go to. Usually this means a country whose politics and policies conflict with our own. It also can mean a country where, as Americans, we will be assigned a government minder to stay with us through the whole trip, or where our route will have to be registered beforehand. Both are true of Iran, but that doesn't bother me. I'm hopeful that our minder will be as happy to have Americans to talk to as we will be to have an Iranian to discuss our preconceptions with. I foresee camaraderie and hope for a spirit that understands the letter of the law just enough to sidestep it.

These hopes are in the future, though, and at the moment, when the Turkish border police raises his eyebrow to question why I'm still standing at his window, I start to sweat. Picture me as a bug, my multiple antenna bristling and waving left, right, left, scuttling for shelter while also trying to inspect everything around me. I'm so distracted as I head toward Iran that I trail my headscarf along the new black tarmac. It's the stares of armed guards that remind me my scarf is not where it belongs. Mortified, I swirl the length of fine blue cotton around my back and over my head. In this regard I know what I am doing, having studied online images of Iranian women for appropriate variations on the theme of hair coverings. Mindful that I'll not be given a second chance in the arena of modesty, I cross the scarf ends under my chin and fling them over my shoulders, to help it stay in place. Bernard has no such issues, both because his hair is sparse and because he's a man. He does, however, tote a camera with a bulky wide-angle lens. His ostensible excuse for slinging the camera over his shoulder is that he didn't want to tempt anyone by leaving it in the car while we were in a trailer doing paperwork. I know him like the gray hairs on my head, however, and I know he's done his own clever practicing, to wit, taking photos with the camera at his side as he walks, without needing to bring it to his eye to check framing. As he saunters behind me, I hear the telltale click and hope the next one I hear will not be the click of a rifle safety being released.

Iran's trailer is nicer than any in my ranch town's trailer park. Inside, I approach the glass booth that says PASSPORT CONTROL in English and Farsi. It's empty. I do a loud clearing of the throat, say a cautious hello, peer surreptitiously through windows, but no one appears. So I sit in one of three new plastic chairs and adjust my headscarf. Bernard sits next to me. We wait. Nothing happens. To occupy myself I retrieve my camera and pretend to clean the lens while doing my own unobtrusive snapping of illegal photos of the border facilities.

A man dressed in dark trousers and a white shirt comes out of the room across from me. Though there's no badge declaring BORDER OFFICIAL, the way he says "Passports, documents" conveys he's the one to reckon with. This is the moment of truth, the reason I went through all the steps of getting a visa for Iran on my own. If there's something wrong with that ivory page with its intricate purple and green swirls, which has an unflattering thumbnail-size photo of me embedded behind a hologram in one corner, this is where I'll find out. The little blue booklet I hand over, stamped in gold with United States of America, never seemed so precious as right then. The man nods and disappears back into the office.

The trailer door opens to allow in five Iranian women dressed in skin-tight pants and slinky, thigh-length sweaters. Each wears her brilliantly colored silk scarf Grace Kelly–style: pushed back on the head, knotted under the throat. Toenails are glossily varnished, feet sheathed in fashionable sandals. Hands grasp the handles of bulging shopping bags, the kind made of heavy paper with store names in bright lettering. A border guard enters the glass booth, gives each identity card a cursory glance, and waves them through. They are chic, and I envy their perfect headscarves.

Twenty minutes later a handsome Iranian youth in T-shirt and jeans enters the trailer, introducing himself as our government guide. Ignoring my outstretched hand, he leans forward to knock shoulders. "Ramadan," he says, then murmurs hesitantly, not wanting to offend, "And as a woman, you are impure." He says be patient, there's nothing he can do to speed things up, but everything will be all right.

An hour more and the border control medical officer invites me into a small side room, where he questions me solicitously. Do I have a fever? Have I recently vomited? Headaches? Sore throat? He's polite in a detached doctorly way. Then, "Welcome," he says. "I am pleased to speak with an American." Spirits boosted, I return to my plastic chair, primp my headscarf, and wait.

After forty-five minutes, the man who took my passport beckons me into his office. Being an American woman with a slouchy cotton headscarf sequestered in a room with Iranian men strikes me as having great potential for all sorts of awkwardness. And then there's my self-consciousness. Mindful of the chic beauty of the five Iranian women who crossed before us, I feel I am letting my side down. When he motions to our guide to join, it's a relief; I want someone to witness what happens.

Inside the office are four men sipping tea, rifles nearby. One nods his head, another studies his tea glass, the other two eye me like shy teenagers. It's as if they've heard about the being called "American woman," but now that they have one in front of them they're tongue-tied. There are two desks in the room, each with a PC, papers and folders spread about. The passport officer points to my right hand. I think scary thoughts about fingernails and the loss thereof. Then he places a form in front of me and, digging through a drawer, extracts an ink pad, which he opens and hands to me, as if offering snuff. Then he motions what I should do. When I'm done pressing each fingertip into the ink and onto the paper, he hands me a tissue so I can clean my fingers, looking remorseful that he has been the cause of a woman dirtying her hands.

Another forty-five minutes and the man whom I now know is the senior immigrations officer emerges from that office. In halting English, he apologizes for the delay, explaining that Checkpoint Kapikoy is so new their computer link to Teheran and the software to check visa numbers are not yet the best. For which he is sorry.

I can't help but gaze admiringly at my visa, which he shows me has been stamped for entry. When a guard walks over and motions where we should bring our luggage for inspection, the senior officer waves him away. Perhaps he feels things have taken long enough. He points to the exit door. As I walk through into Iran, my headscarf stays in place.

River Boundaries

We bump at 15 mph along the stony road, a brown cliff rising steeply to our left, the great roiling mass of the Panj River flowing to our right. The Panj starts in the high Pamirs, where we are heading, and then flows southwest to join the even mightier Amu Darya, the biggest river in Central Asia. Right now its turbulent slate-gray waters move in the opposite direction from us, and far more swiftly than we can. We are in the Gorno-Badakhshan Autonomous Region of Tajikistan, perhaps fifty yards from Afghanistan, which claims the other bank of the Panj, but I've never been able to launching anything, stone or otherwise, further than twenty feet. When it comes to borders, the Tajikistanis lucked out. On their side of the Panj, the river has deposited sufficient cobbles and gravel for a broad bank to develop. It's enough to hold a road on which two cars can pass in opposing directions, for villages to have space for orchards and fields, for the slopes beyond to be modest in height and gentle in slope. Not so Afghanistan. On their side, cliffs drop straight to the water, and space for villages is scraped from the rubble of landslides regularly deposited at the base of cascade-filled gullies, through which is incised a path often no broader than one donkey.

Hour after hour, for hundreds of kilometers, while Bernard maneuvers our Land Rover along the torturous road, I watch that marvel of a path etched into the brown rocky hills on the Afghan side. Wide enough for two people to walk abreast, for a donkey to carry a reasonable load, in some sections even for a motorbike to proceed with caution, it connects isolated sunburnt, mud hamlets, now green with tall corn, broad fanning trees, and bright fields. I see flat roofs piled high with hay for the winter. A small herd of black and mahogany cows tentatively negotiate the steep gray sand bank for a drink. Even here satellite dishes polka-dot the village scape.

The track brooks no obstacle. It runs at roughly the same line of contour regardless of whether it is a pearl-gray path or an acrobat's delight carved into the side of a russet cliff. A gap over a small cascade is spanned by a short stretch of wood plank bridge. In some steep sections where the rock prohibited engraving a flat path, steps are carved, dry laid with rocks, or patched together with branches.

We have driven east, far in land from Dushanbe. When our road first joins the Tajikistani side of the river, the track is there. We stop across the river from an Afghan patrol post, a small building marked by their black, green, and red national flag. In this place where nothing happens, they notice us immediately. "Hallooooo," we hear. We halloooo in exchange, and wave both arms. A figure holding aloft a rifle waves its stick arms back.

Before leaving the US for this latest drive we secured a visa to enter Afghanistan, planning to cross on foot at the Ishkashim border post. In 2011, the war had been going for a decade, the Taliban had wrought all kinds of destruction on society, monuments, and the economy, and Bin Laden had just been killed by a crack Navy SEAL team in May of that year. There was every reason to believe our application would be viewed with suspicion. Even though we were going to a part of Afghanistan where I didn't expect roadblocks or bullets whizzing by my headscarf, I still expected we'd be asked to prove we had relevant business there, such as journalism or fighting. But no one cared. We just filled in a form, which compared favorably to that from other countries that were not at war, asking for name, address, places we'd visit, personal bank account. Actually, that last one wasn't asked for, but all the rest was, same as any other country fond of knowing who was coming in and why.

Although the south of the country was still riddled with IED explosions and suicide attacks, the Wakhan Valley where we planned to go, a tiny peninsula sticking like an aneurism out of the country's far north, was an enclave of peace populated by Ismaili Muslims. The Ismaili are an offshoot of Shia, which along with Sunni forms the two main branches of Islam. But the Ismaili are unusual in that they follow their own private Imam, the Aga Khan; they're considered quite benevolent and are less hyper-critical than their brethren. I did not hold it against the Aga Khan himself for choosing to reside in France. He was more of an improvements-on-the-ground leader, with a foundation making community improvements, like the guest house we'd slept in two nights earlier, a place that had given jobs to quite a few nearby villagers.

As we continue our drive, so the track continues without a break. It is there when a full ivory moon rises over the village of Kalaikhum, where we eat a plate of cucumber salad and roast chicken at a restaurant above an icy tributary that in any other place would be a major river, but here is a mere thread to the sinuous rope of the Panj. That night we sleep at a simple but clean hostel built for travelers by the Aga Khan Foundation. The track is a constant, there in the morning when we depart, alongside me as we drive. For five hundred kilometers it is as unfailing as a new lover, as steadfast as a diamond jubilee husband. Before dark the next day we reach our second night's stop in Khorog, a lovely inn with grape vines, terraced lawns, and duvets on the bed, where I fall into a restless, enervated sleep as the river flows relentlessly outside my window. And it's there in the morning, as we head sixty miles south to Ishkashim, the border between Tajikistan and Afghanistan.

I notice two men ambling the track in white trousers and shirts, with black vests and caps. One is turned toward the other, perhaps engrossed in conversation, as they move with ground-eating strides. That afternoon I see a small group of boys in black pants and white shirts, some with backpacks. They remind me of schoolboys everywhere, moving at the dawdling pace that indicates they're on their way from school, with important things to hash out before reaching home. A couple of women in black with bright headscarfs linger over each step; they must relish the privacy the path can offer. If the racket our Land Rover makes managing the rocks, potholes, and jagged bits of old pavement weren't so infernal, I'm sure the lilt of laughter would waft across the river, no visa needed.

Through it all, the Panj accepts the tributary devotions of countless lesser, unnamed rivers, their water a pure glacial green that disdains mixing with the Panj's heavily silted gray brown. This mighty river convulses with mammoth rapids, that can only hint at the monstrous boulders that must lie on its bed. Over the ages, they have tumbled from peaks that rise 7,800 sheer feet in front of us, a sere range tinged brown, yellow, and ashen, impossibly barren and convoluted, to an altitude where snow hasn't melted. The river is alive. It bunches and flexes, stretches and coils, like the veins and muscles of a well-oiled Mr. Universe. It proceeds thus for fifteen hundred miles from its birth in the High Pamirs of Tajikistan, and what we have been privileged to see thus far is but a sliver of the whole.

For us it is a glorious two days on what must surely be the most remarkable road in one of the most extraordinary places we have ever been. The river's movement seems to transport us through the centuries, to give breath to the ancient stones around us. We are captivated by a sense that time has stood still here while at the same time being yanked writhing straight out of the river's depths into the twenty-first century. And the mighty Panj flowing onward out my window reminds me that not all borders are gated and stationary. Some flow, though they are not fluid.

We continue onward into the High Pamirs, along the Pamir Highway, where the rivers are sapphire and emerald with rapids of white frosting, spanned only occasionally by a pedestrian bridge made of slats wired together and secured on either end by rocks and old cables. In the not-so-far distance, twenty-thousand-foot peaks are crowned with the first deep snow of a coming winter.

When we pull off the road where two trucks are parked, I give a sidelong inspection to a local war dog, so named because they guard the herds and fight off wolves, and also are set to fighting each other. This one is a massive mastiff, his black-tipped beige coat matted, his leonine black head ignoring me, though I can see immediately that one side is caked with old blood and the eye on that side is winking shut. We head into the White Fish Café, intent on their one eponymous dish: small white fish, sautéed so crisp we can tear each six-inch fish apart with our fingers and crunch into it, swallowing delicate bones and sweet flesh. Three tureens of yak yogurt topped with a skiff of orange butter fat are curing on the stove in the low-ceilinged room where we sit on the floor on red woven carpets. A big bowl of yogurt is brought for us, along with a china pot of tea. The yak yogurt is sumptuously rich and, when plied with sugar, makes an excellent dessert. However, the cushions around us smell of too many stinky feet and sweaty bottoms—or vice versa—so we do not linger longer than it takes to devour four fish, a flat round of local focaccia-like bread, and many spoonfuls from the yogurt bowl.

That night we reach a homestay on Karakul, Tajikistan's largest lake, a deep blue splash on an endless flat brown plain at thirteen thousand feet. I'd asked about a place to stay while we were filling the Land Rover tank with diesel from a jerry can after lunch. When the jerry can owner indicated a grimy hovel behind him as our proposed lodging, I pointed to my watch to explain it was too early for us to stop. Through gestures—pointing out where we were on the map and searching for the place names he mentioned—I helped him pinpoint for me that the next guest house was on Karakul's eastern shore, about three hours drives ahead. I then handed him a pen to write the name down, not at all sure this would result in anything but him pocketing the pen to sell later. Having a place name written by a local has helped us find where we're going on many of our trips, though it doesn't always work, as not all locals can write. This time fortune is with me, as he hands back my notepad with a little drawing including dots to denote a village, and X to denote that the guesthouse is next to the road on the village edge, and mountains to denote mountains (this last unhelpful since we're in the Pamirs, with mountains everywhere).

The map is a charm, with the guest house exactly where the X among the dots suggests. When we pull in, the mountains beyond are curtained in heavy clouds. Our well-equipped car is a sure sign that we are travelers and the mistress of the house steps outside to welcome us, ushering us out of the chill air into the entrance/kitchen/living room of her home. It's wonderfully warm inside where we remove our shoes so we can slouch on cushions and carpets strewn around the raised platform across from the stove. Our host brings us small bowls with handmade steamed noodle dumplings filled with potatoes. We tear chunks of bread and dip it in the local honey and a surprise bowl of strawberry jam. We drink more black tea. It is bitter and hot.

Meanwhile our hosts set to heating their new shower cubicle, a six-by-eight concrete hut with a dung-burning stove above which is welded a ten-gallon tank with a spigot. Two hours later our host beckons me with a small wave of his hand. I follow him out into the cold, eager and uncertain, taking the towel he hands me as we walk on pebbled dirt through the deepening blue dusk. With shy courtesy he opens a creaking metal door, pulls a chain to illuminate one bulb, and salaams goodbye.

The stove has heated the room and it's a delight to strip down, fill a small pot with scalding water, splash some cold water from a bucket into it to perfect the temperature, and pour the resulting mix down my front and over my back. Every once in a while, I splash water onto the stove, which releases a burst of steam. It's a bath, shower, sauna, and steam room all in one. A generator keeps the bulb bright till 8:00 p.m., after which it's literally lights out. We sleep on piles of futons on the floor with flowered quilts thrown over us, in a room with quilts on the walls and ceiling. It's like bedding down inside a flamboyant, flowery bubble. I dream of rippling rivers and ribbons of road carving through rumpled peaks which scrape a sky so vast and blue it can conjoin divided countries.

Missed It

GAURIGANJ, NEPAL TO INDIA, 2012

What if you knew a border was there somewhere, but couldn't find it? I'm not talking about terrifying mistakes, like those made by hikers along Iran's border some years ago. I'm referring to an ordinary border between friendly countries . . . of which you are not a citizen. A border where everyone but you can pass so freely that there are no longer signs saying STOP HERE, or CUSTOMS, or TURN BACK, no outposts with razor wire-topped gates like Iran and Afghanistan, no Kyrgyz officials dressed like the local shepherds they are, idly smoking next to the meek fire of a charcoal brazier, no armed guards as in China. I wish I couldn't answer that question, but I can.

My education began on a sunny early October day in southeastern Nepal. To our crash course in border mistakes I brought an overweening desire to make progress, a smattering of carelessness, and considerable hubris stemming from eight thousand miles of driving during which we'd successfully entered and exited ten other countries far less friendly than these two. Hell, we were border connoisseurs. If we knew anything at all we knew that this border would be a quickie, an in-'n'-out of the simplest order.

Looking back, I can pick out the hints that I should have attended to. There was the hut on an otherwise building-free corner, with three soldiers relaxing on chairs in front of it. Each had a rifle across his lap. As we drove by I noticed one had a two-way radio hooked to his thick black leather belt. The street crowds skirted the group, their body language broadcasting, "I have no business with you and you none with me, so let's ignore each other," the universal idiom of those who want to remain invisible to officialdom. I didn't digest what I'd seen; I didn't even chew it over. I wiped my hands of it and tossed it out my open window, more intent on helping Bernard avoid grazing a pedestrian than pondering what I'd just noticed.

Next, there was the cluster of low gray buildings with a scrappy lawn bordered by thick-leaved plants bursting with juicy red and yellow blossoms. On a stretch of road monotone in its beige dust and dirt, this very greenness and trimness spoke of a gardener hired especially to prune and water the shrubbery. Such sprinkling and snipping were a luxury no ordinary citizen could afford. And then there were those two men in sandals, slacks, and button-up shirts without rips, talking on their cell phones. As we drove by, the chubby, balding one slammed his open palm hard on our car's hood, making a loud bang.

"Speed up," I shouted to Bernard, afraid we were being accosted by street bandits. My analysis made sense to me. I knew we were somewhere near a border. I also knew from enough border crossings to fill the twenty-six pages in my original passport and require twenty-six more, half of which were already used, that people always have stealable items on them in such places. They have extra cash, are returning home with purchases, or are carrying special items to sell. Borders are a prime area for petty theft and I had no desire to swell an already-bloated crime statistic.

We scooted away from the two hooligans. When they ran after us as fast as their sloppy thongs would allow, I knew we'd made the right decision to escape while we could. A slow five minutes later, during which we dodged stop-start vehicles picking up walkers and dropping off riders, the thugs reappeared, this time on a motor scooter. The thin one was driving, the chubby one inveighing into his cellphone. His face was flushed, his mouth gaping and puckering like a gasping fish as he ranted about something to someone. "Probably calling in thuggish reinforcement," I said to Bernard, pointing out the impending perpetrators. Darting close enough to touch our car, the chubby one banged on the Land Rover's rear door. It made no sense. Why would ruffians, even inexperienced ruffians, make their dire intentions so clearly known?

Now they were shouting at the pedestrians to clear the way. They pulled alongside, the chubby one pounding on my door as I hurriedly rolled up my window. From behind the glass I could see him mouthing something at me. I was the bad monkey in a cage, he was the kid outside making faces. I refused to look at him, staring straight ahead instead, cringing, expecting him to grab the door handle and be hauled forward with us. If he did, we'd only be able to shake him by hurting him. Escape was one thing, damaging a body, chubby or otherwise, quite another. I had no stomach for the latter.

While Bernard wove the Land Rover through cars, cyclists, and walkers as fast as he could without crushing anyone, I twisted in my seat to make sure we'd lost them. As I turned around, I caught a large billboard out of the corner of my eye. It said INDIA. "How interesting," I thought to myself as I sighed with relief that the scooter-riding goons were no longer in view. "India's advertising for itself in Nepal." On the narrow pavement, the traffic going our way was clotted with pedestrians. In the opposite direction was a long line of cargo trucks at a standstill, engines idling, drivers out of the cabs spitting paan and sipping Dixie cups of chai. "How odd," I thought to myself again. "Those trucks should be moving since they're already clear of the border."

Just as I began computing the math that added one INDIA billboard to miles-worth of stationary trucks, the scooter reappeared. This time chubster and his slender sidekick were not to be denied. They zoomed around us and braked to a halt broadside in front, blocking our way. For a second I entertained the notion that these thieves were inordinately brazen to hold us up not only in broad daylight, but with hundreds of people around. But when the fat one stuck his arm through Bernard's still-open window and tried to muscle out the car keys from the ignition, I knew something else was up.

His face was livid. Soon Bernard's was, too, as he batted and punched the man's arm away, shoving it forcefully back outside. The two of them grappled with each other, grabbing at biceps, pinching at shirt sleeves, slapping away hands, neither going the next step of making a face assault, but not backing down either. "Get away," I screamed. "Leave us. You cannot have our keys!" I reached across Bernard for the window handle and began rolling it up till the short man outside could no longer reach in. Bernard finished the job.

Relegated to the exterior, the two men commenced slamming fists on the doors and hood, screaming in fury while at the same time jabbing numbers into their cell phones. We sat inside, watching pedestrians come to a standstill and then move slowly forward in politely distracted fashion, staring somberly at the shouting men and avoiding eye contact with the two of us imprisoned in our car. Their grim faces conveyed that we were in deep trouble. I remembered the advice of the friendly bystander in Orchha some years earlier, who had circumspectly alluded to what would happen to a driver who'd crashed into our car if we allowed the police to take him to their station. So I knew what was crossing the mind of every one of those wary and watchful bystanders . . . that were it they in the vehicle and not we foreigners, broken limbs and smashed skulls would be the order of the day. There were looks of hope and of horror on those faces. They understood something I was still denying: that we had run the Nepal border and were illegally in India.

My heart leaped and collided with my brain when Bernard said, "I have to get out."

"No Bernard, don't!" I pleaded. More and more men were edging ever closer to the car, roiled by the imminent possibility of someone being sent to jail or perhaps beaten right there. A vision of Bernard disappearing, pulled to the ground within their slowly agitating midst, flashed inside my eyes.

"Here, keep these," and he handed me the heavy bunch of Land Rover keys, which I put in my purse, figuring that was a place as close to my body as possible without being part of my skin, and therefore protected from being grabbed or pulled away. Unless things got really bad.

Bernard smiled out his window and pushed open his car door. As he did so the crowd gave way in a long rippling sigh. He walked over to the chubby man who stood on my side of the car and leaned in, making it obvious he was happy to chat. The man shoved him forcefully back, waving and shouting into his phone all the while. Truck drivers, foot travelers, villagers heading to market, all stopped their journey to enjoy the new local diversion: us. I sat in the car, windows closed, doors locked, rigid with nervous anxiety. The sun beat down on the roof, raising the temperature in the sealed interior until sweat dripped down my spine and dampened the back of my thighs.

When the chubby man finished spewing his outrage into his phone he rounded on Bernard with fury, thrusting his face close, his anger raising him on tiptoes as he pointed to us, our car, his motorbike, and shouted, spittle flying, "Passports! PASSPORTS!" If letting him take the car keys was anathema to us, giving over our passports to the man so recently believed a thief was even more so. Bernard shook his head. The man jabbed his phone for another call, appearing to be as flustered by Bernard's refusal as by his own apparent lack of English. Deciding that if Bernard were going to jail, I would go with him, I got out of the car, too. The crowd exhaled a gasping *ohhhh* when I emerged. For a second I thrilled at being the extra spice in this roadside drama.

A small blue sedan arrived from the direction we'd come and three men in pressed shirts and creased trousers got out. The others immediately relaxed, relieved to give responsibility for us and our transgression to these more senior officials. They huddled together briefly and then a slender man with lank black hair detached himself from the cluster. "Sir," he said, his voice polite but tinged with irritation, "Do you know where you are?"

Bernard knew the answer to that one. "Nepal."

"No, sir. You are in India."

"India? But we haven't crossed the border yet." I hid my eyes, not wanting to give away what I'd seen.

"Indeed you have, sir. And why is that? Why did you not stop when this gentleman here signaled you to? Why did you ignore him when he tried to stop you?" His pitch rose to strident.

Bernard looked at me. I am the trip navigator. It is my responsibility to notice things like country borders and deal with them. My shame and the implications of my *faux pas* kept me tongue-tied. I lied by shrugging my shoulders in commiseration, too embarrassed to admit my mistake, too frightened to say a word.

"You will come with us now."

We looked at the crowd crushing into the car. "We can't leave the car," Bernard said.

"Of course not, sir," said the official, showing a reasonable side that gave me a moment of relief. "My guard will ride with you. Madam will ride with us."

That they were separating us did not bode well. I rely on Bernard's sense of propriety in these situations, on his calm assertions that all will be well, especially if I would stop my dithering. When things leap beyond my control in a foreign country I become alarmed, which leads to me being judgmental and acting inappropriately. He relaxes into the adventure. His willingness to treat everyone as an interesting friend is what got us out of the bribe-influenced clutches of Siberian police. I wanted to be nowhere but by his side. My desires were not to be consulted, as the official was already holding open the passenger door of his sedan and a guard was adjusting his rifle to climb into the passenger seat of the Land Rover. We entered our respective vehicles. The crowd raised a collective moan as our doors shut.

We drove back several miles toward Nepal. When we pulled down that drive bounded by lawn and flowers I couldn't help turning to the official and telling him, "So *this* is where the Indian border entry offices are. Why aren't there signs for it?" I played all innocent and troubled by our mistake, setting the scene for us to be viewed as hapless travelers. He was having none of it.

"Madam, if you had paid attention to the indications of my assistant," and he pointed to the chubby man perspiring happily in the back seat, "We would not now have this trouble." Every time he referred to our troubles it was like an electric shock zinging through my body, a reminder that while he seemed diplomatic he had a duty to fulfill. I had no idea what sort of punishment border running entailed. This could wind up being the delay to end all delays.

Outside the border control building we moved into parade formation, the senior official in the role of drum major, Bernard and I in the middle smile-and-wave positions, chubby motorbike flunky and armed guards bringing up the rear. "No one's handcuffed us yet," I whispered to Bernard. "That must be a good sign." Lowly civil servants sat at battered desks, drowning amongst high, untidy stacks of forms. They looked up and then abashedly ducked their heads as we walked by. Down one dim gray hall we marched, hard right down another, passing open doorways through which I could see crowded desks, too many people in too small a space for the desultory ceiling fans to keep cool. A sweet-sour mix of ink, old sweat, and humid paper was heavy in the air.

The Indian official ushered us into his office. Only the chubby man was allowed to remain, while a chair-wallah was sent to bring us seats from a neighboring bureau. "So," our officer turned interrogator began, when we were all seated. "You understand that you have left Nepal without following formalities. And that you entered India without permission." We nodded. "This is a serious matter." We nodded again. "Passports please." We handed them over.

He thumbed through them in leisurely fashion, seeming more inter-ested in visas for Afghanistan, Iran, Turkmenistan, China, and others, than in inspecting our entry stamp for Nepal and our lack of entry stamp for India. "In India we do not take this offense lightly."

"But everyone was crossing without stopping," Bernard said, with utmost politeness. "We thought we were supposed to do the same."

"Ah. Well, what you saw is correct. For Nepali citizens. And Indian citizens. Because our two countries have such an agreement. I believe you are neither," he finished, tapping our US passports on his desk like a pack of cards. Now I understood the persistent stream of foot traffic. It was open borders between the two neighbors, easing trade barriers and improving border relations—and shopping opportunities—for those who lived nearby.

"That is wonderful! It's nice to be good neighbors," I exclaimed with honest enthusiasm, as if chatting with the president of a home owner's association. I rolled my eyes to express just how tiresome border formalities could be, then quickly blinked as I realized now was not the time to disparage formalities of any sort.

"And you have a car," the official continued. "Your car is from . . .?"

"UK," said Bernard, aware that he was instantly complicating matters further. For what would two American citizens be doing with a British-registered car? It was all highly suspicious.

To buy time, or prolong his afternoon's enjoyment, the officer summoned a boy who'd been idling in the dark hallway. "Chai?" he asked us.

"Absolutely," we answered together. I took this as my secret silver lining, since not once in all our times in India has Bernard ever drunk the local tea. He hates it. Sipping tea together seemed to bode well. Once you've extended hospitality as a host, or partaken of local hospitality as a guest, the rules change, as in my book it then becomes impolite to impose harsh sanctions. And Indians are very polite people.

Perhaps sensing the anxiety that was seething below my twitching exterior, the officer turned to me. "Madam, to relax please," he said to me in a kindly tone. "It is all right. You are here now. We will discuss the matter." I took this to mean that jail might not be in the offing after all. But we had run the border. Surely we would be made to pay, in one way or another.

He turned to Bernard who, as the male, was worthier of his questioning. "Now, tell me why you are driving this car and where you are going." Bernard launched into how we'd started forty days earlier in Istanbul, crossing ten countries before arriving in Nepal. That we had only a few days more to drive before reaching our terminus in Kolkata. That we were not only capable of proper border etiquette, but diligently observant about following it.

The officer became expansive as we waited for the chai-wallah to return with tea. We were the best thing that had happened to him in a long time. We told him about journeys we'd taken in the Land Rover, which led him to digress from the travels to discuss the manly subject of car mechanics with Bernard. The boy returned with a tin tray bearing four small glasses, serving the officer first, us second, chubby man last. The officer was fascinated by it all, pursing his lips, nodding, sipping loudly from his shot glass of sweet milky black tea. We followed suit, alternately slurping and talking, relieved to have found a point of common interest other than that we were scofflaws.

"You must agree, sir, madam," he said, nodding apologetically to each of us in turn, "we have a problem. But what to do?" I waited for some sign of the size bribe he would accept, a discretely scrawled number, an insertion of hand in pocket. His hands stayed still. Everyone waited. He spread his arms wide on the table, seemed to take a decision, and said, "We must look in the Land Rover."

"Oh my god," I hissed to Bernard as he led us back down the hallway. "He's going to make us empty the car. That's the punishment. He has all day, we don't, and he knows it."

"Shhh!" Bernard hissed back. "I think he's looking for a way to save face." I did not believe Bernard. There was an opening here if only we could see it, something that would enable us to dodge the oncoming train wreck of unpacking the Land Rover and enable us to get back on our way. I could think only bad things. One calamity was that while the officer plied us with tea and questions, his minions had stashed drugs in the car, which they would now discover. Another was that he would order the car not only emptied, but dismantled, which would take a day at least. I couldn't even imagine how long it would take to put back together, let alone if it even could be.

We gathered around the car, more guards and minor border officials emerging from offices to join the viewing party. They were all attired in the manner of the minor functionary, loose-fitting shirts ragged around collar and cuffs, slacks that were too long and scuffed around the edges, sandals. The senior man took up his post behind the car, gestured to Bernard to unlock the back door, stood with his hands clasped behind his back. Not for him to sully his fingers picking through our goods. A soldier heaved Bernard's big green duffel out and set it on the ground. My blue one joined it. Boxes with tools, cookstove, and spares, our nylon collapsible chairs and a jaunty tri-color umbrella still in its protective plastic sheath, followed. I prayed my duffel would escape their notice. If they were to unzip it they would find several days of dirty laundry, including lingerie, plainly visible on top.

But the officer wasn't interested in our personal items. He wanted to see car parts. Bernard opened the main tool box filled with orderly rows of shining wrenches, sprocket fittings, and screw drivers. The functionaries leaned in as one, eager to see the miraculous repair kit, so many tools owned by one man who wasn't even a garage mechanic. Now it was the cookstove's turn. Bernard demonstrated how to light it, we held the little coffee pot aloft, I opened the jar containing powdered coffee, holding it out for any who wanted to sniff. Realizing there was a packet of cookies in the stores, I opened it and offered it to the officer. After he happily took two I gave the packet to the man next to him, gesturing for him to help himself and pass it around.

Next the officer stalked to the front and had Bernard open the hood. Bernard adores engines and is always willing to explain what he knows. He began pointing out the location of various engine essentials to the officer, who nodded and pointed and stroked his chin. "Very good car," he said. "Very good!" It appeared to please him that the vehicle he'd captured was in such excellent shape, as if it were a credit to him and his position that such a fine car was now in his clutches. He walked back around the car, peering through the windows at Bernard's camera cases and our jackets on the rear seat, noting the mammoth pink bottle of Indian shampoo I'd stuck in the netting behind. Bernard was now fully in the spirit of displaying the car, so he unlocked the side door and revealed the mini-fridge inside. I took out a half-empty bottle of mango juice, that morning's refreshment, and passed it around. No one dared drink, but everyone smiled to feel the cold bottle in their hands.

After an hour of this show and tell the officer looked around. He, too, seemed at a loss for what to do next. After some reflection he called over the guards and spoke to them briefly. Then they left his side and headed for us. "This is it," I thought. "I wonder if my sister will fly over to get me out of jail. So I can then get Bernard out of jail."

"My guards will escort you to the Nepal border station. I will give them a document with my stamp, explaining that while it looks as though you are coming in, you have actually already come in. That you went out even though you didn't mean to go out and now you are back and should be allowed in. Again."

"But can't we cross here? Now? We're right here." I said, at risk of being annoying by pointing out the obvious. "And with the proper paperwork, there wouldn't be any problems, would there?"

The officer looked at me as though I had lost my mind. "Madam, we cannot let you cross here. This border is only for locals. Only. For. Locals," enunciating as if speaking to a three-year-old. Bernard and I stared at each other in shock, trying to comprehend how we'd managed to skip a border that we technically couldn't have crossed. "You will have to go back to the main road and from there to Mechinagar. I am sorry for this. It is the only way."

Sorry? At that moment, though sentenced to a one-hundred-fifty-kilometer detour that would take four hours, I could have hugged the man anyway. But I hid my enthusiasm, not wanting to unmask him as lenient on criminals. Instead I shook his hand and thanked him politely for his understanding, noting we appreciated his assistance in getting us back on the right road. Bernard walked back inside with him to get our laissez passé, two men, heads together, hands explaining, talking cars.

HERE AND GONE

PREAMBLE

Is travel as I perceive it impossible to capture anymore? Has it become something we long for, accomplished by others who were lucky enough, intrepid enough, or foolish enough to get out in the world while there was still newness to brave? It's easy to make a case for this, because after all everything's been discovered. It takes no imagination whatsoever to understand that wherever you are nowadays, someone has been there before you, done it before you, seen it before you. So here's the question: If there's nothing left that's new, then why bother going at all?

I have a lot of time to think about such things, because so much of the travel I do is, well, pleasant. Unsatisfyingly so. For days, nothing sparks my curiosity. Worst of all there's no Hogwartsian transfer of me from my placid passenger-seat existence through that invisible veil to the infinitely charismatic, magical other side that I *know* is there.

It's odd then how, just when I have reached the fullness of despair, when my mutterings alternate between, "How did I get myself into this again?" and "I swear this is the absolutely final time I will ever get in a car for a long road trip," layered with imprecations of "Would someone please just shoot me now," the wand is waved. I'm not talking about major drama, like a march of ten thousand Muslim schoolchildren in Hyderabad, or a landslide blocking our road in Bolivia, though those have happened to me, too. What occurs is more subtle, as if I'm slowly waking from a soft Valium-induced sleep. (And, yes, I know exactly what that feels like because a doctor prescribed Valium for me after some surgery, and I'm nothing if not a good patient when it comes to doctor's orders.)

When that magic moment turns its sweet face to me, I am usually fidgeting in the passenger seat, scenery out of focus, mind sedated by the miles, perhaps trying to alleviate the numbness that has beset my buttocks, when there it is—a dirt side road in Myanmar for example, nondescript in every way . . . Except that there are three school children walking down it, the tallest shepherding two smaller ones who dally and then tumble forward to catch up, like barn kittens out for their first exploration. Where are they going? And why now?

Of course I could make up an answer and that'd be that. But what bewitches me is that here, now, there's a voice shouting, "Follow them!" And suddenly nothing is more important to me than finding out where this moment in their life may lead them, me tagging along behind. In terms of travel lessons learned over many mundane miles, here is one thing I know: If I can find the question, then I have an opportunity to discover, if not the specific answer, then something. And that something could be anything. I'm not talking major discoveries like John Hanning Speke's "Ah-ha!" moment as he got his feet wet at the source of the Nile. I'm talking about a chance to lift the corner of that veil and step through to the other side, to be *in* the life around me rather than watching it go by.

"Stop," I yell to Bernard. Although I'm the navigator, he will hesitate. I know this man like I know the pores on my nose and like those pores there are things about him that will never change. For example, he is hard-wired to move forward, so when I tell him to stop I have to project rational firmness of the sort implying he disobeys me at his peril. Firmness that I would use if, say, I saw a piano falling toward him from the tenth floor and told him to move. And rationality that is benign and simple to comprehend, yet unarguable, such as, "It'll be good to stretch our legs," which is the truth if not the whole truth.

A quick U-turn and we're scuffing the dust as we wander behind those kids, looking into front yards, wondering what the job of that skinny horse might be and why he isn't out doing it. The kids make a right turn and we hesitate, looking left instead, and realize we're in front of a monastery, its yard weedy and derelict, a wood ladder with broad rungs leading to the raised living area. And now a monk appears at the top of the ladder, beaming in that warm, accepting way monks have, which makes me feel I am the only person of merit in the whole world, that he's been waiting all this time just for me, that the infinite rightness of my presence is a granting of what surely was the monk's most fervent prayer.

"Come up," he gestures. "I will make you tea." His quarters are cavernous, easily holding two hundred cross-legged devotees, its teak floor exhaling musk, vanilla, and smoke. It's airy in the monk's cavern, though at present filled with little but peace and a small stove. And some jars stuffed with pale dried plants. "I am a medicine man," he explains, before I've even stared at the jars. "The villagers. Anything they have, I help them." A wizened woman brings us a tea tray. "A servant," is my thought, followed by, "a monk would not have a servant," neither of which do I let pass my lips as actual statements. As it happens, this monk is in tune with my thought waves. When the woman kneels to place the tray on a low table between us he says, "This is my mother," and "there is my sister."

A notion that I am in the presence of true support and selfless gratitude flits through my mind. Has each woman sacrificed her personal pursuits, devoting her life to the well-being of the blessed son and brother? At this moment I definitely want to know the answer. But how to pose the question in a way that disguises my blatant curiosity under the cloak of appropriately friendly interest? I wrestle silently with my inner boor patrol. Boorishness is something I've been sensitive to ever since our first trip to India, when my drip-dry clothes and sturdy American limbs made me feel like Shrek in the valley of the Barbie dolls. The patrol warns me to keep my mouth shut on pain of being drenched in embarrassment.

I sip monk tea, or monk's mother's tea, a mildly tannic, slightly bitter brew. I hesitate to take the offered sugar, which I know has cost them precious *kyat* (Myanmar currency). And I feel, as I always do in these situations, mildly distraught that I have nothing with me to share with our host. I review all parts of my body, hoping for some ache or ailment to assert itself so I can with honesty ask the medicine monk for advice and possibly pay him for a fusty plant or two. But I'm fine, really, and I can't lie to this gentleman who has so genially taken us into his home, his bedroom, his prayer area, his meeting hall, because I realized from the subtle, head swiveling snoop I did on entering, that this one room is all those things.

Dust motes float in a shaft of sunlight. The mother busies herself with a broom in a far corner and the sister's slippers whisper across the floor as she brings us a small packet of cashew biscuits. Leaves rustle under the house. A warm puff of breeze brings the sweet oily scent of the morning's fried doughnuts, the standard Myanmar village breakfast. My breathing slows until I barely want to stir myself to drain the little puddle of cool tea now left in my small porcelain cup.

And there you have it, the reason I travel as I do: So that I can whirl with chance, my senses wider open than they were a moment ago. Some will say that the purpose of travel is to be in an exotic setting, defying risk, thrilling to the extraordinary. I understand that for many travelers, the fundamental rationale for travel is precisely that next high. But the problem with always seeking a high is that what satiates one time will not be sufficient the next time. Shock and drama are stimuli and the very nature of stimulation is such that the next go-round requires more in order to get the same reaction. If you're a shock and drama traveler, you'll always want to surpass what you got last time: more peril, more of the bizarre and alien.

For me it's never been about that high, because fundamentally I am a person who is unhappy with anything remotely cliffhanging in nature. In those *Road Runner* cartoons I watched as a child, if Wile E. Coyote were hanging by his claw-tips from the edge of a cliff, I rooted for him *not* to fall. Why do I travel? To live the similarities in the differences. To share in the most commonplace activities with someone whose days are as different from mine as silk is to steel. And in sharing a brief moment of ordinariness together, to participate in the full normalcy of life.

Tailored

KOLKATA, INDIA, 2013

A globule of sweat drops from the soft, pendulous chin of Kurshad Alam. It lands on a bolt of crisp cotton fabric casually splayed open on a glass countertop for me to admire, to crinkle in my hand, to, if Kurshad has his way, have made into a shirt.

Even before it has fully permeated the fabric, leaving a darkened aureole in a sea of checkered pink, I can see another drop ready to depart from Kurshad's left jowl. This one is part of a rivulet with its source somewhere in Kurshad's thinning black hair, which meanders through his wispy black sideburn to join similar trickles coursing down the smooth, dark-as-tobacco-juice skin of his plump cheek. The drop hangs suspended for a moment before splashing with a near-audible plop onto the fabric. I can only imagine the havoc Kurshad would wreak on all this material if he were a Labrador retriever and shook himself.

The heat and humidity of this Kolkata morning are so normal to him that he doesn't even notice the splotches that now rivet my eyes to a color which I otherwise don't much care for. As for me, I stand a respectful distance from the counter, so that my own rivers of sweat will sully nothing but my own clothing. Fingering his back pocket, Kurshad extracts a carefully folded square of pocket handkerchief, of a fine, near-translucent white cotton. He delicately pats it over his face, on his fleshy ears, and his roundly feminine chin.

Sweat drops temporarily solved, Kurshad gently caresses the fabric. "It's beautiful, madam," he says in his soft voice with a slight lisp. He looks down at me from his bulky height, but only briefly, a man so immersed in the pleasures of textile that he is blind to any physical discomfort. A hazy yellow light penetrates the large plate glass shop windows of his narrow shop, casting a mild sheen on the material which now draws his gaze back like a magnet. Outside, cars honk and motorbikes beep in the ceaseless clamor that is Kolkata. Saried ladies glide by on mid-morning errands. Rickshaw-wallahs heave their bodies left and right on stick-thin legs, pedaling heavy loads for delivery. Inside, two old ceiling fans whir quietly, moving the moist air about in a desultory attempt to cool.

Kurshad unfurls more bolts, the better for me to assess their shirt-worthiness. "Look at this one," he says. "Feel it, madam." And he pushes the fabric into my hand as if insisting I take another piece of cake. "This cotton is softer than that one. Lighter. Better for hot weather. You prefer it?" This third-generation haberdasher, who proudly shows me the tintype of his grandfather and father, knows fabric so well it's as second nature to him as breathing.

A young man joins us. "My son, Wasim," says Kurshad. "The fourth generation. He will take over the business from me," he finishes with pride. The relationship between the two is obvious, as Wasim has the same skin harking back to their Parsi (Iranian) origins, the same quiet voice, the same sweating as his father. But where Kurshad's dark eyes now have a bluish tinge of age, Wasim's are still piercingly black. And where Kurshad's head is balding and looks like a vinegar-boiled egg, Wasim is the generation that skips male-pattern-baldness, with a thatch that is glossy, wavy, and thick. His full lips smile at me, nearly purple like his father's. "Madam," he says, pressing my hand softly between his. "A pleasure."

Wasim reviews the counter, now strewn with the conservative cottons I prefer for my travel shirts, along with fine wools for trousers. "Allow me to show you some other whites." He is courtly, earnest in his endeavor to please me. In my opinion, there's no travel day that can't be improved by a white shirt. And since I may travel for two months at a time on far-flung road trips, I have a bottomless need for white shirts. I choose to ignore the obvious inconvenience of white for a pleasure so intense I'm willing to put up with the fact that I may make that shirt instantly unwearable if I take a sip of black currant juice at just when our Land Rover hits a speed bump. As Wasim now heaves bolts of fabric off the shelf, flings them out, sweats, hefts, and flings some more, I realize I have barely scratched the surface of possible textures, weaves, and weights of white cotton.

Kurshad retires to a small scratched desk kept company by three chairs, an oasis of furniture in a store that is just scarred linoleum on the floor and two walls stuffed to the ceiling with bolts of fabric. Squeezing his ponderous body into a modest swivel chair, he slowly leans back, as if testing whether the springs will hold his weight one more time. A gentleman arrives. "My friend," Kurshad gestures to him and to me, glad, apparently, to have us both there. Then he waves his hand mildly in the air. Five minutes later a chai-wallah appears with two small glasses of steaming sweet milk tea for Kurshad and his caller. The two men sucking noisily on their burning tea makes my forehead burst out in sympathetic beads of sweat. Not having a handkerchief, I use my wrist as a mop cloth.

Wasim begins my measurements, slowly wrapping a flexible tape around my neck, next from my shoulder to my armpit, then down my spine. The bust measurement looms. It feels improper to have an Indian man do this. Without batting one of his long-lashed eyelids, around my back go Wasim's hands and over my bust goes the tape. "Thirty-three," he says quietly. "And a half." There. It's done. He circles my waist. "Thirty." Then he goes down to my hips. "Forty." How embarrassing. I seem to have become a pear.

My measurements are nothing to anyone in this shop other than a dimension defining what to cut and where to insert needle and thread. That's what their lives are about—Wasim, Kurshad, and the three runners who dash to and from tiny stitching rooms in the warren of streets nearby, bearing bolts of fabrics, returning with samples for fittings. It's the shirt, the jacket, the trousers, not the body in it. They gaze as fondly at gauzy cottons lying limp and exhausted as they would a recently loved mistress. A fleshy palm fondles rough linens exuding a scratchy coolness, caresses tweedy slate and blue wools, suitable for the cold weather of their British customers, a climate entirely unimaginable to them.

"Come back to tomorrow at eleven," Kurshad says. "This hour is fine for you?"

"Oh, no, no, no. I'll come in the afternoon. No rush for the morning."

He waves away my stuttering objections, in which I strive to give the cutters and stitchers more time to create my garments. Kurshad is quietly insistent. "Yes, yes. Eleven is perfect. You will try everything." He beams me a beatific smile, waggling his head just once to indicate that, since we are now in agreement, he is happy. "And we will have tea."

Red Carpet

I wish I'd dressed for the occasion. But no one mentioned at 7:00 a.m. that morning that I was about to cross paths with the president of Myanmar. And then there was that red carpet luring me onward. What choice did I have? Ignoring the proffered hand of the boy holding our long boat, I stepped carefully onto the splintered dock, removed my sandals, and strode off down that scarlet strip.

Don't let that red carpet mislead you. This was not the Kodak Theatre in LA, not even close. It was mid-March and we were on a skiff ride through floating gardens and delicate waterborne hamlets of teak and bamboo houses posing precariously on stilts above placid shallow blue canals, where house cats gaze out over the water from boat ramps, dreaming of trees and birds, where children as young as four use child-size paddles to help steer the family canoe. Unlike those villages, living examples of how we all would be living had not Noah's flood receded from Ararat, in this particular spot children were running everywhere. If I were them and lived in a watery world, I'd be just as excited to be on a patch of dry land bigger than my five-hundred-square-foot hut.

It was a special event that we stumbled into that morning at Alodaw Pauk Pagoda on Inle Lake. The president of Myanmar was coming. And here I thought they'd rolled out the red carpet for me! Mothers in everyday longyis, women in the traditional burgundy and silver weave of the local Intha tribe, men in short-sleeve white shirts, police in creased olive uniforms, and soldiers in blue camouflage mingled and chatted in small groups. The women carried small paper yellow, green, and red Myanmar flags; sparkling cut-glass hair ornaments held their shining black hair in intricate twists and buns. The soldiers slung AK-47s and the police each had a pistol on their hip. No one had a camera or a cell phone. This was Myanmar, where such items exist only in the hands of the cosmopolitan wealthy.

Once on the red carpet, I gave myself up to wherever it wished to lead me. I knew I couldn't go wrong with that approach. After all, the president would soon be striding the same frayed threads as me. Wending my way through this oldest shrine on the lake I *oohed* at the sparkling gem-encrusted, Shan-style Buddha for which the shrine is famous. And I *aahed* at its neighboring Buddhas, covered in real gold leaf.

The carpet, though, kept distracting me with its scratchy texture and curling edges ready to trip me if I didn't watch my step. It would have been more comfortable—and safer—to walk on the cool white marble tile. After a brief tour of the Buddha and his lesser mates, I settled in the shade of a side-stuppa to await the president's arrival with the locals.

I asked around to find out when the president was due. Not that anyone spoke English. I conveyed my question by pointing at the sky and then pointing at my watch. Everyone had a word or two in answer. "Sometime soon," one said. "In an hour, or a half hour, or by noon," gestured others. Thus enlightened, I shared cookies with the kids, played games with the girls, waited, took photos, waited.

Scattered about the pagoda terrace were several welcome groups, each in their assigned place around the shrine. Men lounged in the shade of nearby pillars, spitting red betel juice from packets of kun-ya stuffed in their cheeks. It was a festive occasion and everyone seemed happy to have the extra time for socializing, until finally, no president in sight, the welcome groups slowly began to disperse, drifting to the teashops on the other side of the pagoda. Eventually I drifted that way, too, and squatted on a low plastic stool along with everyone else. Waiting had raised an appetite and I made quick work of some crunchy, hot potato-stuffed samosas.

Unexpectedly, as if blown by a gust of wind, everyone lifted off their stools and wafted over to a low wall. Yes, the faint sound of a helicopter could be heard. With measured pace, they returned to the arrival area, on the other side of an arched bridge from the heli-pad. To help the presidential chopper land safely, soldiers lit damp piles of brush to create a smoke wind sock. The red carpet sections were given a final dusting with stiff reed brooms, while a man tried to uncurl the carpet edges and made sure they overlapped so as not to trip the presidential feet. Someone carried a tall stack of blue plastic chairs to the shade of a scraggly tree, where they were set up for the assembled dignitaries who would greet the president.

Then fingers pointed to the northwest. There it was, a bulky white helicopter, Russian made, wheels out for landing. All the Intha lined up on one side of the carpet, as a six-person band squatted on a hump of grass and tested their flute, drums, and cymbals. Suddenly, the tribeswomen were separated from the men and instructed to line up on the opposite of the carpet; the double tribal line made for a more impressive sight. Children clutched their mothers' hands, and everyone who'd been sitting on the far side of the pagoda came over to our side, to watch the landing.

The helicopter was closer now, and the band struck up their first tune, shrilling and beating out a welcome. An official noticed an unsightly, half-empty bag of concrete near the red carpet and ordered it hidden behind a wall. Paper flags were given practice waves, grannies raised babies high, white-shirted men took their seats as the helicopter came closer, slowly descending.

And then, and then . . . the helicopter made a lazy circle and flew away. One minute the president's arriving and an entire village has turned out to receive him, the next minute he's changed his mind and left.

In this lovely lake heaven, full of floating green gardens, giant egrets resting on lily pads, and fishing skiffs as delicate as an eyelash on a teardrop, no one seemed at all miffed. The chairs were stacked, the ladies wandered off, heads together, arms around each other's waist, the men spat their red spittle, the dignitaries called for their long boats to return to shore, and flags were collected for another occasion.

It's not every day that a president comes to visit, but I suppose it's happened before that he fails to arrive.

The Tired Deva

KOLKATA, INDIA, 2013

Her feet are strewn with orange marigold blossoms and plastic bags. Shreds of crinkled paper from exploded firecrackers and clay shards from broken oil lamps that long ago burned out lie scattered across the wood stage on which she stands.

Perched on her blue painted podium, Lakshmi seems to have lost her normal calm and loving expression. But then, it's been a long, hard night of revelry so she has every right to look weary. Despite that, her fine red sari still shimmers with gold thread, and her filigreed and enameled gold crown is perfectly upright, fanning around the long, tousled black hair that frames her face and hangs to her waist. A full-length marigold garland draped round her neck is all she has left from the festivities.

In spite of Lakshmi's sleepless night, the golden skin of her plump cheeks still glows and the only shadows under her enormous, wide-set black eyes are ones made by the thick rim of kohl outlining her eyelids. I never looked so good after an all-nighter.

Hip cocked, head slightly tilted, an expression of benign resignation playing across her face, she offers me a lotus held in her hennaed hand, gold and pearl bangles lying still and silent on her wrists. That lotus isn't all she holds. Nestled like a wriggling baby in the crook of her left arm is a bulbous red vessel shaped like a snowman, its fat belly and round head topped by a pointy hat. Legend says it's full of gold, though from the outside it's impossible to tell. Yet Lakshmi betrays no concern that in this destitute part of Kolkata someone might rob her. Perhaps that's because her pet owl sits on a conch shell by her side. In terms of godly rides, he's not as powerful as the elephant or lion that accompany some of her kind, but he can certainly fly her away if she's threatened. That's his job.

If Lakshmi weren't a plaster statue, her bee-stung ruby lips would surely now open in a yawn, stifled by the desultory lifting of a limp wrist. Her kohl-rimmed lids would bat once or twice. "What do you want from me?" she'd ask. "I'm just a goddess. Don't I, too, have a right to rest?"

On this morning after, the street in front of her is filled with locals and Kali devotees. While Lakshmi stands ignored amidst the litter, some early risers—or late revelers—cluster around chai-wallah stands. Others gather under clouds of smoking, spiced oil, which rises from the blackened pans of nearby street food vendors. One such slaps wide disks of potato into a thin batter, then drops the coated slabs into the oil where they sizzle and puff into crispy soft pillows, to be sprinkled with chili powder and salt, wrapped in a square of newspaper, and handed to a hungry customer. Beggars take up their places in front of the gates leading in and out of Kalighat Kali Temple. Two young girls in ragged shorts and T-shirts squat by a communal water tank in the middle of the street. Opening the rusty tap, they wet the bristles of their tooth brushes and commence morning ablutions under the gaze of a thin old man in a white dhoti who sits cross-legged on a nearby stoop, his navel-length white beard carefully combed, one hand clutching, claw-like, the knobbed end of a walking stick.

Last night Lakshmi herself was the focus. Twelve hours ago, the street was filled with the sharp crackling of fireworks, as revelers and worshippers jostled shoulders and jabbed elbows to get close enough to Lakshmi to offer her food and sweets. Under a perfumed shroud of incense, the crowd chanted her 108 names, repeating prayers and singing devotional songs. On that brightest night of the year, under a moon gorged to fullness, in this poorest of poor sections of Kolkata, who wouldn't sing and chant and pray and revel and plead with Lakshmi to descend to earth, to replace a year's-worth of anger and stagnation with optimism and renewed ambition, to take away the darkness of poverty.

But now it's daytime, and Lakshmi does not seem quite up to the monumental task of bestowing prosperity on all. At least not yet. And not in the face of the Black One, the powerful goddess Kali across the street, she of the three eyes, the four arms, the black face, the lolling tongue, the blood-smeared face and breasts.

Daytime is Kali's time and there's a clotted line of pilgrims pressed hip to rump around her temple, eyes trained in blissful concentration, measuring the distance to the temple corner, and from there the door that will admit them into Kali's divine presence. Undeterred by her terrifying form, they consider Kali the kindest and most loving of all Hindu goddesses. To them she's the mother of the whole universe, a great protector, and they are here to lay their personal difficulties at her feet and ask for help. Despite that everyone has a problem so insurmountable they cannot fix it themselves, the mood is festive. Everyone seems relieved that soon enough their burdens will be lifted, or if not lifted, at least soothed by Kali's maternal interest. Lakshmi may have the power to answer prayers for prosperity, which is helpful to some. But others have more complex, or more mundane, problems better suited to Kali's ample heart and capacious powers. Given the long line for Kali, and the empty stage around Lakshmi, it seems Kali's your go-to goddess when faced with one chance to ask for the world and maybe receive it.

So, at least, might be the reasoning of the young woman who sits on a straight-backed chair under the Kalighat Temple sacred banyan tree. Eyes closed, she keeps her head lifted to receive droplets of water sprinkled on her and the baby kicking on her lap. The sprinkling is done by a crone in a faded sari, who rhythmically paces back and forth between the woman and a bucket of water, completing a simple choreography of dip, sprinkle, pray, dip, sprinkle, pray. Most likely the water in the bucket was taken from the street spigot, but now, by virtue of its proximity to the sacred tree, it has a derived ability to bless.

Perhaps the young woman has come in thanks for having her prayer for a baby answered. Or maybe she's here for another go, hoping now for a second child, eager not to tamper with the formula that worked the first time. Perhaps her seat on the chair under the sacred tree has nothing to do with the baby and she's there because her husband's ill or her mother-in-law's too mean, or she's lost her way. The tree and Kali, goddess of infinite knowledge and inner purity, will fix it. For a small fee.

Behind Kalighat Temple, next to the Harkath Tala where bulls and goats are sacrificed, a priest gently hugs a black billy goat to his chest. The small goat has been washed, its coat now moist, its delicate hoofs and softy curling horns patent leather shiny. Strangely, it is neither writhing nor squirming to escape, but instead seems to snuggle deeper into the man's warm, enfolding arms. The remains of a recently nibbled hay meal are on the ground nearby. This is a happy, well-fed goat who is pleased with life. He doesn't know that the good times are about to end.

An incoming tide of devotees surges through a gate, but the goat stays calm, as if hypnotized by the hum of mantras from inside the temple. Soon it will have its throat slit while the devotee who paid for the sacrifice croons his prayers to Kali. Interesting trade, one goat for improvements in one person's life.

Even if Kali ignores the prayers, the goat is not wasted. Its meat will find its way to the temple's charity kitchen. Later, when rice from a vast cauldron is dished into the plastic bags and bowls brought by the homeless, they will also have a spoonful of goat stew to moisten it. For now, those same homeless sit patiently outside the temple, and there are far more cupped hands outstretched than there are hands reaching into a pocket or purse for a spare coin.

Back at Lakshmi's deserted stage, a cur with the fine beige coat and pointy snout that are standard issue among Kolkata's pariah dogs, noses through the detritus at Lakshmi's feet. His jaws snap in excitement as he uncovers a sweet. He rips at the waxy paper, shaking his head to loosen the wrapping. Too hungry, he bolts the bit of pastry, paper and all, then sits on his bony haunches, considering the morsel that will go a small way toward filling his empty stomach. Lakshmi may be tired, but she doesn't play favorites.

Come Back!

PUERTO CISNES, CHILE, 2008

Turning left off the Carretera Austral, we find ourselves driving down a gravel road bound so tightly by steep slopes that it's barely wide enough for one car. On both sides giant ferns tickle the car, immense rhubarb-like plants try to hug us, and masses of delicate, magenta fuchsias wink and nod, everything dripping from the myriad tiny springs spraying gossamer silver threads through the foliage. When we reach the bay, the road literally is hacked out of the cliff, sea below one side, sheer walls above the other. I'm on the sea side, where it's apparent that if we drop off the edge we'll be gone forever. This strikes me as so awful a fate that I squeeze myself away from the door, hoping by this maneuver to put an extra few inches between myself and the water that will flood through if we plunge into the ocean.

The cliff road dead ends in the fishing village of Puerto Cisnes, where we'll stay the night. In the sheltering dusk, the darkly forested slopes that wedge Cisnes between hills and sea recede. We get out of the car to stretch our legs with a stroll on the shore. Yellow and blue dories, those deep-bellied fishing boats, recline on the damp sand left by low tide, like pebbles in a fisherman's palm. The sun lingers on the horizon, a hot orange spotlight on the dogs romping and tossing kelp in the air.

Next morning, our old Avis Pathfinder seems to be sliding toward the bay, despite that it's parked on level ground. "Bernard, you realize we drove seventy-eight hundred miles from Beijing to Paris and never once had a flat? And now, with a rental car, we get a flat tire. Can you believe this?" But neither of us is aggravated, because a flat tire is a novelty, something new to deal with. And besides, we're in a civilized place with a choice of family-run breakfast cafés. And if there's one thing that I know from life in general and road trips in particular, it's that a meal can improve just about every-thing. We offer a nearby tire repair man the whole day to patch the tire, eat a mound of scrambled eggs and toast washed down with rich coffee, and hire a boat with attendant captain to take us to Chile's largest island, Isla Magdalena, an hour and a half offshore.

As we motor out over the rolling swells of the deep blue ocean, we pass floating cages connected by steel walkways. They stretch out in an endless line, parallel to the mainland. At first, I think they're traps waiting to be emptied. But they're large, perhaps thirty or more yards long, and they're anchored in the bay. "Salmon farms," says Miguel, our young captain, with disgust.

A Puerto Cisnes native, Miguel is a man of medium build and natural authority. His green polo, baggy brown trousers, and sockless loafers are relaxed enough to make approaching him for conversation easy, yet formal enough to reassure me he's used to being in command of the boat. I am still that person who doesn't trust the ocean not to do its worst with me, and it's important for my peace of mind to know that I'm with someone who'll get me back to shore safe and dry.

Miguel's black hair, shaggy and glossy, blows off his forehead as he squints into the west, and he stands loose-limbed at the wheel, one arm making modest course corrections as naturally as breathing. He tells us that in the recent past, Cisnes was a thriving independent fishing village. Until the Carretera Austral was built, the villagers' main connec-tion with the outside world was via the weekly mail boat. When the Chilean government sold fishing rights for the local waters to Spanish industrial fishing enterprises, those companies went at it with gusto, profit in mind, overfishing the waters and putting the formerly self-sufficient local fishermen out of business. Then, with perfect timing, the salmon-farming enterprises moved in. Norwegians set up the first ones, and now there are hundreds. They offered everyone good jobs and people were happy for the pay. After all, they couldn't make a living fishing on their own anymore. But working on a salmon farm requires being away from home for twenty-day shifts. What seemed to us a pristine coastline was horrifyingly polluted. And what struck us as a charming, isolated village was actually a community under terrible strain, divided between inviting in more farming operations in order to boost incomes versus finding a way to return to the independent fishing life in order to salvage traditions.

Isla Magdalena is a national park, and the fantasy I've created for our day is that we'll have a chance to walk around on fertile, shadowy paths once our private launch docks there. As we approach, one thing becomes clear: if ever there were 608 square miles that did not need the protection of national park status, Magdalena is it. Magdalena's rocky shoreline is primed to create a shipwreck and the inland flora rising 5,446 feet to the peak of Mentolat Volcano is so tightly knit that to promenade through it would be like walking through a felt hat. I doubt any government official ever set foot there to investigate exactly what they were protecting.

From the water, though, the island's shoreline is beautiful, in a nature-left-to-its-own-devices way. Delicate branches weighted with fuchsia blossoms dangle like plump pink and magenta fingers toward the water's edge. Wild grapevines wrestle with smaller shrubs, smothering them in a passionate, tangled embrace. We drop anchor in a quiet lagoon of calm aquamarine water, where Miguel lowers a small skiff. He clambers down a rope ladder, leaving us on board. "Watch," he says. Paddling a short distance away he flings a cobweb of fishnet onto the water with a broad flourish. It's so lacy and light it lingers on the surface as if loath to sink. As it disappears, he lets the current drift him back to the boat, where he lashes the skiff to the side. "Salmon escape from those cages," he says, climbing back on board. "We catch them all the time."

"And I bet you don't return them to the farm manager, do you!" I say and we all laugh, though ruefully. I'm not sure whom I'm rooting for: the wily fish that has managed to escape its captivity, or our captain—and us—who wouldn't mind a dinner of flapping-fresh salmon.

Miguel pulls a bottle of chilled mango juice from a small refrigerator, pours us each a glass and the three of us sit on the little deck at the prow of the boat nursing the cool nectar, sun warming us, the gentle rocking and slapping of waves lulling us to silence. Suddenly the net seems to be yanked down by a hidden hand. "I think we've got one," Miguel shouts, springing up to look. "Maybe even two," he adds, while the net jerks and the skiff to which it's attached bounces like a bathtub toy. Forgoing the rope ladder, Miguel does a pirate leap from deck into skiff and paddles out to the edge of the netting circle, which he carefully pulls in hand over hand. The net rises, a black filigree necklace sparkling with crystal droplets. As the last of it clears the water's surface, we see two silvery salmon, ten pounds each, thrashing in the bottom. Miguel stands, legs apart for balance, broad grin on his face. "Dinner!" he yells. "For all of us." He holds up the netting to display the wiggling trophies so Bernard can photograph. I suspect his happiness is magnified knowing he's gotten some of those corporate salmon for free.

Puttering back toward the port, Miguel asks if we'd like to stop by the place where he grew up, describing a spit of land with vegetable garden, orchard, livestock, and, best of all, his parents. I nudge Bernard with my elbow. "Family farm. Let's go, no?"

When I was young, I read Hans Christian Andersen's fairy tales. Over and over again I would immerse myself in the story of "The Red Shoes," "The Snow Queen," and "The Emperor's New Clothes." The one that captivated me most was "The Little Match Girl." I grew up in an early twentieth-century Dutch Colonial house with a yard surrounded by azaleas and rhododendrons, and massive apple trees left so long untended that they were big enough to hold both a playhouse and a swing. My existence was secure, with parents who doted on me and a sister who willingly played pick-up sticks with me and let me tickle her in the bath. I never had any sense of being without. Yet I strongly identified with Andersen's shivering young pauper, her naked feet blue from cold on that wintery New Year's Eve. Growing up, we were the only Jews in a neighborhood of Mafia-connected Italian Catholics. We were expected at the table at 6:30

every evening, when all the neighborhood kids were let loose to play on the street before dark. We wore shorty shorts to their Bermudas, ate goulash to their pizza. And in my early elementary school years, I spoke with an accent picked up mimicking the English of my French mother and Austrian father. That my teacher thought it appropriate to make me stand at my desk repeating words in proper American did not help my self-esteem. I wasn't poor and I didn't sell matches, but I definitely felt like an outsider looking in.

On a road trip, that sense of not belonging dyes my perception of each day. Though he's never spoken about it, I know Bernard feels this as well, because we are as one when it comes to visiting people's homes in foreign places. We have tacitly agreed that it's the first of two ideal ways to banish the frustration of otherness and bring about the ease of belonging, the second being watching a soccer match on the TV of a local bar.

Now, Bernard nods enthusiastically. Miguel drops anchor offshore from the family home built on a swatch of green lawn up a short slope from the shore. Set back from the lemon-yellow house are rows of gnarled trees and behind them, jungle, of the same opaqueness as that which covered the islands we passed on the *Evangelistas*.

As we crowd into the little skiff, a school of dolphins surfaces to escort us to the dock where his parents wait. His mother, mousy-haired and grandmotherly in a cotton dress cinched around her broad middle with an apron, is ebullient, spreading her arms wide to welcome us. Barely introduced, she grabs me to her bosom in a prolonged hug, then places my chilled hand in her warm one. Her palm is both pillowy and rough, her fingers gripping mine like a vise. Miguel's father, tall like his son, looks like he's adopted Bernard, linking arms and bending his head as he enunciates, "Welcome!" in English. For the next hour we roam the property arm in arm, hand in hand, inspecting the house they built themselves, walking the freshly weeded rows of their vegetable garden, identifying herbs, playing "How do you say this in Spanish and here's what we call it in English."

Above the garden is the orchard of apples, pears, apricots, and plums, guarded by a majestic old plum tree. Miguel's mother stretches her stout self to pull a plum off a low-hanging branch, tests it, wipes it on the front of her dress, offers it to her husband by whose side she had hacked away at the forest by hand for over five decades, clearing it foot by aching foot for their homestead, eventually creating enough pasture for a small flock of sheep and thirty cows. "We planted this when we moved here," she says, casting a flirtatious glance at her husband, as if they were newlyweds. "Before any of this ground you see had been cleared. Before the salmon farms. Before my husband could no longer make a living fishing." She pauses and I see a brief tremble in her lips. Taking a deep breath, she says, patting his arm, "Now he fishes only for the two of us." The mother pulls more plump, soft purple plums the size of walnuts from the branches and offers them around. I take the last two. Her cupped, upturned palms are empty now of fruit and I see the hazel skin, tough and deeply creased. More than her words, they tell me of building something from scratch that would endure, of what it took for her to stand by her husband when he lost the only livelihood he ever knew. I'm standing in a veritable garden of Eden peopled by an arthritic Adam in baggy brown trousers and his stout Eve in a shapeless shirtdress, both in rundown shoes that have already given more than a lifetime of service. We crowd into the tree's shade and eat the fruit, sweet juice dripping down our chins, while bees buzz lazily in the grass, drunk from the rotten plums fermenting at our feet.

Distracted by the pleasures of our visit, we don't notice a storm has blown in. While we've been inspecting parsley and tomatoes, the morning's placid seas have turned rough. Now, heaving swells are slamming against the dock. A quick glance at the scudding dark clouds and a quiet but firm *debemos irnos* from the captain, is all we need to jump into the skiff and paddle with great vigor back to the boat. The captain quickly weighs anchor. A moment ago, he was just a son, his round face boyish, but his authority is such that it doesn't even occur to me to question his decision to head back to port in the growing storm. Instead, I batten myself down in the mid-ship cabin and assert a firm grip on the little table within, which is tightly bolted to the floor. Looking steadfastly at the bounding horizon, trying to will my stomach to be still, I see Bernard up on the seesawing bow. He's perched on a coil of rope, his face upturned to the wind that slashes droplets of salt water across his cheeks. After a while, thinking some fresh air would help, I stick my head out the cabin door. It takes just a second for the wind to whip off my P2P cap.

This is not just any cap. It's a garment whose very existence is testimony to what can happen when you see a door, push your foot through, and shove it open. I watch wide-eyed as it skitters across the deck. Briefly, very briefly, I consider dashing after it, even plunging over the deck rail in pursuit of this bit of head gear so weighted with significance. In the moment it takes me to sternly talk myself down from diving into the surging waves, the ivory-colored cap is lost from view.

I stay on deck contemplating the leaden horizon. A bullwhip of wind and spray lashes my face, salting my lips, startling me to clarity. That it's not about me or about travel, about sameness or difference, about difficult or easy, about going away or returning. The haiku master Matsuo Basho synthesized it as he wandered Japan in the mid-seventeenth century. Basho was a master at reducing complexity to a few words and what he harmonized in a few syllables is profound in its simplicity. I understand it now: that the journey itself is home.

ACKNOWLEDGMENTS

I am grateful for the generous and open hearts of many. All those I have met on my travels, whether mentioned in this book or not, have enriched these stories through their willingness to pause whatever they were doing when I appeared, to share with me a coffee, perhaps a tale or two, and to pull back the curtain to show me their life for those precious hours.

Jane Rosenman helped me shepherd singular tales into a cohesive book with an uncanny ability to understand the soul of what I wanted to share.

At Skyhorse, my editor Lindsey Breuer-Barnes inspired me through her faith in my storytelling. It is no exaggeration to say that without her this book would not exist.

And always, Bernard—because when the cosmic caller in the square dance of life calls out "Now do-si-do, then allemande left, and walk your partner home," his is the arm I want around me as we stroll on.

ABOUT THE AUTHOR

D ina Bennett was born in Manhattan. After five years as a PR executive, she joined her husband's software localization company as
senior VP of sales and marketing. The two worked side by side until they
sold the firm in 1998 and abandoned corporate life for a hay and cattle
ranch. Since then she has untangled herself from barbed wire just long
enough to get into even worse trouble in old cars on more than 100,000
miles of far-off roads. She is the author of *Peking to Paris*, and she has lived
in Colorado, Oregon, and now France.